Praise for *A Vanished World*

"Masterfully tells of a time when Muslims, Christians, and Jews coexisted and flourished religiously, intellectually, and civilizationally."

—John Esposito, author of
What Everyone Needs to Know About Islam

"Lowney tells the tale of coexistence, and its eventual unraveling, with detail, delicacy, and verve. . . . This bold and compassionate articulation of medieval Spanish history, with its complex interactions among Jews, Muslims, and Christians, speaks directly to contemporary international crises."

—*Publishers Weekly* (starred review)

"A coherent and exciting history...Chris Lowney successfully brings the story of medieval Spain to a wider audience and draws out of this rich history important lessons for the post-9/11 world."

—*Christian Science Monitor*

"Lowney's accomplished work comprehensibly covers medieval Spain and connects the country's past to its present."

—*Booklist*

ALSO BY CHRIS LOWNEY

Heroic Leadership:
Best Practices from a 450-Year-Old Company
That Changed the World

A Vanished World

Muslims, Christians, and Jews
in Medieval Spain

Chris Lowney

OXFORD
UNIVERSITY PRESS

OXFORD
UNIVERSITY PRESS

Oxford University Press, Inc., publishes works that
further Oxford University's objective of excellence
in research, scholarship, and education.

Oxford New York

Auckland Cape Town Dar es Salaam Hong Kong Karachi
Kuala Lumpur Madrid Melbourne Mexico City Nairobi
New Delhi Shanghai Taipei Toronto

With offices in

Argentina Austria Brazil Chile Czech Republic France Greece
Guatemala Hungary Italy Japan Poland Portugal Singapore
South Korea Switzerland Thailand Turkey Ukraine Vietnam

First published by Free Press, a Division of Simon & Schuster, Inc.

First issued as an Oxford University Press paperback, 2006
Oxford University Press, Inc., 2006
198 Madison Avenue, New York, NY 10016
www.oup.com
ISBN-13: 978-0-19-531191-4

Library of Congress Cataloging-in-Publication Data is available

7 9 10 8

Printed in the United States of America
on acid-free paper

Contents

A Vanished World

Chronology for A Vanished World

Year	Christian Spain		Muslim Spain		Key Events		Culture and Religion
600	476–711 Visigoth Rule						632 Muhammad 636 Isidore of Seville
700					711 Muslim invasion of Spain		
800			756–788 Abd al-Rahman I		778 Charlemagne ambushed (basis for *Song of Roland*)		
900			756–1031 Umayyad Dynasty 912–961 Abd al-Rahman III		850–859 Córdoba martyr-activists		857 Ziryab 859 Eulogius
1000			976–1002 Almanzor 1009–1031 Umayyad dynasty collapses		997 Almanzor sacks Santiago		c. 1003 Pope Sylvester II (mathematician) 1013 Abulcasis 1056 Samuel ha-Nagid (general)
1100	1065–1109 Alfonso VI		1086–1144 Almoravid Dynasty		1085 Alfonso VI captures Toledo 1094 El Cid captures Valencia 1095 Pope Urban II launches Crusades		1100—*Song of Roland* 1185 Ibn Tufayl (*Hayy Ibn Yaqzan* author)
1200	1217–1252 Fernando III 1230 Léon and Castile permanently united 1252–1284 Alfonso X		1147–1228 Almohad Dynasty		1170 Order of Santiago founded 1212 Las Navas de Tolosa (Muslim army defeated) 1236 Fernando III captures Córdoba 1248 Fernando III captures Seville		1187 Gerard of Cremona (translator) 198 Averroes c. 1200 *Poem of El Cid* 1204 Moses Maimonides 1240 Ibn Arabi (Sufi mystic)
1300	1369 Enrique (II) kills Pedro the Cruel		1232–1492 Nasrid Dynasty rules Granada		1348–1350 Bubonic Plague sweeps Europe 1391 Anti-Jewish riots		1305 Moses de León (*Zohar* author)
1400	1469 Isabella marries Ferdinand 1474–1504 Isabella the Catholic				1481 Spanish Inquisition begins 1491–1492 Muslim rule ends (Granada surrender)		
1500					1492 Jews must convert or emigrate 1492 Columbus reaches Americas 1502 Muslims must convert or emigrate		

Key: A single year denotes an event's occurrence or an individual's death. Dating of medieval events is an inexact science, and the dates shown should be considered no more than close approximations.

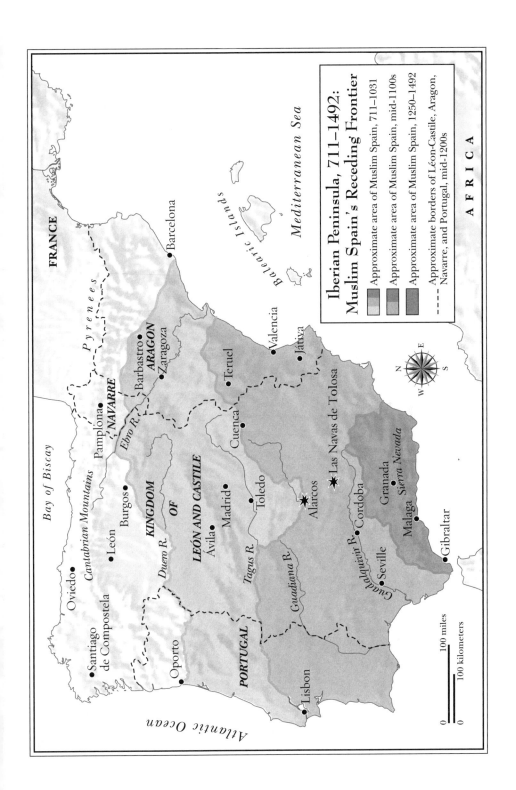

Iberian Peninsula, 711–1492:
Muslim Spain's Receding Frontier

Approximate area of Muslim Spain, 711–1031
Approximate area of Muslim Spain, mid-1100s
Approximate area of Muslim Spain, 1250–1492
– – – Approximate borders of Léon-Castile, Aragon,
        Navarre, and Portugal, mid-1200s

FRANCE

Bay of Biscay

Atlantic Ocean

Mediterranean Sea

AFRICA

Pyrenees

Cantabrian Mountains

Balearic Islands

Oviedo

Santiago
de Compostela

León

Burgos

Pamplona

NAVARRE

Barbastro

ARAGON

Zaragoza

Barcelona

KINGDOM
OF
LEÓN AND CASTILE

Duero R.

Ebro R.

Avila

Madrid

Cuenca

Teruel

Valencia

Játiva

Toledo

Tagus R.

Las Navas de Tolosa

Alarcos

Guadiana R.

Guadalquivir R.

Cordoba

Seville

Granada

Sierra Nevada

Malaga

Gibraltar

PORTUGAL

Oporto

Lisbon

N
W   E
S

100 miles
100 kilometers
0
0

Jews, Christians, and Muslims, as we know, come from different religious traditions, but have many ties to each other. In fact, all the believers of these three religions refer back to Abraham . . . for whom they have a profound respect, although in different ways . . . If there is not an amiable peace among these religions, how can harmony in society be found?

From believers, from the representatives of religion, from persons who have spent so many years of their life in meditation on the sacred books, the world is waiting for a world of peace.

Pope John Paul II, April 30, 1991, to a conference
of Christians, Muslims, and Jews

Preface

On a sunny March morning in 2004, as Spanish commuters converged on a Madrid pulsing with the gathering energy common to rush hour in every large city of the world, ten bombs shredded four commuter trains. Nearly two hundred persons died within seconds, and Spain earned the dubious distinction of hosting the worst terrorist attack ever inflicted on mainland Europe.

But *who* had attacked? Government authorities immediately fingered ETA, acronym for a notorious separatist group boasting a decades-long résumé of terror in the cause of prying their Basque homeland from the grip of Spain's federal government.

Then the plot thickened. Authorities backpedaled as ETA's political wing disavowed Basque involvement in the tragedy and Islamist terrorists proudly claimed responsibility. The world shuddered to wonder whether the masterminds of the September 11 attacks on New York's twin towers had inaugurated a transatlantic phase of their gruesome campaign.

Spain had never suffered a worse terrorist incident, but she had suffered far bloodier days. For more than seven centuries, ending in 1492, Spain had been divided into a Muslim-ruled south and a Christian-ruled north. After one of the deadly clashes that punctuated crusading attempts to reclaim all Spain for Christendom, a jubilant monarch exulted, "On their side 100,000 armed [Muslim] men or more fell in the battle . . . [But] unless it be a miracle, hardly 25 or 30 Christians of our whole army fell. O what happiness!"

The Muslim extremists who claimed responsibility for Madrid's train bombings may well have been recalling that bloody medieval day. They justified their attack as "settling old accounts with Spain, the Crusader." In fact, the murky circumstances of March 11, 2004, eerily

1

echoed Spain's medieval past in other ways. By blaming Basque sepa-
ratists for bloody havoc wrought by Muslim terrorists, government
authorities had unwittingly reversed a monumental, nine-hundred-
year-old propaganda injustice. *The Song of Roland,* by many estimates
the medieval era's greatest epic poem, climaxes with a Muslim sneak attack on a Christian army. Though such an ambush did actually occur,
Basque bandits perpetrated the heinous assault, not the Muslims so
roundly vilified in the *Song of Roland. Roland's* twelfth-century anti-
Muslim recriminations lingered; repeated again and again as decades
piled up into centuries, they acquired the timeless certainty of the epic
itself. Thus, medieval Muslims wrongly blamed for Basque transgressions gave way to twenty-first-century Basques wrongly blamed for
Muslim violence. Both episodes, medieval and current, were freighted
with the same heavy undertones of Muslim-Christian enmity.

I visited many of the places commemorated in the *Roland* saga in
late September 2001. With the New York twin towers attacks still an
open wound on the human psyche, I rattled around tourist sites scared
empty of tourists. Spain's churches, monuments, language, and literature are richly redolent of a unique, multifaith heritage. Muslims,
Christians, and Jews had worked, worshipped, and interacted in Spain
on a scale unparalleled and even unimaginable elsewhere in the medieval West. As I pondered the wound inflicted on my own native city
of New York, I wondered what these medieval Christians, Muslims,
and Jews might teach us in a twenty-first century still plagued by enmity among adherents of the world's three great monotheistic religions.

Discerning medieval Spain's lessons is no straightforward task. Madrid's police investigators had it easier in March 2004. After dispassion-
ately sifting shards of train wreckage and forensic evidence, they pieced
together an objective narrative of that fateful day when so many innocent lives had been callously swept away on a late winter morning in
central Madrid. Picking through the artifacts of humankind's shared
medieval story is less easy to do. Medieval Spain's poets, historians, and
chroniclers were anything but dispassionate. They peered at events
through the prism of their own sacred books and beliefs. They manipulated religious rhetoric to pursue political agendas and vilified as enemies those who professed a different faith. They bore long-nursed

grievances of their countrymen or coreligionists. They chose starting points of their liking when tracing the convoluted drama of their past, leading to narrative journeys that ineluctably corroborated their sympathies.

We're too often guilty of the same. As our Muslim, Christian, and Jewish neighbors argue the righteousness of their respective causes, we readily pounce on their oversimplifications, prejudices, and self-interest; we're less quick to subject our own hearts and minds to the same exacting scrutiny. We believe we already know how the Muslim, Christian, or Jew "ought" to feel; we have little need, therefore, to listen to his or her story. We focus on the dogmatic differences that divide us, seldom considering that we are united in common worship of the same God of Abraham.

Roland the medieval epic hero rallied comrades for battle by boiling down Muslim-Christian confrontation to conveniently simple terms: "The pagans [Muslims] are wrong and the Christians are right." Such simplicity certainly appealed to Roland's warrior colleagues, and Madrid's terrorists of 2004 undoubtedly reassured themselves in some similar fashion.

Medieval Spain's enterprising, devout, imaginative, ambitious, and adventurous men and women forged a civilization that in many ways far outshone those elsewhere in Europe. They almost built the peaceful, common society that we must learn to build. But by clinging unblinkingly to the perceived black-and-white certainties of their respective causes, they all but destroyed the very wonder they created.

We risk the same, the stakes now higher. Technology has shrunk our world. Our globe has become, in some respects, no different from those tiny medieval Spanish villages where Muslims, Christians, and Jews rubbed shoulders on a daily basis. Technology delivers us each day the ideas, beliefs, and culture of those a half-world away, and technology renders us capable of instantaneously inflicting damage on those whose ideas offend, on a scale that would have been inconceivable to these medieval Spaniards.

All the more urgent, then, that we learn to heed wisdom sacred to Muslim, Christian, and Jew alike. Jesus told listeners that the greatest commandment was to love God above all things and "Love your neighbor as yourself." He was, of course, echoing Yahweh's revelation to Moses atop Mt. Sinai. The Quran frames one starkly relevant dimension of that commandment for troubled modern times: "Whosoever kills an innocent human being, it shall be as if he has killed all humankind."

Introduction

In 711 C.E., some ten thousand Muslim invaders from North Africa engineered a stunningly abrupt conquest of 5 million on the Iberian Peninsula. Spain became the first—and so far only—Islamic state to take root on mainland Europe. The Muslim usurpers vanquished Spain's Visigoth monarchs, descendants of northern European barbarians who had seized control of Iberia more than two centuries earlier. Spain, once a shining jewel of the Roman Empire, had suffered under these Visigoths the economic and cultural stagnation that later historians dubbed the Dark Ages.

Under Muslim rule Spain shone once more, her economy resuscitated and cultural life revived. Thanks to reinvigorated trade and technological advances unrivaled across Europe, daily life was transformed as exotic new species like cotton, figs, spinach, and watermelon burgeoned in fields nourished by new irrigation techniques. While Spaniards under Muslim rule luxuriated in hot water soaks at local bathhouses, one chronicler sniffed at the primitive hygiene of Europeans elsewhere, "[who] do not keep themselves clean and only wash once or twice a year in cold water. They do not wash their clothes once they have put them on until they fall to pieces on them."

With its hundred thousand residents, the emir's capital of Córdoba dwarfed every other city in Europe. His 400,000-volume library may well have sheltered as many books as all Christian Europe combined, shelving among its treasures long-lost Western wisdom and exotic new ideas from the East. Where Europe's scribes had been reduced to copying and recopying the few classical texts that survived barbarian pillage, Islam's scholars now introduced Europeans to Hindu-Arabic numerals, higher mathematics, new medical techniques, and fresh approaches to philosophy.

5

While Córdoba's emir ruled unchallenged throughout most of Spain, Christian rulers stubbornly clung to a narrow strip of the country's desolate north, nursing resentments that would stoke a *Reconquista* (Reconquest) in later centuries to reclaim the peninsula for Christendom. When political infighting fractured al-Andalus (the Arabic name for the Muslim-ruled part of Spain)* into more than two dozen small municipal kingdoms by the 1030s, a resurgent Christian north reasserted itself. Through centuries of back-and-forth warfare, Christian kingdoms clawed back chunks of frontier no-man's land before seizing Toledo, one of Islam's crown jewel cities. Christian momentum then stuttered as North Africa's Almoravid dynasty invaded Spain in the late eleventh century, propping up their faltering Muslim coreligionists. A few decades later, Almoravids were supplanted by a more fanatical North African Almohad dynasty, who intensified the increasingly bitter religious rhetoric now dividing Muslim and Christian Spain while briefly shoring up Muslim sway over Iberia's south.

But neither Almoravid nor Almohad could hold back the steadily encroaching Christian tide. In the early decades of the thirteenth century, Christian kings claimed the great Muslim commercial centers of Valencia, Seville, and Córdoba. By the mid-thirteenth century the ta-

---

*An introductory note on terminology, names, and approach: Like many popular treatments of medieval Spain, this one sacrifices terminological precision in the interest of readability and simplicity. The terms "al-Andalus" and "Moorish," "Muslim," and "Islamic" Spain all synonymously refer to that portion of the Iberian Peninsula under Muslim control at any given point during the medieval era. Conversely, "Christian Spain" and "the north" connote regions controlled by Christian rulers. "Iberia," "Spain," and "the Peninsula" refer to the whole Iberian Peninsula. "France" is used as a shorthand—and anachronistic—reference for the lands that, during much of the medieval era, would more accurately be called kingdoms of the Franks.

Numerous complications accompany the use of shorthand labels for medieval Spain. The boundaries of al-Andalus and Christian Spain were never exact and ever fluid, expanding or shrinking with military success or failure. Terms like Muslim and Christian Spain can each imply a homogeneous monolith, which was never the case. Christian Spain, for example, was a patchwork of kingdoms (e.g., León, Castile, Aragon, Navarre) that remained independent throughout some or all of the medieval period before falling under unified leadership in the Spain of today (Portugal effectively established its independence in the mid-twelfth century). There were always Christians, Muslims, and Jews in both Christian and Muslim Spain; indeed, Muslim Spain early on sheltered many more Chris-

bles had turned completely: the Muslim rule that once blanketed Spain was hemmed into a pocket of land surrounding Granada. Now it was Muslim princes who gamely struggled to maintain a foothold in Iberia. Over two centuries passed before their dreams finally withered as their food stocks vanished during a punishing siege of Granada in 1491. This last bastion of Muslim power surrendered to King Ferdinand and Queen Isabella just months before Christopher Columbus was dispatched on the voyages of discovery that ultimately left the Spanish flag waving over half the world known to Europeans.

Ferdinand and Isabella undertook another stunning initiative during 1492, forcing their Jewish subjects within a scant four months to embrace Christianity or depart Spain forever. Families were separated in the frantic rush to settle affairs; one Judah Abrabanel subsequently learned of his son's forced conversion to Christianity: "He is lost. That is the thought that sickens, strangles, slashes me; that is the razor, sharper than any barber's blade, that rips the membrane of my aching heart." In one dizzying year, Ferdinand and Isabella exterminated Muslim power from Spain, expelled her Jews, and added Columbus's New World to their domains.

Alone among nations, Spain has alternately suffered and exulted

---

tians than Muslims. Moreover, Islamic, Christian, and Muslim properly refer to religions and religious beliefs and can be applied only loosely—and imprecisely—to geography, government, and culture, as is done throughout this and similar works. Though the term "Moor" became synonymous with "Muslim" among medieval Christians and is used here as such, the word probably referred originally to the Mauri, the inhabitants of Roman Mauritania.

No popular history can comprehensively treat every important event and character; this one focuses almost exclusively on the succession of kingdoms that ultimately came to dominate Spain: Asturias-León-Castile. Many important figures and episodes are admittedly lost in this simplified approach, most notably the fascinating history of the realms of Aragon.

To render Hebrew and Arabic names more accessible, they are reproduced here without diacritical marks, and familiar anglicized forms are used when they exist (e.g., Averroes for Ibn Rushd). Such forms are typically rooted in Latin corruptions of Arabic proper names. Romance names are retained except where an alternative has become familiar (e.g., Ferdinand and Isabella). Each faith maintains its own system of dating history; this work uses C.E. for the Common Era beginning in the year traditionally associated with the birth of Jesus.

through this impossibly panoramic sweep of human history, bridging the ancient world to the brink of the modern: the barbarian invasions and implosion of Rome's empire, the rise of Islam and foundation of the only substantial Muslim state in western Europe, a crusading Reconquest, *jihad,* Spanish Inquisition, and Columbus's discovery of a New World. How we in the West got ourselves to where we are today, for good and for ill, is a question that inevitably (if improbably) leads to medieval Spain. So does the heritage of most citizens of the Americas and, by some estimates, nearly half of Israel's Jews. One gnarled root of our religious animosities stretches back to medieval Spain, as does a more nourishing root of much modern religious wisdom.

This book is not a conventionally styled history of the kings, battles, and dynasties that delivered Spain from 711 to 1492, history that has been better and more comprehensively told by many others. Instead, this work makes medieval Spain's alternately thrilling and horrific stories of adaptation and conquest the backdrop to explore the engagement—and, too often, the collision—of the world's three great monotheistic faiths for the first time on Western soil.

Medieval Spaniards were tossed by the Muslim conquest into an ocean of clashing religious cultures and were utterly ill-equipped by modern standards to navigate such uncharted waters. Most Americans understand that there are many religions in the world, have considered the virtues of religious tolerance, and have been exposed to the principle of church separated from state. Such notions were as alien to the medieval mind as Einstein's theory of relativity. Yet, at their best, these medieval Spaniards somehow accommodated each other's beliefs and lifestyles in ways that humanity's later (and supposedly more enlightened) generations have often been hard-pressed to match, much less surpass.

Medieval Muslims, Christians, and Jews were challenged not only by encountering one another, but by rediscovered works of classical philosophy outlining invigorating yet frightening new ways of thinking. Brilliant twelfth-century Spaniards like the Jewish Moses Maimonides and the Muslim Averroes dared wonder whether their beliefs and sacred scriptures stood up to rational dissection. For the first time in a millennium—arguably for the first time *ever* in systematic fashion—they and others flexed the glorious power of human reason not merely to justify but also to *scrutinize* the assertions of the Quran and Bible. They asked questions that still challenge us: What is the proper relation between God's law and human laws? Did God really create a world in seven days, or are those scriptural stories about God and Creation anything more than merely, well, *stories*?

Other devout Spaniards eschewed philosophy's neatly parsed syllogisms to delve into mysticism and spirituality. The soaring meditations of the thirteenth-century Jewish kabbalist Moses de León and of Sufism's "greatest master," Ibn Arabi, are regarded by many scholars as the pinnacle of mystical spirituality in their respective faiths. Overall, medieval Spain's encounter of faith with reason proved part blissful marriage and part bitter clash, prompting crises and condemnations that left indelible imprints on all three faiths. Medieval Spaniards helped turn humanity to revolutionary trajectories in mathematics, medicine, spirituality, astronomy, philosophy, and theology. But those revolutions lurched along nervously in medieval societies that preferred revealed religion's certainties over freewheeling speculation. By reviving European intellectual life, Spain helped push science toward Galileo's radically true theory of a sun-centered universe, yet medieval Spain's tumult equally helped shape an early modern Europe where religious authority would not yield to science.

So three intertwined stories unfold in the chapters that follow: the first is Spain's passage from ancient kingdom to flourishing Islamic state to the broad outlines of the Spain we recognize today; second is the unique collaboration and collision of the world's three great monotheistic religions on European soil; and third is the struggle to engage religious faith with rediscovered reason. Human history was forever changed by the encounter of the three religions; each religion was forever changed by encountering the others; and each in turn was changed by its confrontation with human reason.

These intertwined stories are told where possible through the words and personalities of the protagonists who created and destroyed the multicultural, multireligious experiment that was Spain. Some are well-known names, like El Cid, Charlemagne, Moses Maimonides, and Ferdinand and Isabella; others are lesser known but no less extraordinary characters, like Isidore of Seville, Averroes, and King Alfonso X. The medieval chronicles and epics that survive today disproportionately represent a Christian point of view, confirming the old adage that history is written by the victors. Yet the stories told by these Christians to galvanize their coreligionists or commemorate their triumphs will at times grate uncomfortably on modern Christian ears.

This is, of course, exactly why reflecting on our past illuminates our present. Medieval Spain may distantly echo our own, often failed efforts to foster successful twenty-first-century multireligious societies. Spain, too, suffered religious jihad, was horrified by martyr-activists who provoked their own deaths, and saw traditional cultures trampled by a technologically superior society. But medieval Spain offers no facile lessons learned. Alternately romanticized and demonized by historians, Spain was neither utopia nor dystopia but a bit of both, often at the very same moment in the actions of any one conflicted person.

Although popular histories often portray a Reconquest where zealous Christian Crusaders relentlessly hurl themselves against an equally monolithic Islam, the thirteenth-century Christian king Alfonso X embodies the more complicated reality that ambitious rulers often chose allies opportunistically, not as religious affiliation might dictate. Self-interest motivated Alfonso to wield religious rhetoric as a cudgel when it suited and to ignore it when it didn't. He generously supported Jewish scholars who helped bring the world's wisdom to his Spanish kingdom, from Aristotle and astronomical treatises to the Talmud and Quran. Yet respect for his Jewish translators and Judaism's holy books yielded to a harsher inner voice when the same Alfonso mandated the death sentence for any Christian subject "so unfortunate as" to convert to Judaism. In the final act of his contradiction-wracked reign, the Alfonso who once crusaded against Muslim North Africa concluded an alliance with the same Muslim dynasty to wage war on his own wayward son, a Christian prince.

Not coincidentally, the tensions that tore medieval Spain were mirrored in the schizophrenic image of her chosen patron, Santiago (St. James). James was—and is—never far off in the Spanish imagination. A thousand-year-old route of pilgrimage snakes across northern Spain to Santiago de Compostela, by tradition the resting place of James's earthly remains and, after Rome, Europe's most important pilgrimage site. Spain's churches everywhere enshrine James's image in altar pieces, paintings, and sculptures. One discomfiting depiction occasionally appears in churches along the pilgrim route: James bestride a horse, his muscular right arm swinging a sword down upon a turbaned, darker-skinned figure cowering beneath the rearing steed's hooves. The iconography is as clear today as it must have been to thirteenth-century pilgrims: this is *Santiago Matamoros,* St. James the Killer of Moors (i.e., Muslims), patron of the crusading Reconquest. James the Muslim Killer embodies one strand of this story: religiously grounded hatred that shredded medieval Spain and still haunts humanity.

Yet, instead of this violent killer-apostle, a statue of a more serene St. James stands sentinel at the great cathedral in Santiago de Compostela. *Santiago Peregrino* (St. James the Pilgrim) wields no sword, bearing only a walking staff. Pilgrim visitors celebrate their arrival by laying a hand on the base of the column supporting the statue. James appears to return the embrace, as the visitor's hand slips into an inch-deep imprint worn into the rock by millions such contacts over hundreds of years. In the most tangible way possible, each day's arrivals join their hopes, wishes, and prayers to those of centuries of pilgrims and tourists who have preceded them.

A famous medieval sermon explains that James the Pilgrim is armed and defended only by the great law of charity: to love neighbor as self, a command revered by Muslims, Christians, and Jews alike. James the Muslim Killer finds his alter ego in James the Pilgrim; while the former inspires the hateful frenzy of war, the latter engenders the reconciliation and concord that proceed from love of neighbor.

What the Muslim killer would accomplish by the sword the pilgrim would achieve through charity and goodwill: unification of a divided peninsula. Muslims and Christians pursued the dream of unity for centuries, battering each other up and down the length of a mountainous, river-sundered Iberian Peninsula that, ironically, seems destined by its geography for anything but unity. Spain's interior topography bumps along disjointedly. Mountain ranges guard her French border, shadow pilgrims trekking to Santiago, and frame the picturesque backdrop for Granada's romantic Alhambra palace. A vast interior plateau, the *meseta* or "table land," sprawls across half the peninsula. Most of Spain's many rivers meander east-west paths of least resistance through this roller coaster terrain, dividing the country into horizontal slices. Even her climate frustrates all who would seek signs of unity. Parts of the arid south are cousin to North Africa and other semidesert lands rimming the Mediterranean; parched Granada, long-time capital of Spain's Islamic civilization, treasures its few cupfuls of rainwater each year. In soggy contrast is the north's Santiago de Compostela, reminiscent of water-logged Britain or Ireland, where deep green mossy life carpets a region drenched by some seventy inches of annual rainfall.

Still, despite this vertiginous, river-sliced interior that is often too wet where it's not too dry, countless medieval Spaniards were captivated by the vision of uniting this land. Only one source of division proved ultimately insurmountable. Though Muslims, Christians, and Jews all worship the same God revealed to Abraham, that common bond paled in their eyes before the differences dividing the three faiths.

It's the unique blessing and curse of the human animal to be able to perceive *one* or *many* and to focus consequently on what unites us or on what divides us. The wildebeest trudges through life alongside fellow wildebeests, never pausing to wonder whether the Tanzanian border or membership in the wider animal kingdom should mean anything. Only the human can know himself or herself as a person, Basque, Jew, believer in God, Spaniard, and human being. And only the human animal judges some allegiances more vital than others, or *exclusive* of others.

These three religions share not only a lineage back to Abraham but also the ritual practice of pilgrimage. Long before ninth-century Christians first journeyed to Santiago de Compostela, devout Muslims were traveling to Mecca for the *hajj* and devout Jews to Jerusalem for the pilgrim festivals of Passover, Weeks, and Booths. In all three faiths, the pilgrim's journey metaphorically embodies deeper human yearnings. Every pilgrim journey is by definition one of hope: the hope of reaching a destination successfully and the more profound hope that one's life will be bettered for the experience.

Like the pilgrim pressing forward toward a destination, James the Pilgrim symbolizes an inherently hopeful vision of history that is common to Judaism, Christianity, and Islam: the journey forward of flawed humankind toward some promised land or brighter future, "where God will wipe away every tear from their eyes." In stark contrast was the belief prevailing in other ancient civilizations that human history was essentially cyclical. Spring verdure inevitably yielded to fall and wintery death before renewing itself year after year, just as night ever followed day following night. Why not human history? The Latin poet Virgil imagined humanity relishing periodic, fleeting golden ages where peace reigns on earth before "new wars again shall arise, and a mighty Achilles be sent to Troy." The Greek Pythagoreans observed the planets ceaselessly whirling in their orbits and theorized that humanity, too, would revisit the same spots in our own perfectly cyclical journey through history.

All three monothestic traditions reject this purposeless wheel of history sung by Virgil and calculated by Pythagoreans, where humanity chases its tail, ultimately getting nowhere. Yet, though no medieval Spanish believer *preached* so pessimistic a worldview, all too many *lived* it by answering the siren call of James the Muslim Killer, patron of all those aggrieved parties who generation after generation would nurse old hatreds and perpetuate the cycle of violence suffered and vengeance sought. James the Muslim Killer's hateful march back toward some unrealistic, idealized past conflicts with the pilgrim's hopeful march forward toward some better future.

James's two conflicting images—killer and pilgrim—have nothing to do with the saint himself and everything to do with his devotees. Medieval Spain's Christians projected their hopes and hatreds onto their patron, transforming Santiago into a reflection of the best and worst of themselves. Medieval Spaniards struggled to dominate Spain even while transforming her into Europe's cultural, economic, and intellectual marvel. Here was a land of love and hate, pointing the way forward for humanity, yet going round in circles. Medieval Spain offers the modern age questions, not blueprints. Will we focus on the one or the many, on what unites us or on what divides us? Do we follow James the Pilgrim or James the Killer? Will we lead humanity forward under our collective watch, or will we merely add our own violent chapter to that endlessly recurring and sorry cycle of history imagined by the ancients?

Medieval Spain's Muslims, Christians, and Jews embraced and rejected each other's faith traditions and customs, fought alongside each other and against each other, occasionally tolerated their neighbors and somehow forged a golden age for each faith. They allow us some glimpse of what a common society might look like. Their glory was their joint accomplishments; their tragedy that they could not see and preserve what made those accomplishments possible. They haltingly blazed humanity's trail toward tolerance and mutual respect before finally veering into an overgrown thicket of religious enmity and intolerance. Humanity has never completely found the way back. Medieval Spain might help point the way.

1. Spain Before Islam

Imagine a world in which one person could know everything worth knowing. And imagine a world in which everything worth knowing filled a mere few hundred pages. Archbishop Isidore of Seville was such a person, and seventh-century Europe such a world.

Lest Isidore be accused of vanity unbecoming an archbishop, he himself never claimed to be the Man Who Knew Everything. Rather, it was his friend Bishop Braulio of Saragossa who gushed that Isidore's seventh-century encyclopedia comprised "well-nigh everything that ought to be known." Unfortunately, few of Isidore's contemporaries perused that encyclopedia. There were few Europeans to begin with, only a minute fraction of them literate, and books were rare treasures.

Today's Spain enjoys a population of some 40 million. Isidore's Spain was a far lonelier place, with perhaps only a tenth as many people; imagine Utah's sparse population scattered across an expanse twice as large. The written word was an impenetrable mystery to the overwhelming majority of these 4 or 5 million Spaniards. Organized education was nonexistent, save for a few monastic or cathedral schools that labored to equip clerics with the rudimentary skills required for church rituals.

Though Spain's (and Europe's) literate population was tiny, the medieval "publishing industry" struggled to service its few readers. A modern printing press effortlessly churns out many thousands of volumes each day; a medieval scribe would be lucky to turn out two in a *year.* That was after he and his monastic brethren invested sweaty hours of soaking animal hide, scraping away fat, and stretching, curing, and drying the skin to produce serviceable vellum parchment. No wonder the few texts emerging from this labor-intensive process became precious items. Whereas bibliophiles today might scoop up a handful of used books for the cost of a hamburger, a ninth-century manuscript would have cost the equivalent of "fifteen pigs or four mature sheep."

Spain's illiterate majority was deprived of Isidore's intellectual cornucopia, but they also were spared the depressing realization that they lived in a Dark Age. Perspective was hard to come by in an era when most Europeans knew little of the world beyond the next village and little of the past save what their parents recalled. No Spaniard knew that he lived in a country of some 4 or 5 million people, much less that Spain had sheltered many more before devastating plagues ravaged much of Europe's population. The plummeting population had plunged Spain's (and Europe's) economy into a depression that was exacerbated when barbarian hordes breached the Roman Empire's borders, disrupted trade, and strained the empire's resources to the breaking point.

What was unknown to Spaniards made little practical difference to their daily lives. Peasants scratched out meager livelihoods; surviving the next winter was their major preoccupation. Their horizons were bound by their village and its environs, just as it had been for parents, grandparents, and great-grandparents. Surviving to a first birthday was no mean feat, and celebrating a fortieth a better than average achievement. The outside world seldom visited them, and they seldom visited the outside world. For all they knew, the world was proceeding as the world always had.

Through the curse of literacy, Bishop Braulio knew better. The few books in his library made reference to classical scholars who had blazed a more enlightened path forward for humanity's earlier generations. But while Braulio knew names like Aristotle, Galen, and Ptolemy, he also knew that most of their works had long since vanished from circulation, presumably lost forever. Nor had Braulio's century spawned intellectual lights to replace those of ancient Greece and Rome. Most civilizations harbor at least the illusion of progress, that humanity is somehow struggling forward under their generation's collective watch. Braulio was permitted no such illusion, and Isidore became for him a beacon from humanity's happier past: "God raised [Isidore] up in recent times after the many reverses of Spain (I suppose to revive the works of the ancients that we might not always grow duller from boorish rusticity) . . . we apply to him the famous words of [Cicero] 'While we were strangers in our own city, and were, so to speak, sojourners who had lost our way, your books brought us home, as it were, so that we could at last recognize who and where we were.'"

Ironically, this Isidore who outlined "everything that ought to be known" revealed relatively little about himself. He was born in 560. His parents died young. He had two brothers who both became priests and rose to the rank of bishop. It's difficult to imagine any one family duplicating this episcopal achievement today, but such feats were less astounding in the cozier confines of medieval Spain, where relatively few well-connected, well-endowed, and literate families surfaced regularly in influential church or state positions.

It is generally assumed that Isidore was raised in monastery precincts overseen by his much older brother, Bishop Leander. One might imagine a lonely childhood spent mostly in the company of monks and the precious texts they copied and preserved. The scholarly environment clearly absorbed Isidore, who eventually authored over a dozen major treatises on everything from arithmetic to Holy Scripture to monastic rules. In between sentences he somehow found time to cope with the countless administrative headaches that inevitably plague a bishop.

The encyclopedic work known as the *Etymologies* was one pinnacle of his scholarly career. Braulio's compliment that it includes "everything that ought to be known" seems at first glance no exaggeration. Isidore's chapter headings map out a comprehensive catalogue of human knowledge: "size of the sun, size of the moon, acute diseases, legal instruments, the seasons, Old and New Testaments, God, monsters, human monstrosities, serpents, worms, small flying creatures, shields, helmets, the circus, gambling, peculiar costumes of certain peoples, head ornaments for women, girdles, footwear, cooking utensils," and so on. Isidore telescoped this encyclopedic gallop through human learning into a relatively slender volume. Centuries before, Greek and Roman attempts at encyclopedias had yielded far bulkier tomes. Pliny the Elder's first-century encyclopedia sprawled to some 2,500 chapters. But Isidore lived in an age when, sad to say, the pool of human knowledge was slowly evaporating. Simply put, humanity knew less than it had six centuries earlier, in Pliny's day.

Scientific method was many centuries in the future, and Isidore did little more than absorb the sources at his fingertips and regurgitate what struck him as plausible. Early in the work, Isidore shares the relatively humdrum observation, "An even number is that which can be divided into two equal parts, as II, IV, VIII." Within a few pages, however, he has departed math's timeless certainties for a fantastic tour of human monstrosities:

> The Cynocephali are so called because they have dogs' heads and their very barking betrays them as beasts rather than men. These are born in India . . . The Blemmyes, born in Libya, are believed to be headless trunks, having mouth and eyes in the breast; others are born without necks, with eyes in their shoulders . . . They say the Panotii in Scythia have ears of so large a size that they cover the whole body with them . . . The race of the Sciopodes . . . have one leg apiece, and are of a marvelous swiftness . . . in summertime they lie on the ground on their backs and are shaded by the greatness of their feet . . . The Antipodes in Libya have feet turned backward and eight toes on each foot.

Seville's conscientious shepherd, apparently fretting that this freakish catalogue will render his readers susceptible to believing all sorts of nonsense, closes the chapter by warning against gullibility: "Other fabulous monstrosities of the human race are said to exist, but they do not; they are imaginary."

Isidore and his contemporaries may not have known as much as the Romans and Greeks before them, but what they *thought* they knew was marvelous. Long before the scientific revolution's rational dissection of natural phenomena turned textbooks into soporific tomes, here was a world of wonders great and small. Isidore's encyclopedia sang of a blazing sun racing across the skies each day, and "after it comes to the west and has bathed itself in ocean, it passes by unknown ways beneath the earth, and again returns to the east." No less entrancing is the lowly bee, "skillful in the business of producing honey . . . they flee from smoke, and are enraged by noise . . . A good many have proved by experiment that these spring from the carcasses of cattle."

Still, before dismissing what passed for seventh-century knowledge, one pauses to wonder how well current wisdom will stand up over an equivalent interim. Today's cutting-edge science and technology may by 3400 C.E. seem no less buffoonish than some of Isidore's assertions appear. How will that glorious artifact of twentieth-century technology, the gas-powered automobile, strike Earth's citizens fourteen centuries hence as they tool around in whatever contraptions they've engineered to navigate a planet long since sucked dry of fossil fuels? Indeed, who even *one century* from now will consult an encyclopedia assembled in 2004? Who today can even *find* an encyclopedia composed in 1904?

Unlike 1904 encyclopedias, Isidore's *Etymologies* was consulted a century after its composition, and two centuries later, and eight more centuries later still. No less than ten editions of the *Etymologies* were published after the 1400s, a striking compliment to this beacon of light shining forth from the Dark Ages. Across a full two-century sweep of the intellectually barren early Middle Ages, Isidore stood alone as western Europe's only major compiler of secular knowledge. When contemporaries eulogized him as *saeculorum doctissimus* ("the most learned of the ages"), it was not sentimental puffery; there were few other candidates.

Isidore would have been greatly surprised to find scholars consulting his works in the 1500s, as he almost certainly doubted the world would last so long. In the late 500s, Pope Gregory the Great had taken stock of humankind's bleak prospects and solemnly moaned, "The world grows old and hoary and hastens to approaching death." There's every indication Isidore shared His Holiness's outlook. Like many Christian apologists before him, Isidore envisioned history unfolding according to a divinely ordained design. Starting with creation's seven days and continuing with venerably vital Adam, who sired a son at age 230, Isidore charted history's path with striking precision. As he wrote in the 630s, Isidore calculated the world's exact age to be 5,825 years. He dots humanity's time line with a curiously chosen panoply of the famous and infamous: Homer was at work during the world's 4,125th year, Plato in its 4,793rd; Cleopatra (5,150) and Nero (5,266) also merit mention. (In fact, only eight centuries separate Homer [c. eighth century B.C.E.] from Nero [d. 68 C.E.], not the thousand-plus years Isidore supposed. Thus, Isidore overestimated the glorious era of the ancient Greeks and Romans, while shrinking the thousands of years of pre-Homeric civilization into a scant four millennia.)

Vastly more important than this mere tally of years was history's underlying pattern. Though Isidore frequently parroted the few classical works at his disposal, his vision of history notably departs from those pagan sources. Aristotle had noted the planets' ever repeating orbits and ventured in oddly matter-of-fact language the extraordinarily depressing conjecture that "probably each art and science has often been developed as far as possible and has again perished." Round and round. Going nowhere.

Isidore demurred, instead hearkening to the fifth-century Christian bishop Augustine, who saw history unfurling purposefully through time toward the goal of creating a City of God on Earth. God had initiated human history by breathing life into Adam's nostrils in Eden; Adam had fallen, but humankind was inexorably making its way back to the Creator. Mighty Rome and all other earthly kingdoms would yield in time to a greater empire dominated by the Christian virtues, "whose king is truth, whose law is love, whose measure is eternity." As Augustine saw it, this Divine City of those following God's will was steadily gaining ground and would win increasing sway over humankind in preparation for that moment when Jesus would return in glory to judge the living and the dead.

Like his mentor Augustine, Isidore imagined the drama of human history unfolding in seven great epochs paralleling the biblical days during which God had created all earthly things. As Isidore wrote, the world was deep into what he considered its sixth and (ominously) final age before the figurative seventh or Sabbath day, when the redeemed would rest in God. This sixth age had begun with Jesus's nativity in 5211 and had already stretched far longer than humanity's fourth or fifth eras. Indeed, only the age of long-lived Adam and the other biblical greats had endured longer than a millennium. Still, if Isidore was preparing his readers for the approaching climax of this old and hoary world, even the Man Who Knew Everything didn't dare pinpoint the precise date of the Lord's long-anticipated second coming, for, he tells us, "The remainder of the sixth age is known to God alone."

Although Isidore did not know when the world might end, he was pretty sure that his beloved Spain would be center stage, ruled over since the late fifth century by a dynasty of one-time barbarians known as the Visigoths. To his credit, Isidore admirably restrains himself from excessively fawning over his native country in his *Etymologies*—encyclopedias are objective, after all—but he more than compensates in another work, the *History of the Kings of the Goths*. Its very first sentence rushes right to the chauvinistic point: "Of all the lands from the west to the Indies, you, Spain, O sacred and always fortunate mother of princes and peoples, are the most beautiful . . . You are the pride and the ornament of the world, the most illustrious part of the earth . . . you are rich with olives . . . your mountains full of trees, and your shores full of fish."

Much of Isidore's *History of the Goths* seems an exercise in what modern generations would call spin doctoring. The Visigoths had become protectors and supporters of Spain's Christian Church by Isidore's day, and Isidore thought it in the Church's interest to support the Visigoths by burnishing their reputation. This was no easy task, even for the Man Who Knew Everything. For the Visigoths were not really Spaniards, nor, when first reaching Spain during the early fifth century, had they professed the Church's version of Christianity, nor, finally, had Spain prospered on their royal watch. Bishop Braulio had wistfully lamented Spain's "many reverses" over preceding centuries. It fell to Isidore to convince readers that the same Visigoth rulers who had presided over those "many reverses" were worthy of "the most illustrious part" of a world now deep into its decisive sixth age.

That the Visigoths were themselves immigrants hardly made them oddities in Spain's ethnic paella pot. African Iberians and northern European Celts had been filtering into Spain for centuries before Christ's birth. Jews from the Near East may have established small trading communities as early as the first century C.E. The Peninsula remained a polyglot amalgamation of ethnic fiefdoms until the Romans' bruising two-century struggle to incorporate Spain into their growing empire. They labeled the new region Hispania, and their soldiers, bureaucrats, and commercial immigrants further spiced Iberia's ethnic and cultural stew. Over time, most Peninsular tribes assimilated Rome's language and ways. But while the Romans may have believed that Hispania was one cohesive administrative unit, proudly independent peoples at Iberia's fringes saw things differently. Galicians still considered themselves Galicians, Cantabrians were still Cantabrians, and, most notoriously, Hispania's Basques spoke their own ancient language and ignored the dictates of whoever claimed to be governing the Iberian peninsula.

A new immigrant wave was unleashed when Rome's increasingly porous borders allowed northern and eastern Europeans to seep, then flood into the empire from the third century onward, some of whom eventually found their way to Spain. The newest immigrants were not sophisticated Romans but unruly barbarian tribes of Vandals from the Baltics, Germanic Sueves, and Alans from the Russian steppes.

The Visigoths were latecomers to this multiethnic society. Like Vandals and Sueves, they arrived as barbarian invaders, hailing from the southern Baltic region and slowly wending their destructive path toward Spain. In 376, Emperor Valens granted some 100,000 Visigoths permission to settle within the empire's borders in Thrace (i.e., the southeast Balkan region near today's Greek-Turkish border). After straining Thrace's overextended foodstocks, the Visigoth horde stooped to bartering their retinue into slavery in exchange for dog meat, in desperation driving the exchange rate as low as one human Visigoth for one Roman dog. Ever more talented warriors than farmers, the Visigoths lashed out, engaging Rome's legions in 378 and slaying the same Emperor Valens who only two years earlier had permitted their resettlement. Valens had lived to regret allowing the Visigoths into his empire, but he hadn't lived to regret it long.

The Visigoths slowly worked their way west, in 410 crowning their destructive road show by sacking Rome itself. This time it was Emperor

Honorius who had cause to regret: Rome could have bought off the Visigoth sacking for "30,000 pounds of silver and 5,000 of gold, 4,000 silk robes, 300 purple-dyed furs, and 3,000 pounds of pepper." It would have been a bargain. Refusing to indulge the gaudy, spice-loving, extortionate Visigoths cost Rome dearly.

The inexorable Visigoth drift westward toward Spain was driven alternately by hunger, innate wanderlust, and, by no means least, sheer ambition. All three motives were likely at work when the Roman emperor Honorius, still presiding over his now ransacked capital, managed to bundle the Visigoths off to quell an uprising in Gaul (France) as his allies or *foederati*. After vanquishing the rebel forces, the Visigoth king settled in to rule sizable chunks of France and Spain himself. Though the Visigoths were nominally subject to the emperor, one chronicler was closer to the truth in supposing that the Visigoth king Athaulf "wanted to obliterate the Roman name and to make the entire Empire that of the Goths alone and to name it . . . Gothia." Though Gothic Empire may have an intriguing ring to modern ears, the Visigoths were never powerful enough to pull off so grand an imperial ambition. Frankish tribes eventually routed them from France and, to Iberia's dubious fortune, Visigoth ambitions were forever after limited to Spain, a land they dominated right up to the day of the Muslim invasion.

Isidore set out to rehabilitate the suspect pedigree of this Visigoth dynasty in the *History of the Goths*. They were a long-wandering, barely housebroken barbarian tribe of perhaps 200,000 lording it over an Iberian Peninsula of some 5 million. Their résumé, long on marauding and pillage, was short on any skill relevant to reviving an Iberian economy that had been deteriorating during the empire's centuries-long death throes. The Visigoths had seized a few shards of an empire they themselves helped shatter, and they had no clue how to reassemble the pieces.

The Visigoths' Christian credentials were also spotty. Their wanderings had exposed them to teachings peddled by Arius of North Africa, who taught that Jesus was not quite divine, but not quite human either—neither one of us, nor coequal with God the Father. Arius's formula has intuitive appeal: the Christian Jesus, truly God yet truly human, is a mystery that even today astounds and baffles believers. Still, though it may be easier to grasp the notion of Jesus as an in-between figure, it was (and is) a notion heretical to orthodox Christians.

Though the Arian heresy may seem an arcane squabble, Arius's legacy endures in Christian worship (even though his name is rarely recognized). His heresy prodded worried church fathers into global convocation at Nicea in 325. They hammered out the Nicene Creed, which (as refined slightly later that century) is recited faithfully at countless Sunday worship services by Roman Catholics, Anglicans, Lutherans, Calvinists, Eastern Orthodox, and other Christian denominations.

Though Arianism was condemned early in 325, it incubated in the Visigoth nation for centuries, and Visigoth carriers infected those they encountered in their European wanderings. Christianity itself was an emerging religion, rather suddenly thrust upon Europe's pagan populace when Rome adopted it as its state religion in the late fourth century. Those in the empire's more remote outposts were often illiterate, save for an overwhelmed cleric barely able to form the words of church rituals, much less plumb their theological depths. Once virus-like heresies took hold, it wasn't easy to flush them out. Spain's episcopal elite, however, were distressed that their monarchs spouted such heresy. And Church hierarchical discontent was something a Spanish ruler ignored at his peril. Few besides clerics were literate, and they therefore assumed inordinate importance not only as shepherds of the Christian flock but as advisors to princes and governors.

Visigoth monarchs needed all the support they could muster to assert authority over restive factional chieftans, ever rebellious Basques, and remnants of barbarian tribes. The Visigoth kings' Arian beliefs cost them the full-throated support of Spain's influential churchmen for nearly a century. In 589, all was set right at the Third Council of Toledo, presided over, coincidentally, by Isidore's brother, Archbishop Leander. The Visigoth king Recared, motivated by genuine faith, political savvy, or more likely some combination of both, led Visigoth Arian bishops in confessing Jesus Christ true God *and* true man. His profes-

sion ushered in intensely cozy church-state relations. Isidore reports
that divine blessings immediately rained down: "With the help of his
newly received faith, Recared gloriously waged war against hostile peoples," winning so convincingly that "No victory of the Goths in Spain
was greater than or even comparable." Isidore was calling history as he
saw it, or at least as a Christian apologist might see it.

But orthodox Christian belief and military might were not enough
to stitch together a fraying Iberia. Few merchants dared travel the
splendid roads inherited from the Romans, long ago scared off by, ironically, these very same Visigoths and their barbarian ilk. The Peninsula
had sunk into a subsistence economy. In fairness, one cannot blame the
Visigoths for all Spain's ills. The whole Roman Empire had stalled
under the cumulative weight of plague, barbarian invasion, inflation,
overtaxation, overextended military commitments, and inept leadership.

Braulio was right in anguishing over Spain's "many reverses" and
steep slide toward "boorish rusticity." For all his rhetorical resourcefulness, not even Isidore could conjure up a rosier Spain than the one that
limped along one century before Islam's arrival. The Visigoths had kept
Spain from reverting to its pre-Roman patchwork of smaller fiefdoms.
They held Spain together but could not endow her with prosperity.

Isidore's *History of the Kings of the Goths* tapers off in 625 C.E. He died
a decade later without finishing his encyclopedia. Despite Braulio's as-
surances to the contrary, the encyclopedia had deprived readers of at
least one fact that "ought to have been known" as Spain drew near its
all-changing eighth century: neither Isidore nor his contemporaries understood that a religious movement swelling up from the Arabian
Peninsula would soon unleash a wave across the Near East. It would
swamp the Holy Land, the Egypt once ruled by pharaohs, and the Near
Eastern provinces of mighty Byzantine and Persian empires. This wave
would soon enough crash down upon Isidore's own Spain as well,
washing away his neatly constructed world where Christian Visigoth
kings would make Spain a new Rome and reign gloriously until the end
of the world's sixth age.

Visigoth rule would be swept aside, and so would much else that
passed for fact in Isidore's *Etymologies*. Isidore sang of a sun that coursed

through the skies and bathed itself in the ocean; but the new civilization would bring Spain long-lost astronomical treatises that would reawaken Europeans' desire to scan the heavens with less poetic, more rational eyes. Isidore taught his contemporaries shortcuts for doing arithmetic on their fingers; this new civilization would introduce Europeans to the wonders of algebra and trigonometry. Isidore's encyclopedia made room for outlandish chimeras, but found no room for the prophet Muhammad and the very real revolution he ignited. Had Isidore lived a few generations later, Muhammad's followers could have told him that impossible creatures like one-legged Sciopides and dog-headed Cynocephali were products of fevered, overly fertile imagination. Muhammad's followers would know: before reaching Spain they had visited the lands supposedly inhabited by these fantastic creatures, not as tourists but as conquerors.

Isidore was right about this much: a great empire would replace the Romans in Spain, but it would be a *Muslim* empire rather than the Visigoth dynasty whose praises he sung. Isidore had gushingly reassured his Spanish compatriots, "After many victories all over the world, [they] have eagerly seized you and loved you: they enjoy you up to the present time amidst royal emblems and great wealth, secure in the good fortune of empire." In one sense, he was right about that as well: armies *did* seize and love Spain amid great wealth, but it was *Islam's* warriors rather than the Visigoths who accomplished such glories. Muhammad's followers were to wrest Spain from the Visigoths by force, imposing their rule on a nation too fragile to resist. And though Islam's invaders, like Visigoths and Romans, numbered a tiny fraction of the population they conquered, they would dominate Iberia for centuries.

Like the Arian Visigoths, Muhammad's followers professed beliefs anathema to those of the Christians they conquered. The Arian Visigoths believed Jesus's patrimony divine and his mother a uniquely exalted woman; so, according to their own nuanced formulation, did Muhammad's Muslims. But Muhammad's followers never embraced the faith of their vanquished hosts, as the Visigoths had. Perhaps for this reason, Isidore's Christian successors never lionized the Moorish conquerors as stewards worthy of Spain. Yet, unsung or not, they accomplished what Visigoths never could: they lifted Spain from her

Dark Ages gloom and depression, making her worthy of Isidore's boast: "the pride and the ornament of the world, the most illustrious part of the earth."

Isidore closed his *History of the Goths* by singing the martial praises of the Visigoths: "In the arts of war they are quite spectacular." What army could ever conquer such a people?

Spain would find out soon enough.

2. The Moors Conquer Spain

"Our God and Your God Is One"

In spring of 711, Tariq ibn Ziyad led seven thousand North African raiders into southern Spain. King Roderic rallied Spanish troops to repel them but was routed by Tariq's much smaller army. By late fall, Tariq surmounted token resistance to capture Toledo, the capital; its archbishop and most citizens had fled in panic before Islam's advance.

And so, with relatively little bloodshed and even less fanfare, Christian Spain became Muslim-ruled Spain before winter fell in 711.

The Visigoths had given too few Spaniards good reason to die in Spain's defense. They had alienated Spain's Jews, for example, who had lived and worshipped there for centuries while nomadic, barbarian Visigoths were still wandering Europe. Spain's Visigoth rulers hardly invented anti-Semitism, but they embraced it fervently, heaping ever more creative opprobrium on the Jews. Visigoth legislation forbade Jews from marrying Christians or owning Christian slaves, proscribed circumcision, outlawed observance of Jewish holy days, and ultimately offered Jews the stark choice of conversion, exile, or slavery. Penalties were severe, if sadistically creative: any man assisting at a circumcision rite risked mutilation of his own male organ. By some barely discernible anatomical logic, the equivalent penalty for a woman abetting a circumcision rite was mutilation of her nose. In the late 600s, the bishop Julian of Toledo, said to have been partially descended from

Jews himself, had put such laws in the chilling context that Judaism itself "had to be cut off, since it was like the cancerous part of the body, before this harmful disease, could be passed on to the healthy parts."

The Visigoths had also alienated Spain's nobles and magnates. Because the Visigoths had never successfully established the principle of hereditary monarchy, each royal death typically triggered an unwieldy succession scramble. Half-election, half-confirmation of the king's designated heir by warlord-nobles, the one predictable result of this unpredictable melee was an intriguing nobility forever vying for influence when not backstabbing political enemies. In fact, so many Visigoth kings were dispatched to a higher reward by disgruntled courtiers that the odds of a natural royal death hovered slightly below fifty-fifty for long stretches of the late sixth and early seventh centuries. No wonder seventh-century Wamba, deemed wisest of the Visigoth monarchs, refused the crown until threatened at sword point.

Roderic, last of these Visigoth kings, started his woe-filled reign inauspiciously in 710. One disgruntled contender for the throne formed a breakaway kingdom. The ever restless Basques also acted up, drawing Roderic far from his capital to quash insurrection in the remote, mountainous northeast. Through luck rather than military intelligence, Tariq ibn Ziyad chose this propitious moment to launch his invasion in 711. From North Africa's port of Ceuta it was a short Mediterranean crossing to the landmark that still bears his name: Gibraltar (*Jabal Tariq*, "Tariq's mountain"). Chroniclers credit Tariq with the gutsy gesture of burning his ships on the spot and weaving his soldiers' resulting dilemma into a stirring oratorical exhortation: "Whither can you fly,— the enemy is in your front, the sea at your back. By Allah! There is no salvation for you but in your courage and perseverance."

Notwithstanding the chronicler's cinematic recrafting, the invasion force that conquered Spain was in all likelihood only a reconnoitering expedition. Who would purposely pit an invasion force of seven thousand against a Christian Spain numbering 5 million? When Tariq's initial probes met little resistance, he kept going. Minor towns along the Mediterranean coast fell. While he wreaked havoc in the south, Roderic toiled away in the northeast Basque country, not only caught off-guard, but about as far removed from the crisis as he could have been.

Eighth-century warfare played out in slow motion compared to today's high-tech, long-range pyrotechnics. Messengers slogged hundreds of miles north to apprise Roderic of the unhappy developments down south. Roderic's bedraggled army, already worn down by the Basques, trudged through Iberia's interior to engage Tariq in a decisive final stand. Tariq must have assumed his prospects were dim, because instead of racing inland to capitalize on early victories, he nervously hugged the coastline, as if contemplating inevitable retreat to North Africa—perhaps employing those very same boats that later chroniclers reduced to cinder and ash. Retreat never became necessary. Roderic's army was routed near the Guadalete River in July 711. The last king of Visigoth Spain reigned scarcely a year.

Later Muslim chroniclers depicted Tariq's few thousand arrayed against a wildly exaggerated estimate of a hundred thousand Spanish defenders. The tenth-century Ibn al-Qutiyya portrayed the wily Tariq attempting to even the odds through psychological warfare. After one victory, his men round up the Spanish dead and "boil their flesh in cauldrons" as if preparing to devour the slain. Tariq orchestrates this bit of theater before Spanish prisoners that he subsequently frees. Predictably, they spread the word that Spain's invaders are ruthless man-eaters. "And God filled [the Spaniards'] hearts with fear," weakening their resolve to battle Tariq's cannibalistic horde.

Roderic had no standing army to speak of, and few Visigoths who fought alongside him could have afforded full battle regalia, which might have cost the equivalent of fifteen or more cows. His military complement would have been a ragtag, ill-coordinated bunch motivated not by allegiance to some vague ideal of Visigoth Spain but answering the summons of their own regional chieftan. Foot soldiers faced Tariq's band without helmet, armor, or sword; indeed, they counted themselves lucky to carry even a lance and crude shield.

Roderic's forces were ill-equipped and exhausted ahead of the decisive battle, but in fact, the Visigoths had lost the war long before 711. Roderic depended on Spain's nobles to answer his war summons, but he and his predecessors had done little to secure their allegiance. Some nobles stayed home. Of those who showed, the disaffected command-ers who guarded Roderic's flanks simply wheeled round and headed home at the first whiff of battle, whether from fear, treachery, or a cold calculus that it just wasn't worth it. The war was also lost through the Visigoth persecution of the Jews, who largely welcomed the Muslims, if not quite as liberators, then in the hope that anyone was preferable to the brutal Visigoths. Most of all, the Visigoths were defeated by their own inability to bring prosperity to Iberia. Resistance might have been greater had more Iberians felt they had something to lose.

Still, take nothing away from Tariq, for every battle that's lost has also been won. At the vanguard of an empire every bit as large as Rome's, assembled in a fraction of the time, he represented the dawn of a new imperial age in Spain, though not the Visigoth Empire that Isidore fondly expected. Yet few in Spain, or anywhere in Christian Eu-rope, knew anything about this new imperial power or what motivated them.

Nor are there indications that eighth-century Spaniards cared to un-derstand better the beliefs that motivated the Peninsula's new overlords. Some Christian chroniclers assumed that the Muslim invaders adhered to some heretical Christian sect, much as the earlier Visigoth invaders had professed Arianism. But to Tariq and his fellow Muslims, it was Spain's Christians who swore corrupted beliefs, as an Arabian desert merchant trader named Muhammad had warned in preaching a new religious movement based on total self-surrender to God's will. Some 170 years after Muhammad's death, Tariq incorporated Spain into the very wide swath of territory known as the *dar al Islam* ("abode of Islam"). Muhammad's vision had inspired Spain's conquerors, deeply influenced their statecraft, and guided their interaction with non-Muslims.

Nothing of Muhammad's early life suggests a nascent empire builder. He was born in 570 into a respected, albeit impoverished clan, affiliated with an influential Meccan tribe. Orphaned young, he en-tered the caravan trade that criss-crossed the Arabian Desert. He mar-ried well and prospered, raising some half-dozen children, though only one survived him. Muhammad was well-respected, nicknamed al-Amin (the trustworthy one) for his judgment and negotiating skills. He was a religious man, though never trained to serve as a religious leader. In fact, Islamic tradition holds he was an unschooled illiterate, and Muslim believers see the literary grace of their sacred book, the Quran, as confirmation that the work is exactly as the Prophet Muhammad called it: a *quran,* Arabic for "recitation." Muhammad claimed to compose nothing, at least not in any traditional sense. Rather, he faithfully recorded divine revelation imparted over twenty-three years through the agency of the archangel Gabriel.

Muhammad periodically retreated to Mecca's surrounding hills for rest and prayerful recollection. Once while praying in a cave on Mt. Hira, he was overwhelmed by a disembodied voice commanding him to "recite." At first attributing the frightening experience to evil spirits, he later understood himself a prophet chosen to receive and disseminate God's revelation—the One God revealed to Abraham and the prophets, the same God proclaimed by John the Baptist and Jesus. Though popularly regarded today as founding a new religion, Muhammad understood himself to be preaching the same faith revealed to the other great prophets, as the Quran relates: "The same religion has He established for you as that which He enjoined on Noah . . . and on Abraham, Moses and Jesus." The Jewish and Christian disciples of these earlier prophets had strayed, perpetuating corrupted beliefs and interpretations. Now Muhammad, last of this prophetic lineage, preached to those who had misinterpreted, never heard, or willfully ignored God's message. He professed Islam (Arabic for "surrender") to God's will, calling all to the example of Abraham, Jesus, and those others who had marked themselves as, to use his terminology, true Muslims (Arabic for those who "surrender" or "submit" to God's will).

Though the three great monotheistic religions spring from the same Abrahamic root, profound—and irreconcilable—dogmatic differences separate them. The person and nature of Jesus is one stark fault line. Christians understand Jesus as the Christ (God's "Anointed"), prefigured by Old Testament prophets as the Messiah for God's chosen people. The Jewish community still waits faithfully for the promised

Messiah's coming, not identifying Jesus of Galilee as the Anointed. In Islam, Jesus is no less but no more than a human prophet of uniquely exalted patrimony, conceived when the Divine Spirit entered Mary. The Muslim Jesus is not God, but human, and Jesus's Christian followers strayed by elevating him to divine status after his death. In so doing, they not only erred but blasphemed the One God by associating the merely human with the Divine. With Tariq's arrival these three religious fault lines intersected in Spain as nowhere else in the West.

Islam's essence is elegantly spare. Five principles are articulated as pillars of the faith. The first is the defining belief invigorating Muslim life: there is no god but God, and Muhammad is the messenger of God. This pillar illuminates the other four: the devout Muslim prays five times daily; donates alms to support the poor, widows, and orphans; abstains from food, drink, and sexual activity from sunrise to sunset during the month of Ramadan; and journeys on pilgrimage to Mecca at least once, health and finances permitting.

Muhammad's core messages didn't sit well in seventh-century Mecca, a cosmopolitan city straddling trade routes linking Arabia, the Near East, and Africa. Far more than a happily situated oasis turned trading center, its physical and spiritual heart was the Kaaba, an imposing cubic stone structure that by Muhammad's day had already been a pilgrimage destination for centuries. Islamic tradition cites Adam as the first worshipper at this site, with Abraham and his son Ishmael not only worshipping there but refining the Kaaba's structure. In Muhammad's day, representations of no fewer than 360 idols surrounded the Kaaba; Muhammad, like the Hebrew Bible's patriarchs and prophets, branded idols false gods and insisted instead on exclusive worship of the One God.

Muhammad's message was fraught with political overtones. Peace was ever tenuous in a region where scrappily independent tribes treasured their autonomy and resisted any imposition of external authority. Muhammad's insistence on supplanting the Kaaba's panoply of tribal gods threatened a delicately balanced social order. What's more, Muhammad proposed allegiance to Islam as the bond superseding all others, including the tribal loyalty that had always claimed paramount allegiance from any Arab.

Islam shook every rung of Arab society. At its pinnacle were the prestigious Umayyad clan, who wielded enormous authority as the Kaaba's
guardians. Their status was undermined by Muhammad's rejection of
polytheism. Islam not only rattled Mecca's elite but rallied its downtrodden, as Muslims were enjoined to support the poor and widowed.
Muhammad's unyielding commitment to social justice rebuked a society that spared scant consideration to its marginalized members.

Thus, Islam's implications stretched far beyond personal religious
belief. Though Islam's defining act was a personal confession of the
One God, its social vision encompassed the whole believing family.
Muslims were exhorted to create the *umma,* a community of believers:
"Ye are the best of peoples, evolved for mankind, enjoining what is
right, forbidding what is wrong." Individual Muslims surrendered to
God's will by living Islam's five pillars, but the Muslim community
shouldered a broader responsibility to enjoin what is right and forbid
what is wrong. This Quranic mandate implied the power to set laws
and enforce them. The cleavage of church from state remains problem-
atic even in Western democracies buttressed by the Gospel's famous
maxim to render to Caesar what is Caesar's. Such a notion was deeply
antithetical to Islam's vision of a religious state empowered to mold a
moral society, and even today Muslims disagree—at times violently—
over the proper intersection of state and religion.

Muhammad was hounded from Mecca by tribal leaders desperate to
quash his revolutionary message. His embattled circle undertook a
two-hundred-mile journey to Yathrib, later renamed Medina (Madinat
an-Nabi, "the city of the prophet"). The Muslim calendar begins with
this *Hijra* (emigration) to Yathrib: year 622 of the Common Era, year 1
to Muslims.

Each Muslim mounts an inner *jihad* ("struggle") to live Islam's precepts faithfully, but it became inescapably clear to these early believers
that their jihad also entailed literal, physical struggle. From the outset,
Muhammad's followers had to fight for their lives and for the right to
worship the One God. These embattled early days inevitably colored
Islam's worldview. The Quran portrays a world starkly divided into dar
al-Islam ("abode of Islam") and the forebodingly named dar al-Harb
("abode of war"). The two coexist uneasily; there is no buffering middle

ground. Even as the Quran unambiguously demands religious tolerance for Christians and Jews, Muslims also find the admonition to "Take not the Jews and the Christians for your friends and protectors; they are but friends and protectors to each other." The Quran prepares Muslims to defend the dar al-Islam and preserve the community of believers: "Let those fight in the cause of Allah who sell the life of this world for the Hereafter."

Military victories, savvy tribal diplomacy, and swelling enthusiasm for Muhammad's message won the upper hand for Islam. Within a decade he returned triumphantly to Mecca. The Kaaba's idols were destroyed. By Muhammad's death in 632, large swaths of the Arabian Peninsula were unified in professing Islam. This Arab unity spurred a flurry of conquest of lands beyond the Arabian Peninsula as the aggression that once fueled internecine tribal feuds now turned spectacularly outward. Muslim warriors overran great chunks of the storied Byzantine and Persian empires that had long dominated much of the Near East.

The lure of war booty undoubtedly stoked the frantic pace of conquest. But Quranic precepts endowed military ambition with a profounder purpose: "To him who fighteth in the cause of Allah—whether he is slain or gets victory—soon shall We give him a reward of great (value)." Still, Islamic rule's relatively light touch often induced threatened states to sue for peace rather than fight. Unlike history's many thuggish conquerors, Islam's armies shunned the blood sport of indiscriminate pillage. Diplomatic ultimatums typically preceded the threat of military onslaught. Islam's warrior-diplomats promised peace and protection in exchange for allegiance and annual tribute. Submission was undoubtedly humiliating, but typically enabled potentates to save both their heads and their jobs. The Muslim invaders were few in number and lacked bureaucratic infrastructure. With constrained resources and limitless ambitions, they had no choice but to co-opt the governmental bureaucracies they inherited. The more intriguing challenge the invaders faced was what to do with the *gods* of those they conquered.

Islam wasn't the first empire to face this dilemma. Rome had long ago overrun many of the same territories Islam now claimed, but with a crucial difference. Pagan, polytheist Rome saluted an abundance of deities and saw no harm in allowing subjugated peoples the comfort of their own familiar gods, provided that taxes were paid, conscripts funneled to Rome's armies, and Rome's own deities honored, including her semidivine emperor. Indeed, alien gods were not only tolerated but harvested for import: Greek Apollo won a cult following in Rome, as did Isis from Egypt and the great mother Cybele from Asia Minor. The apparent bottom line: if gods are already many, adding a few more to the pantheon presents no inherent contradiction.

One subject nation stood uneasily apart from this divine league of nations. The Jews' very first commandment underscored the jealous Oneness of their God: "I am the Lord your God . . . you shall have no other gods before me." For a Jew to waft incense toward a Roman deity was tantamount to utter renunciation of his or her defining belief. Jews refused to comply with Roman ritual observances, and relations with their overlords became wary and notoriously prickly.

Ironically, conquering Muslims faced a similar dilemma as conquered Jews. Islam's central, nonnegotiable tenet is monotheism: there is no god but God. If God is One, gods cannot be many. And that simple, plain fact of monotheism complicated things for conqueror and conquered alike. Granted, conquerors like Muslims enjoyed rather more options for dealing with this dilemma than did the conquered Jews.

The later history of the Roman Empire presented one approach for monotheistic conquerors dealing with polytheist subjects. The emperor Constantine had renounced Rome's pagan ways to profess Christianity in the early 300s, beginning the Empire's slow transformation to monotheism. The famously benevolent tolerance extended by the once polytheist empire evaporated completely in 395, when the emperor Theodosius urged Rome's subjects in no uncertain terms to embrace his own Christian faith: "And those who don't, since in our judgment they are foolish madmen, we decree that they shall be branded with the ignominious name of heretics . . . They will suffer in the first place the chastisement of divine condemnation and in the second the punishment of our authority."

Muslim conquerors chose a different approach. Islam offered tolerance, albeit a restricted tolerance of second-class citizens whose liberties were curtailed and who paid supplemental taxes for the privilege. Muhammad had taught that both Christians and Jews were *Ahl al-Kitab* (People of the Book). Their mistaken dogmas notwithstanding, they worshipped the same God of Abraham as Muhammad's own followers. The Quran unambiguously instructed the Muslim faithful, "And dispute ye not with the People of the Book . . . but say, 'We believe in the revelation which has come down to us and in that which came down to you; our God and your God is One.'"

Islam's success in quickly defusing Christian resistance across Spain might have had something to do with the tolerant surrender treaties they sculpted, like this one accepted by the Christian prince Theodomir of Murcia:

> The latter [Theodomir] receives peace and the promise, under the guarantee of Allah and of his Prophet, that there will not be any change in his situation nor in that of his people; that his right of sovereignty will not be contested; that his subjects will not be injured nor reduced to captivity, nor separated from their children nor their wives; that they will not be disturbed in the practice of their religion; that their churches will not be burned, nor despoiled of the objects of the cult found in them . . . He and his subjects will have to pay each year a personal tribute of one dinar in specie, four bushels of wheat and four of barley, four measures of malt, four of vinegar, two of honey and two of oil.

The swift conquest and generous treaties might suggest a new era of good government dawning in Spain, from bumbling Visigoths to enlightened, efficient Moors, but the early reality hardly measured up to any such promise. Spain's new rulers succumbed to the same infighting that had so hobbled the Visigoths. Tariq ibn Ziyad's military heroics undoubtedly qualified him for an important role in Islam's newest province, but if politics' first law is not to screw up, its second is not to upstage the boss. Musa ibn Nusayr, governor of Islamic North Africa, arrived in Spain more peeved at his lieutenant than thrilled at the conquest. He thrashed Tariq with his riding crop, rebuked him for overstepping his authority, and demoted him.

Musa himself was soon after summoned to Damascus, effectively
Islam's global capital as residence of the caliph. Musa is said to have
arrived with four hundred noble Spanish hostages in tow, his caravan swollen with gold, jewels, and booty. The gaudy show didn't im-
press the caliph. Europeans today may regard themselves as the epitome
of progress and sophistication, but the world looked different from
eighth-century Damascus. Europe was remote, impotent, and backward. Spain was no vital cog in a master plan to dominate Europe; it
was simply another peripheral province, and not a very attractive one,
to have fallen under dar al-Islam. Musa was deemed an overreacher and
paraded around Damascus with a noose around his neck, then side-
lined into career-ending oblivion. Musa's son Abd al-Aziz, left behind
to tend Spain, succumbed to a worse fate than either Tariq or Musa. He
took the vanquished king Roderic's widow as a wife (Roderic's daughter in other accounts), sported a crown, and required supplicants to
bow upon entering his presence. It irked his lieutenants to see Abd al-
Aziz so seduced by the trappings of Western-style kingship; they murdered him.

No fewer than twenty governors ruled al-Andalus in the subsequent
forty years, some surviving only months. The momentum of conquest
had kept Islam's warriors united in the face of their enemies. But once
momentum slowed and external threats dissipated, fissures erupted
amid the victors. Tariq's invasion force had been largely composed of
North African Berber tribesmen. Not so many years before Tariq unleashed these Berbers on Spain, they themselves had been futilely attempting to ward off Muslim invaders. Fairly recent converts to their
conquerors' faith, they were enticed to Tariq's expedition more by the
promise of booty than the dream of enlarging dar al-Islam. Though the
Berbers bore the brunt of the fighting in Iberia, the Arab elite claimed
the plum jobs, the lucrative war spoils, and the most fertile lands, con-
signing the Berbers to Spain's inhospitable highlands. It was a none too
subtle reminder that the Berbers were second-class citizens in Islam's
unspoken but undeniable ethnic hierarchy. Though Muhammad had
pronounced all Muslims equal under Islam, Arabs were proving more
equal than others.

The dry tinder of Berber resentment sometimes sparked into outright rebellion during these tumultuous early decades. And when not preoccupied with restive Berbers, Arab governors were often plagued by infighting among their own elite. Islam's unifying vision had not blunted the old tribal loyalties, especially those pitting northern against southern Arabs. Berber-Arab and Arab-Arab tension spawned revolt, civil war, and conspiracy. Syrian mercenaries invited to crush one Berber uprising found Spain so much to their liking that they stayed; after quelling the Berbers, they turned on al-Andalus's governor. In one particularly gruesome episode of this farce, one Arab faction murdered an aged ex-governor and crucified his corpse for good measure, hanging it between a pig and a dog. Islamic Spain had picked up where Visigoth Spain left off; inept Visigoth rule had been traded for equally ineffective Muslim hegemony.

Even as governors came and went in this obscure outpost of Islam's vast empire, no Christian forces mounted a serious threat to Muslim rule, and none would for centuries. By 720 Islam had subjugated most of Iberia. Christian princes clung to power across a narrow sliver of northern Spain. Occasional Muslim forays against these holdout princes were half-hearted. Who cared about the little strip in the north? There were no towns of note and few people; it was wet, cold, and mountainous, everything that was distasteful to Arabs accustomed to an arid desert climate. Even the Romans had never totally subdued the north, and it had hardly impaired their ability to rule. Muslim governors saw little reason to waste valuable time and resources on the Christian north.

The north may not have been worth much trouble to Spain's new rulers, but a far different account entered Christian lore. The ninth-century *Chronicle of Alfonso III* sings of a certain Pelayo, swordbearer and distant relative of the defeated King Roderic. Pelayo retreats to the mountainous far north rather than submit to Muslim rule. There on Mt. Auseva near Covadonga, he and a brave few comrades mount a heroic stand in 722 against a massive army of 187,000 Moors.

Shockingly, the noble Pelayo receives little succor from Spain's Christian hierarchy, who might have been expected to abet resistance.

Over and above the looming threat to their cherished Christian faith, their cushy ties to royal power were also jeopardized. Yet when one traitorous Christian bishop counsels Pelayo's guerrillas at battle's eve, he offers frank advice in lieu of encouragement: "Heed my warning and recall your soul from this decision, so that you may take advantage of many good things and enjoy the partnership of the Chaldeans [i.e., Arabs]."

Despite the bishop's lesson in realpolitik, brave Pelayo remains undeterred. A wondrous battle ensues. Although God's human representative had done little for Pelayo, God Himself now steps into the breach. Stones launched from Muslim catapults "turned back on those who shot them." Those Muslims not slain in battle were hurled from a mountain miraculously engulfed by an earthquake-like tremor. The chronicler warns his skeptical readership, "Do not think this to be unfounded or fictitious. Remember that He who parted the waters of the Red Sea so that the children of Israel might cross, also crushed, with an immense mass of mountain, the Arabs who were persecuting the church of God."

This warning notwithstanding, historians find little evidence for a battle of Covadonga. Guerrillas undoubtedly resisted Islamic rule, relying on familiarity with the harsh mountain terrain to elude and ambush Moorish pursuers. But these engagements fell short of Covadonga's mythic scale. At a minimum, the convincingly precise casualty tally of 187,000 would have been many multiples of Spain's total Muslim population at the time. The Muslim chronicler al-Makkari depicts Pelayo's Christian guerrillas as an insignificant, pitiful band of thirty starving resistance fighters, who had "no other food for support than the honey which they gathered in the crevices of the rock which they themselves inhabited, like so many bees."

However insignificant the real skirmish, it supplied an invaluable mythic kernel. Those who fought attributed no cosmic import to their resistance, but, after decades and centuries of retelling, a vital link was established: the Visigoths had been Iberia's rightful rulers, no matter that they themselves had been heretical invaders before the Moors. Pelayo was a living link to the Visigoth dynasty, which lived on as his descendants ascended to rule kingdoms in Spain's Christian north.

They not only had the right and the duty to reunite Spain under Christian rule, but Pelayo's glorious victory proved they had the innate mettle and courage to do so.

Even as the chroniclers were lauding Pelayo, another seed of the still germinating myth of Christian Spain's vigor had already begun blossoming in a remote corner of Spain's fertile north.

3. Santiago Discovered
in the Field of Stars

The opening scene of the New Testament Acts of the Apostles relates a startling occurrence. The risen Jesus gathers his disciples, and, "as they were looking on, he was lifted up, and a cloud took him out of their sight." Before ascending, Jesus imparts this final instruction: "You shall be my witnesses . . . to the end of the earth."

The apostle James, Santiago in Spanish, took the instruction literally. His purported remains are today venerated in the small Spanish town bearing his name, Santiago de Compostela. It lies a few dozen miles from the end of the earth, or so it seemed to Roman legionnaires surveying the outer limits of the province they had named Hispania. One promontory was so wild, wet, windswept, and utterly godforsaken that it struck them as *Finis Terrae* ("end of the earth" or "land's end").

The name stuck. Many centuries later, pounding Atlantic breakers still leave Cape Finisterre wild, wet, and windswept, though hardly godforsaken. What Romans once deemed a remote land's end came to exert irresistible appeal for hundreds of thousands of Europeans with the resources and courage to journey there. For that Spain can thank Santiago.

Whether James ever actually visited Spain and whether he today lies buried not so many miles from Cape Finisterre are two very separate questions, the truth behind each obscured by the misty haze that arises when history, faith, and superstition collide.

James's Spanish sojourn is only slightly more mysterious than his scant New Testament profile. We know he was one of three preeminent apostles. Peter, the rock on which Jesus resolves to build his Church, is undoubtedly the first of the twelve. Although the gospel evangelists never explicitly name James and James's brother John as next in the apostolic hierarchy, their importance is signaled by their uniquely privileged witness to the crucial turns in Jesus's life. Only James, John, and Peter behold Jesus's miraculous transfiguration, where "his face shone like the sun and his garments became white as light." From this pivotal episode Jesus then "sets his face" toward crucifixion and death in Jerusalem. The twelve celebrate a Passover Last Supper with Jesus, never fully grasping the allusions to Jesus's looming suffering and death that seem so obvious whenever latter-day Christians hear the Passion narrative tumble toward its awful conclusion. After the Last Supper, Jesus retreats to pray at Gethsamene; once again the privileged trio of Peter, James, and John accompany him, unaware that Judas's betraying kiss is but moments away.

Peter and John are sharply etched figures in the gospel accounts, but James, in stark contrast, utters not a single solo word throughout the eighty-nine chapters of the four gospels. We are told he is a son of Zebedee and brother of John, the beloved disciple. Mark's gospel nicknames the two *Boanerges*: Sons of Thunder. Although Mark never explains the nickname, Luke's gospel gives grounds to surmise: when Samaritan villagers refuse to receive Jesus, the Sons of Thunder ask whether they should "bid fire come down from heaven and consume the villagers."

How could Jesus's most intimate acquaintances conceive so supremely wrong-headed a response? Children only need a Sunday school lesson or two to catch on to Jesus's instruction to serve others and treat even one's enemies benevolently, yet his tone-deaf inner circle often serve as the supreme archetypes of human frailty and foils for Jesus's unshakable loyalty in its face. Shortly before the Last Supper, the Sons of Thunder stand by mutely (we assume approvingly) while their ambitious mother pitches them for plum roles in the heavenly hierarchy: "Command that these two sons of mine may sit, one at your right hand and one at your left, in your kingdom." Another moment to make Sunday schoolers cringe. Most poignant, the same James, John, and Peter drop off to sleep during their master's agonizing moment of need at Gethsamane, prompting him to despair, "Could you not watch with me one hour?"

The gospel James is a less than flattering portrait. Yet he and his bumbling colleagues eventually find their footing. While huddled away in fearful seclusion and indecision after Jesus's ascension, God's Holy Spirit descends upon them, appearing in "tongues as of fire." The Spirit's gifts include a dollop of courage and good judgment as well. They fan out and spread Jesus's message with zeal and authority, enjoying some success and enduring no little persecution. James is first of the twelve to die for the new faith, some time around the year 42 in Jerusalem.

Spain is mentioned just once in the entire New Testament, and not by the James who purportedly travels there but by Paul, early Christianity's inveterate road warrior. Paul's indefatigable zeal spurs a peripatetic itinerary extraordinary given the primitive exigencies of first-century travel. Starting in the Holy Land, he takes in modern-day Turkey, Greece, Cyprus, and Lebanon. He then sets his sights on more distant lands, writing to the Romans, "I hope to see you in passing as I go to Spain."

Paul fulfills his pledge to the Romans, though not quite as he had envisioned; he arrives in Rome a prisoner. Charged with sedition in Jerusalem, he exercises his rights as a Roman citizen by appealing directly to the emperor. Undeterred by house arrest in Rome, he preaches to all who visit, pious and skeptical alike. Though eventually acquitted of all charges, his life ends in martyrdom when Nero scapegoats the Christian community for a terrible fire that consumes much of the imperial capital in 64 C.E. (the very same fire during which Nero has been depicted as "fiddling," a gloss on the Latin historian Suetonius's account that the emperor sang while watching the conflagration consume his capital).

Only James of the apostolic generation apparently made it to Spain, even before Paul wrote of his ambitions to travel there. Medieval chroniclers portray the Son of Thunder evangelizing Iberia sometime in the decade between Jesus's death and James's own martyrdom, but their accounts rest on dubious foundations. No archaeological artifact provides evidence of James's visit and no contemporary account records it. Indeed, centuries pass before any written record links James to Spain. Only in the late sixth or seventh century do church chroniclers provide the first tantalizingly sparse snippet that James preached in Spain.

Even the Man Who Knew Everything seemed more convinced of dog-headed Cynocephali than James's Spanish mission: Isidore only glancingly refers to James's Spanish journey, in a minor work of debated authenticity. But by the mid-ninth century Church chroniclers' reticence yielded to full-throated promotion, and a new wrinkle embellished the plot. Usuard of Saint-Germain-des-Prés, for example, confidently reported that James not only preached in Spain, but "his most holy remains were translated from Jerusalem to Spain and deposited in its uttermost region; they are revered with the most devout veneration by the people of those parts."

Reportedly, James journeyed from the Holy Land only to meet disinterested disdain in Spain. Despairing of ever making headway in obstinately pagan Iberia, he started for home. He didn't get far; while he rested beside the Ebro River (near present-day Saragossa), the Virgin Mary miraculously appeared atop a radiant column of light. She encouraged him not to forsake Spain so readily, and as a reminder of her continuing patronage gave him a small statue of herself on a jasper wood pedestal. The reinvigorated apostle then redoubled efforts to spread the gospel in Spain. He eventually returned to Jerusalem (and impending martyrdom), but before departing entrusted Mary's precious memento to a now burgeoning community of Spanish believers. They proved worthy guardians of the precious relic. The twelfth-century basilica of Nuestra Señora del Pilar in Saragossa, nearly a football field high and twice as long, exudes a cold, cavernous emptiness except for one chapel continuously pulsing with fervent prayer, where devout Christians revere a statue of Mary in a church housing what they believe to be the jasper pedestal left to St. James by the Virgin.

All in all, whatever James said and did during his remedial circuit of Spain seems to have worked. Fully 94 percent of Spaniards proclaim themselves at least nominally Catholic, making Spain one of Europe's most Catholic countries, trailing only St. Patrick's holy Republic of Ireland and the pope's own Italy.

Of course, Spain today may be one of Europe's most Catholic countries, but much happened between the apostle James's visit and Spain's current Catholic age. Indeed, it was once Europe's *most Muslim* and *most Jewish* country.

If the line connecting James's mission to Spain's present Catholic character seems more jagged than straight, the line that connects James to Spain *at all* is even trickier to trace. Perceptive readers will have noted that James's story doesn't quite hang together. New Testament accounts assure us that the apostle was martyred in Jerusalem in 42 C.E. How is it, then, that his remains are interred in Santiago de Compostela?

We're told by medieval chroniclers that the martyred James's disciples, fearful that his persecutors might also desecrate his corpse, spirited his remains to Spain's Galician coast aboard a vessel hewn from pure marble. (Though not what marine engineers might have recommended, the construction material worthily honors the esteemed apostle.) The Galicians, already relapsed into paganism in the short time since James first preached to them, did not initially welcome the apostle's remains and harnessed wild bulls to drag his coffin back into the ocean. But the fearsome animals turned docile at sight of the casket, inducing the wayward Galicians to repent their pagan ways (and leaving readers to wonder why the suddenly gentle bulls were a more persuasive miracle to Galician eyes than a marble ship that actually floated).

Remote Galicia suddenly boasted an honor bestowed on only one other European location. The city of Rome, treasuring the remains of St. Peter the Apostle, ever reminded the world of the fact, buttressing the bishop of Rome's claim as Peter's legitimate successor. Yet the Galicians somehow forgot that James lay interred in their midst. Devotion to St. James languished; his tomb lay neglected and was eventually forgotten, for centuries, until a lowly peasant-hermit rediscovered the relic in a sequence that echoes Luke's Gospel narrative of the Nativity.

In that account, the high and mighty don't arrive first at Jesus's manger, but the marginalized and lowly. Shepherds "keeping watch over their flocks" are summoned to the stable by angels' songs on high. So, too, a humble hermit shepherd named Pelayo was awarded the honor of rediscovering Santiago's tomb. While tending his flock one night, he was drawn to a field bathed in heavenly light and found James's long-neglected tomb. The local bishop (Theodemir) authenticated the remains through some forensic process conveniently glossed over by the chroniclers. This time Galicia did not forget its saint. King Alfonso II of Asturias erected a small church on the site. Though no date was given for Pelayo's find, the chroniclers' mention of Bishop Theodemir and King Alfonso II places the discovery somewhere between 818 and 842.

Santiago's centuries-long peaceful repose ended forever as his shrine immediately became a pilgrimage attraction. Before the ninth century ended, foreign visitors began streaming there. Over ensuing centuries, Alfonso II's modest church gave way to ever grander constructions, paralleling the shrine's increasing popularity and the town's growing affluence. The town boasted no natural resources, numbered few people, and lay far removed from Europe's trade routes, yet in time became one of Europe's wealthier cities. Grateful citizens rechristened their town Santiago de Compostela in honor of the saint responsible for their new-found prosperity. Although the derivation of *Compostela* is uncertain, a poetically appealing etymology traces the name to the Latin *Campus Stellarum,* the "field of stars" where Pelayo happened upon the tomb. But there is an earthier, alternative derivation: the Latin *compositus* conveys the sense of something buried, as in the distinctly unflattering image conveyed by compost. No wonder "field of stars" is the town tourist board's preferred alternative.

Pelayo's story, improbable though it may seem, evinces a beguiling charm. James's tomb was discovered under the same irenic circumstances as Jesus's birth, associating the apostle James with the themes of peace and goodwill so central to Jesus's message. A simple hermit-peasant made the discovery, symbolically establishing the apostle, like his master Jesus, as champion and patron of society's downtrodden.

Yet this simple tale was also freighted with political symbolism. The peasant Pelayo who rediscovered the tomb bore no relation whatever to Pelayo the valiant guerrilla fighter who purportedly had slain 187,000 Moors thanks to a divinely engineered earthquake. But it didn't hurt the chroniclers' purposes that these two heroes shared a name. Santiago's illiterate pilgrims likely heard both tales more than once in the course of months-long journeys to Compostela, and the two Pelayos inevitably became one in the minds of more than a few pilgrims, thereby linking Saint James ever more closely with Christian Spain's political affairs.

The Alfonso II who built Santiago's first church was king of Asturias, a dynasty that traced its legacy to the guerrilla Pelayo. As northern Spain's small Christian principalities jockeyed for relative advantage over the ensuing decades, the kings of Asturias backed their claims to preeminence by boasting unique credentials: descendants of the Visigoth warrior Pelayo *and* protectors of Spain's holiest relic in Santiago.

As Christian Spain slowly coalesced, Asturias was successively folded into the kingdom of León and then into Castile, which was finally joined with Aragon to form the superpower state that came to dominate all Christian Spain. Asturias's mythic glow—its ties both to the Visigoths and to Santiago the apostle—rubbed off on Castile's monarchs through the ages, onto Queen Isabella of Castile, who, with King Ferdinand of Aragon, in 1492 completed the Christian Reconquest of Iberia by exterminating the last vestiges of Muslim power.

Spanish Christians who dreamed of reclaiming Iberia throughout the medieval era naturally looked to James as their patron. Yet, as the crusading Reconquest gathered momentum, the peace-loving James discovered by a simple peasant seemed ill-suited to warrior needs. The earlier story was accordingly chucked for a far more violent saga that dragged St. James to center stage of the clash between Islam and Christianity that would ravage Spain for centuries. Unfortunately for humble Pelayo, and perhaps for Spain and certainly for James's legacy, a later era not only refurbished his simple story but altered St. James's image radically. The newer, more epic Santiago myth elbowed aside the shepherd Pelayo to introduce a more heavyweight hero. The Pelayo legend seems to have taken shape during the ninth century; the new and improved account began circulating in the early 1100s, when an allegedly

long lost chronicle happened to resurface, according the honor of un-
earthing James's tomb to the brightest star in medieval Europe's royal
firmament: King Charlemagne.

Charlemagne's exploits were well documented by his contemporaries. He expanded and united the Frankish territories, reformed a
Church plagued by dissolute monastic practices, and was crowned emperor in the year 800 by Pope Leo III, grateful for Charlemange's defense of the pope and Church against potential enemies. Yet none of
Charlemagne's contemporary biographers, neither his royal confidant
Einhard nor the chronicler immortalized by the humiliating nickname
Notker the Stammerer, ever reported what would have been the most
spectacular of his successes: discovering James's tomb.

The silence of Charlemagne's contemporaries bothered few if any
Christians as the new, more epic Santiago myth began circulating. Nor
were they upset that a chronicle purportedly written by Archbishop
Turpin of Reims, an advisor to ninth-century Charlemagne, included
sloppily anachronistic references to eleventh-century persons and
events. Pseudo-Turpin's account caught on despite its blatant historical
inconsistencies.

Turpin's Charlemagne was plagued by a recurring dream in which
the Milky Way stretched before him as a dazzlingly starry highway to
the west. Though it may seem fairly obvious that the portent symbol-
ized Charlemagne's heavenly invitation to follow this starry highway,
that interpretation eluded the king. An exasperated St. James finally appeared personally to inform Charlemagne that his long-forgotten tomb
lay at the end of the starry highway. James lamented that its Galician
guardians had lapsed into paganism and lost control of their homeland
to infidel Moors. Thus, Charlemagne was anointed to liberate the
tomb and restore the capricious Galicians to Christianity.

According to the chronicle, Charlemagne responded to the apostolic
summons, marched westward with his army, liberated towns, and inaugurated the very same pilgrim route that thousands would later trace
to Santiago. After discovering the saint's tomb and presiding over Galicia's reconversion, he proceeded to plant his lance in the seashore beyond Compostela, as if to symbolize that he had conquered all the land
from France to the end of the earth.

Spain's Christian princes proved too feeble to defend what Charlemagne had so valiantly won for them. An African king named Aigolandus invaded and captured part of northern Spain, forcing a dutiful Charlemagne once again to rally to Spain's defense. After preliminary skirmishes, Charlemagne's battle with Aigolandus ground to an improbable truce while the two royals debated the respective merits of Christianity and Islam. A persuasive Charlemagne—speaking Arabic no less—secured Aigolandus's conversion.

At the ensuing banquet, Aigolandus saw Christian knights celebrating in luxurious splendor while their Christian servants languished. He recanted his conversion, scandalized that Christians could abide such blatant inequity. Charlemagne rearmed and trounced Aigolandus, whether for his apostasy, his vaguely socialist leanings, or his uncomfortably trenchant observation that Christianity's "haves" seemed to manifest a rather un-Christian complacency about the "have nots." By the chronicle's end, the pilgrimage route to Compostela was once again in Christian hands, and Charlemagne's army gratefully retired to France, for, as Turpin sniffily explained, "The Franks were unwilling to dwell in Galicia, since it seemed to them to be wild."

The Turpin chronicle was soon enshrined among Santiago de Compostela's cathedral treasures, even though the account glorified Charlemagne and France while belittling Spain as too impotent to defend itself. Homegrown hero Pelayo's credit for uncovering Santiago's tomb was snatched away, bestowed instead on the French interloper Charlemagne. But the Turpin chronicle gave Compostela's canons good reason to overlook these indignities: it instructed the world's Christians to pay an annual tithe to Compostela's cathedral and further suggested that the resting places of the three great apostles—St. James's Compostela, St. Peter's Rome, and St. John's Ephesus—should be hailed as the preeminent bishoprics in Christendom.

Compostela thrived but never attained such lofty status. As it turned out, the prescription for elevating Compostela's status was not even penned by the French chauvinist and impostor who had composed the rest of the chronicle under Archbishop Turpin's name, but by a wily Compostela cleric who slipped the promotional material into an edition of the chronicle (in other words, by someone pretending to be the chronicler who was pretending to be Turpin). The resulting Turpin chronicle, though a near total fabrication, served Compostela's canons, the French, and Christendom's nascent Crusader movement—something for everyone except poor Pelayo and the apostle James's peaceful pilgrim legacy.

This much is true: Charlemagne's armies entered Spain, but the circumstances were very different from pseudo-Turpin's reports. No reliable source attests to the existence of this mighty African king Aigolandus. Even if Aigolandus had existed, Charlemagne could hardly have debated him in Arabic. Scholars believe that Charlemagne could read Latin, but his writing skills ranged little beyond scratching out his name in a barely legible scrawl. His court biographer, Einhard, notes that this greatest of medieval Christendom's monarchs kept "writing-tablets . . . under the pillows on his bed, so that he could try his hand at forming letters." The Turpin chronicle also claims that Charlemagne conquered England, news that would surprise British historians. Finally, whether or not a slumbering Charlemagne ever dreamed about the Milky Way, he never journeyed to Compostela. Spain's Christian princes, unaided by Charlemagne, liberated and defended any stretches of the northern pilgrimage route that temporarily fell under Moorish dominance.

But in another sense, the chronicle's essence is as true as its supposed facts are false. The two stories of Santiago are windows into two very different moments in Spain's history and the apostle's cult. Humble Pelayo suited a shrine frequented by individual penitents, sightseers, and pilgrims presenting their private hopes and needs to St. James. But by the 1100s, Compostela was mushrooming into far more than a personal pilgrimage destination, and the very act of pilgrimage itself was changing—to something more akin to war. Santiago was becoming embroiled in a mounting struggle between Christian and Muslim Europe. Pelayo's ninth-century story no longer fit this twelfth-century world.

Others besides Iberia's Christians understood and respected Santiago's grip on medieval Christians. Not long before pseudo-Turpin's work was being circulated in Spain, the Muslim historian Ibn Hayyan (d. 1076) offered a non-Christian's dispassionate assessment of the

shrine and its extraordinary appeal: "Santiago is . . . one of the sanctuaries most frequented not only by the Christians of Andalus, but by the
inhabitants of the neighboring continent, who regard its church with
veneration equal to that which the Muslims entertain for the Kaba at
Mecca . . . pretending that the tomb . . . is that of Yakob [James] of the
twelve apostles."

Santiago's popularity was spread first by word of mouth as each passing year's pilgrim bands set off and returned, and only later by clerics
and chroniclers anxious to bend Santiago's image to their own ends
through elaborate myths. Before the route attained its prominence, visitors to Spain's remote, underpopulated north were far fewer and their
purposes far different from those of later pilgrim generations. One of
those early visitors to the north, a cleric from Córdoba named Eulogius, was received as a guest in a monastery near Pamplona at the
route's eastern anchor near the French border. Given the uncertain dating of the rediscovery of Santiago's tomb, it's unclear whether Eulogius
would have learned of the cult that may have already been developing a
few hundred miles to the west. In any case, he never journeyed to Santiago, returning instead to his native Córdoba, a city that had become
Spain's, and Europe's, most sophisticated, advanced capital.

But Córdoba's prosperity and prominence didn't delight Eulogius; it
worried him.

4. Martyr-Activists

Determined to Die in a City "Piled Full of Riches"

Eulogius reached the Monastery of Leyre, not far from Pamplona, sometime around the year 850. An accidental tourist, he had intended to make his way over the Pyrenees and all the way to Germany, where two of his brothers were being detained for reasons he never fully explains. When political unrest and banditry closed the border passes, the stranded cleric instead visited the region's monastic libraries to acquire texts unavailable in his native Córdoba. The Christian classics, already rare in the 600s, when Isidore and Braulio battled Spain's slide into boorish rusticity, had become rarer still since the Moorish takeover. Eulogius's shopping foray proved productive. His acquisitions included the *City of God*, St. Augustine's classic meditation articulating a vision of human history unspooling inexorably forward toward its happy, peaceful, just climax when society would be governed by God's law and awaiting the Messiah's second coming.

But Eulogius was more deeply impressed by a work unrelated to Christianity, a skimpy, four-page biography of the prophet Muhammad. Eulogius's native Córdoba, teeming with Muslims and Muslim scholars, already figured among the Islamic world's most sophisticated cities. It may seem illogical that Eulogius chose to learn about Muhammad in a Christian monastery in Spain's far north. But Eulogius was neither the first nor certainly the last to learn about "the other kind" from familiar if uninformed sources.

The *Istoria of Mahomet*'s author is unknown. His handiwork demonstrates some knowledge of the prophet's life but betrays a distinctly unsympathetic viewpoint. There are just enough similarities to identify the *Istoria*'s Muhammad as Islam's founder: he is orphaned young; he enters the caravan trade; he marries a widow; he receives revelations, though this account attributes them to "the spirit of error" assuming "the form of a vulture" while pretending to be the archangel Gabriel.

Muhammad is swayed by this satanic perversion and induces countless others to follow. The short biography culminates with an artful parallel to the gospel Jesus, a twist that no Muslim would find in Islam's sacred texts but that every Christian would immediately recognize. Muhammad predicts his own resurrection on the third day following his death. But as his increasingly edgy disciples later stand vigil by his corpse, nothing happens. Worse yet, "dogs followed his stench [i.e. of his rotting corpse] and devoured his flank." The anonymous biographer closes with a moralizing taunt: "It was appropriate that a prophet of this kind fill the stomachs of dogs, a prophet who committed not only his own soul, but those of many, to hell."

It's unlikely Eulogius scanned this account with a critical eye. His upbringing disposed him to believe only the worst about Islam. He recounts childhood recollections of hearing the muezzin summoning Muslims to prayer; Eulogius's grandfather would cup the child's ears with his hands, murmuring a psalm to drown out the muezzin's five-times-daily cry that "God is most great . . . I witness that there is no god but God . . . Come to prayer."

Eulogius returned to Córdoba armed with potent rhetorical ammunition but lacking any clear strategy for using it. With one bold act, a Córdoban Christian named Isaac was to hand Eulogius the opportunity that framed his subsequent life mission.

Isaac had risen within Córdoban society to a prominence that few Christians could rival. He was noble-born, well-educated, and fluent in Arabic. He eventually attained the prestigious rank of *katib adh-dhimma* (secretary of the covenant). Though the role's full duties are unknown, its broad outlines are clear. Iberia's Muslim rulers honored the Quranic mandate counseling tolerance for ahl al-Kitab ("People of the Book"). Christians and Jews enjoyed limited self-government and freedom of worship. As secretary of the covenant, Isaac mediated between the majority Christian community and the minority Muslim authorities, ironing out frictions, negotiating on the Christian community's behalf, interpreting and disseminating regulations, and perhaps overseeing tax collections.

Isaac abruptly resigned this prestigious post for reasons unknown. Immediately thereafter, he joined Christian men and women devoted to an austere regimen of prayer and meditation at the Christian monastery of Tabanos in the hill country a few miles outside Córdoba. While there he conceived an unusual plan that was to affect Córdoba's Christians far more profoundly than any initiative he had taken as secretary of the covenant. Whether he discussed his plan with his monastic community is unknown, though it seems probable in the light of subsequent events.

About three years after his transition to monasticism, Isaac returned to central Córdoba one day in late spring 851. He approached a leading *qadi* (judge), with whom he may have dealt in his earlier civic role. Isaac initiated a discussion of Islam, and then deliberately blasphemed the prophet Muhammad.

Isaac of all Christians understood the implications of his act. He had chosen his setting carefully. By confronting the qadi before the emir's palace, he compounded blasphemy with an affront to Islam's civil authority. The qadi was the public face of Islamic law and in this case a personal witness to sacrilege; his response would be an important signal to all Córdoba concerning one of Islam's most sacred laws. He offered Isaac the chance to excuse his actions by admitting drunkenness or temporary insanity. Isaac assured the judge of his sober state and sober purpose, quite intentionally leaving the qadi little latitude for his ruling.

Blasphemy against the prophet was a capital offense; Isaac was decapitated. His lifeless corpse was left hanging upside down across the Guadalquivir River from central Córdoba to be picked over by scavengers, an unmistakable warning to other would-be blasphemers.

Those scavenged remains may have still been fouling the Córdoba breeze when, two days later, a Christian veteran soldier of the emir's service, one Sanctius, duplicated Isaac's offense and suffered the same fate. Within the next forty-eight hours six more Christians jointly presented themselves to authorities, professing resolve to follow the path of Isaac and Sanctius: "Now hand down the sentence, multiply your cruelty, be kindled with complete fury in vengeance for your prophet. We profess Christ to be truly God and your prophet to be a precursor of antichrist."

Three more martyrdoms followed within the next few weeks. Then, after three months of false calm, the first women offered themselves up. Maria and Flora were both products of mixed Muslim-Christian marriages. Maria's Muslim mother had converted to her husband's Christian faith, and Flora had been raised a devout Christian after her Muslim father's death.

Córdoba's emir and his counselors recognized their grave dilemma long before being driven to the gruesome spectacle of butchering two young women of Muslim heritage. Isaac's act had no doubt struck them as a disquieting but isolated incident perpetrated by a deranged Christian. But the rapidly mounting toll of martyr-activists made clear that the problem would not simply go away. More worrisome for the authorities: the capital punishment they meted out for blasphemy had not deterred the Christian radicals. Indeed, quite the opposite: the activists deliberately seized upon the blasphemy laws to win prominence for their cause. Many centuries before Gandhi marched to the ocean or King to Montgomery, Isaac perceived the power of using the laws of the state to attack the state. But here was civil disobedience of the most vital consequence, akin less to the civil rights campaigner destined for jail than the South Vietnamese monk's sacrificial self-immolation on a Saigon street.

The months dragged on. The pace of martyrdoms slackened but never completely abated. The authorities early on had rounded up and jailed leading clerics and known agitators, with predictable effect. Imprisonment only hardened their resolve; Maria and Flora had concluded their martyr-activist pact while incarcerated.

Córdoba's governors cast about for other measures. The emir contemplated "killing all Christian men and dispersing their women by selling them into slavery." Cooler heads counseled that such precipitate barbarity could only provoke the emir's greatest fear—and exactly what the activists may have longed for: a mass uprising that would transform a fanatic fringe movement into full-blown rebellion by Spain's Christian majority against the Muslim minority that ruled them.

If Spain's governors were among history's first to be tested by determined civil disobedience, they nonetheless handled it more savvily than so many ham-fisted twentieth-century rulers whose thuggish tactics precipitated their own demise. The emir, persuaded against wholesale massacre, chose to pressure the broader Christian community with less drastic, yet deeply painful measures: Christians were dismissed from the civil service; Christian soldiers were deprived of pensions; heavier taxes were levied; churches were slated for demolition. And the protest movement petered out, or so we assume because the reports of activist-martyrdoms tailed off sharply. Approximately fifty Christians sacrificed themselves in the decade following Isaac's bold initiative. Their names and the movement's history survive primarily through the accounts of one man, Eulogius.

Eulogius himself was arrested in 859, charged with harboring an apostate from Islam, and sentenced to a flogging. But after witnessing so many martyrdoms, Eulogius may have sensed his own moment for bravery had arrived—or he may have contemplated the shameful prospect of rejoining Christian society chastened but alive after others had embraced a more drastic fate. So Eulogius, too, denounced Islam. How Córdoba's Muslim authorities perceived the whole martyr movement may be reflected in one court official's response to Eulogius's tirade: "If stupid and idiotic individuals have been carried away to such lamentable ruin, what is it that compels you . . . to commit yourself to this deadly ruin, suppressing the natural love of life? Hear me, I beseech you, I beg you, lest you fall headlong to destruction. Say something in this the hour of your need, so that afterward you may be able to practice your faith."

Eulogius stood fast, and he, too, was decapitated. But with his death the movement lost impetus, or at a minimum lost the leader who chronicled it for posterity. Subsequent records reference the occasional capital punishment for isolated acts of blasphemy, but nothing on the Córdoba movement's robust scale.

The martyr-activists were acclaimed saints in a decidedly less ecumenical age than our own, when anti-Muslim heroes were welcomed by a Church that saw itself struggling against the infidel. Yet they stand uneasily alongside many others Catholicism has recognized as martyrs. True, many Christian martyrs in some sense provoked their death by unwavering public commitment to their faith in hostile environments; early Rome's Christians well understood that brazen persistence in Christian worship could cost their lives. Yet most martyrs have been victims of active persecution: religious enmity and intolerance pursued *them,* not the other way around.

What's more, many strained their wits to prolong their earthly Christian lives; Jesuit infiltrators to Protestant England inspired the word "jesuitical" by surreptitiously roaming the countryside in deep disguise, constructing ingenious hiding places on the properties of sympathetic crypto-Catholics. Once captured, they did their best to outfox their accusers with carefully nuanced testimony at show trials. Only after exhausting every avenue for escape did these martyrs resolutely refuse their last available escape route: abjuring the religious beliefs that endowed their lives with meaning. In Córdoba, almost alone in Córdoba, did martyr-activists deliberately seek out their own deaths by goading so-called persecutors who had tolerated Christian practice and lashed out only when their own Islamic beliefs were vilified.

However awkwardly the Córdoba movement may fit the Christian tradition of martyrdom, more basic questions arise concerning these activists. Simply put, what did they want? What drove them to the most extreme form of protest imaginable? And why didn't their brutal execution arouse widespread public outrage and support among Córdoba's Christians?

Notwithstanding the Quranic mandate to offer tolerance to People of the Book, Córdoba represented a repressive environment for religious Christians (and Jews, for that matter). Laws prohibited the construction of new churches and repairs to existing ones. Religious processions were proscribed, as was the tolling of church bells. Christians and Jews were second-class citizens subject to a special poll tax (the *jizya*). These Christians were descended from Spain's former masters; now they were merely tolerated in their homeland. What's more, they suffered the added indignity of diminished social status: they were reduced to equal footing with the lowly Jews, whom Visigoth kings had once persecuted.

But *living* Córdoba differed from the Córdoba of law codes. If construction of new churches was legally impossible, for example, where had Isaac's Tabanos monastery come from? Eulogius's writings refer to some dozen churches constructed in and around Córdoba in the decades following the Muslim takeover of Spain and razed only during the postmartyrdom crackdown. Legal proscriptions notwithstanding, church bells pealed regularly, judging by Eulogius's complaint that Christians were harassed for making a (holy) racket during worship: "For when the psalmody schedule dictates that we give the signal to the faithful . . . these liars [i.e., Muslims living near the church] . . . listen intently to the clang of the reverberating metal and begin to exercise their tongues in every curse and obscenity."

The martyr-activists' own occupations attest to the opportunities available to Christians under Muslim rule. Isaac entered a monastery after a successful career culminating in a senior government appointment. A martyr named Argimirus had served as a judge in the Christian community. Even Eulogius's own brother served in Córdoba's court until the postmartyrdom crackdown cost him his job. Sanctius was a soldier, one of many Christians to attain prominence in the military. (That the emir so readily bestowed advancement opportunities on Christian soldiers was more a testament to the shaky allegiance of his fellow Muslims: never knowing when Arab factionalism would erupt into open rebellion, some emirs felt more secure surrounded by Christian soldiers than by their own coreligionists.)

Though the martyrs never articulated demands, they presumably longed for respect, greater freedom of worship, enhanced civil rights, and, fundamentally, if unrealistically, for Muslims to depart the Peninsula, enabling Spain to reestablish her Christian identity. Yet the martyrs' dramatic gestures may have been intended as much to shake their coreligionists as Córdoba's Muslim rulers. Eulogius saw his community slipping away from its Christian identity and practices. He may have hoped that the movement would spark renewed Christian zeal.

But the results only confirmed his greatest fears. The limited but real tolerance enjoyed by Christians benefiting from Córdoba's prosperity may explain why the movement never roused wider public support. Simply put, Eulogius's Christian coreligionists liked things as they were. Isaac, Argimirus, and Sanctius were not the only Christians prospering in Muslim Córdoba. And those who were doing well hardly wanted their prospects threatened by the fanatic Christian fringe.

Nor was rejection of the martyr movement limited to secular Christian opportunists. It deeply discouraged Eulogius and fellow activists to learn that their own Bishop Reccafredus had fingered Christian troublemakers and urged the emir to lock them away. As Eulogius's biographer put it, "Bishop Reccafredus fell upon churches and clergy like a violent whirlwind and threw as many priests as he could into jail." When released from prison, Eulogius threatened to stop celebrating mass, the most potent symbolic protest he could conceive against his weak-kneed bishop's complicity with the Muslim oppressors. After Church leaders gathered to discuss the martyr crisis gripping Córdoba, Eulogius angrily recounted that the council president "Bishop Reccafredus moved his tongue against me, heaping insults upon me."

What had Eulogius done? At a minimum, he had publicly identified himself with a cause that Córdoba's Church leaders wished would go away. He had not only chronicled the movement, but in at least one case had counseled and encouraged a would-be activist. He recalled the lash marks borne by Flora as punishment for apostasy from Islam: "I saw the skin of your venerable neck, torn and cut by the lashes of the whip at the time of your persecution . . . And touching it gently with my hand—because I did not think I ought to caress the wound with kisses—I departed from you and for a long time I sighed thinking about it." As Flora contemplated martyrdom, Eulogius steeled her against backing out when faced with imminent, grisly death: "The news of your struggle, passing through nations and peoples, will begin to be known to many."

Flora's death did indeed become known to many, many more over the ensuing centuries than she could have imagined. But it never inspired similar resolve among her Christian contemporaries. Their indifference to her self-sacrifice only confirmed Eulogius's fear that Córdoba's Christians were slipping away—in their culture, in their interests, in their religious devotion, indeed, in their very embrace of Christianity.

Mixed marriages proliferated; Flora and Maria were two of at least a dozen of the martyrs born into mixed-faith households. Christians were embracing Islam in increasing numbers, whether for convenience, in a cynical attempt to bolster career prospects, or moved by genuine faith. Islam's North African and Arab invaders had once constituted an infinitesimal minority of the country they ruled, twenty or thirty thousand Muslims in an ocean of 5 million or more Christians. But the lopsided demographics were rapidly tilting in the other direction. North African Muslims were steadily immigrating to Spain, but far more distressing to Eulogius would have been the steady stream of Spaniards deserting Christianity for Islam. By 800 as many as 10 percent of Andalusians professed Islam, a proportion that more or less doubled over the next two generations. The trend was unmistakable: within another century a majority of Andalusians would be Muslim. By the turn of the millennium the land St. James Christianized was at least 80 percent Muslim.

As if the trend of conversions wasn't sufficiently depressing, Eulogius had other reasons to worry. He surveyed a Córdoba transformed by Islamic rule, "elevated with honors, expanded in glory, piled full of riches, and with great energy filled with an abundance of all the delights of the world, more than one can believe or express." Recall that this assessment was authored by the emir's bitterest enemy, not his public relations staff.

No surprise that this flourishing Islamic society captivated even those unprepared to forsake Christianity. Christians adopted Arabic dress and spoke Arabic. Some had themselves circumcised to accommodate to the new culture. Eulogius's biographer Paulus Alvarus fretted over a younger generation turning away from its traditions, enthralled by the dominant new culture. Alvarus's ninth-century lament previews the similar complaint voiced today in traditional Islamic societies that find their values trampled by media-hyped Western entertainment and culture: "Do not all the Christian youths," wrote Alvarus, "handsome in appearance, fluent of tongue, conspicuous in their dress and action . . . highly regarded for their ability to speak Arabic, do they not all eagerly use the volumes of the Chaldeans [i.e., the Muslims], read them with the greatest interest, discuss them ardently, and collecting them with great trouble, make them known with every praise of their tongue, the while they are ignorant of the beauty of the Church and look with disgust upon the Church's rivers of paradise as something vile."

Córdoba had achieved such prosperity thanks to a fortuitous infusion of royal blood from the Umayyad clan that had long occupied the most prestigious, powerful seat in Islam, its global caliphate. The Arabian Peninsula's Umayyads had wrested control of the caliphate soon after Muhammad's death and maintained unbroken power for nearly a century, ruling first from Mecca and later from Damascus. In 750, the Umayyads were violently supplanted by rival Abbasids, whose first caliph was nicknamed al-Saffah ("the shedder of blood") after his preferred strategy for seizing power and (permanently) removing Umayyad rivals.

One Umayyad prince, Abd al-Rahman, escaped the Abbasid bloodletting, fleeing across the Near East and North Africa before reaching al-Andalus. Once there, he easily sparked an uprising against Muslim Spain's ruling emir. Al-Andalus had endured a forty-year free-for-all among feuding tribal and ethnic factions since the Muslim invasion of 711. Stirring up discontent was simple; picking one's coconspirators was the only challenge, and Abd al-Rahman wisely chose to ally himself with an Arab faction one chronicler described as "a set of men in whose breasts raged the most violent passions."

Abd al-Rahman seized power within a year and reigned for over thirty (756–788). He displayed a lesson or two learned from the Shedder of Blood. After discovering that Abbasid spies had infiltrated his domain, Abd al-Rahman had them beheaded and their severed heads delivered to the Abbasid caliph. The pungent, gruesome gift evoked mixed horror and relief from the caliph: "God be praised for placing a sea between us." The gift served its purpose, inducing the Damascus potentate to adopt a noninterventionist policy toward Spain.

The chroniclers portray Abd al-Rahman as an imposing figure, "always dressed in white" and crowned with a white turban: "His countenance inspired with awe all those who approached him." Awe-inspiring, but not perfect: the chroniclers add the odd details that Abd al-Rahman "could only see out of one eye, and was destitute of the sense of smelling." While Abd al-Rahman's brutality secured his reign, his clear-sighted governance transformed al-Andalus into the marvel that so threatened Eulogius and so charmed his fellow Christians. His reign marked the critical turn in Muslim Iberia's fortunes. Erratic rule yielded to the Umayyads' steadying dynastic hand. In contrast to Muslim Spain's earlier chronic instability, the first four Umayyads ruled for a combined eighty years.

The transplanted Umayyads wasted neither love nor respect on the Near Eastern Abbasids who had usurped their caliphal throne. Spain had long languished as a neglected province at Islam's periphery, beholden to caliphs who spared little time or energy tending to Spain's needs. Now the Umayyads effectively carved Spain away from the caliph's sway. Though Spain's religious leaders continued to profess nominal respect for the caliph who was theoretically Islam's worldwide leader, Spain proceeded to choose her own rulers and largely ignored the caliph's whims. Indeed, within a few more generations, Muslim Spain's leader stopped referring to himself as emir, the title meaning "prince" or "commander" that was customarily applied to provincial governors throughout the Islamic world. Instead, he took to proclaiming himself caliph, a title heretofore reserved to Muhammad's recognized successor, the global leader of Islam's faithful. Muslim Spain's first self-proclaimed caliph, Abd al-Rahman III, was not signaling intent to supplant the caliph then ruling from Baghdad; he was, however, declaring his claim to rule Spain independent of even the pretense of obeisance to foreign rule.

Spain's Umayyads wrested for al-Andalus the independence to navigate its own future, yet maintained its cultural and commercial links with the Islamic world. Arabic remained the language of governance, prayer, and commerce, which facilitated interaction with the wider Islamic world and allowed access to its scholarly advances. Devout Spanish Muslims made pilgrimage to Mecca like Muslims the world over. These journeys inevitably exposed them to new learning, fresh ideas, and business opportunities. Córdoba was not shy about importing the best of those ideas, including Islam's version of high culture. For instance, the one-time slave and accomplished musician Ziryab is said by the chronicler al-Makkari to have created such a stir at the Baghdad caliph's court that jealous rivals threatened his death to force his exile—Spain's gain. Ziryab reached Córdoba in about 822, roughly a generation before the dour Eulogius's fateful trip to Pamplona. While northern Spain's Christians plodded along in their relatively drab lifestyle, talented Córdobans flocked to Ziryab's music conservatory, the first of its kind in Spain. They studied song, dance, and poetry, sometimes accompanied by Ziryab plucking his lute with a plectrum fashioned from an eagle's talon, his talented hand caressed by "the soft down which covers the claw of that bird."

Ziryab had not only created the "Córdoba sound," but also dictated Córdoba style. Pre-Ziryab Córdobans dressed their hair in stylish bangs: "Both men and women, wear the hair over the upper part of the forehead, and hanging down between the temples and the eye." The look didn't survive Ziryab's spell. After noting that Ziryab and his family "all wore their hair parted in the middle, and not covering the forehead, the extremities being placed behind the ears and falling over the temples . . . [Córdobans] all relinquished the old fashion, and adopted that which he had introduced." In other words, bangs were out; the swept-back look was in.

Hairstyles and music were but two examples of wide-ranging genius that spanned cuisine to hygiene. Ziryab taught Spaniards the culinary delight of gathering wild *asfaraj* (asparagus). He discovered a lead extract that "[took] away the fetid smell of the arm-pits" and introduced a primitive bleach to the Spanish market, mixing salts, water, and garden flowers, "through which the linen was made clear and white." Many assume that seasonal couture was a conceit first pushed on mon-eyed society by greedy fashion designers with their media and advertiser sidekicks. Not so. The chronicler al-Makkari informs us that "change of clothing according to the different seasons of the year was another of the improvements introduced by Ziryab." Meanwhile, a Muslim commentator many generations later observed that across Spain's Christian north, "[the Christians] do not wash their clothes once they have put them on until they fall to pieces on them . . . Their clothes are very tight-fitting and have wide openings, through which most of their bodies show."

Much of Muslim Spain was semiarid, and water meant far more than the chance to bathe before applying Ziryab's deodorant concoction. Andalusian farmers couldn't coax rainfall from parsimonious skies, but they learned to hoard and exploit the few drops that fell. Land ill-suited for Europe's water-guzzling staple of wheat began to blossom with more abstemious produce that added color and taste to Europe's bland palette: oranges, lemons, spinach, and watermelon were just some of the crops introduced from the Islamic East. Thanks to Arab ingenuity at coaxing life into bloom from scarce desert resources, Muslim Spain eventually engineered Europe's most sophisticated technologies for tapping, channeling, and distributing water. Elaborate *norias* (water wheels) lifted water from wells, reservoirs, and rivers; clay pots dipped, rose, and spilled in endless succession, powered by draft animals or the force of flowing streams. Extensive canal systems expanded the acreage under cultivation and lengthened the growing season. Water rights were judiciously managed, often by ingenious clepsydras (water clocks) rigged to switch sluice gates open and shut, automatically redirecting water flow from one farmer's canals to another's.

Spanish agricultural and water terminology is studded with Arabisms, testament to Moorish Spain's pioneering introductions: *acequias* (irrigation canals), *azudes* (sluices or floodgates), and *acenas* (water mills). These engineering marvels still awed Christians centuries after their construction. In 1240, King Jaime I of Aragon wrote of cresting a rise to a promontory overlooking Muslim Játiva: "And [we] beheld the most beautiful area of irrigated farmland which we had ever seen anywhere . . . Our hearts filled with pleasure and satisfaction at the sight; and it seemed to us that we should come to Játiva with our army . . . in order to take the castle for Christendom."

Lengthening the growing season and extending acreage under cultivation were vital for medieval societies struggling to lift themselves beyond subsistence. Each agricultural innovation shifted the margin between life and death. Land cultivated more intensively supported larger populations; surplus production freed laborers from farming to specialize in craft works; surplus produce and manufactured crafts became the engine of foreign trade.

Just as al-Andalus looked east for technological inspiration, so too Andalusian traders looked across the Mediterranean to the wealthier lands of their coreligionists. For long stretches of the Middle Ages the Mediterranean effectively became a "Muslim lake," with Muslims ruling not only North Africa and the Near East but island way stations like Sicily and Crete. The medieval commentator Ibn Khaldun boasted that by the tenth century, "not a single Christian board floated on [the Mediterranean]." No wonder Córdoba's Christians were drawn to all things Islamic, and no wonder Eulogius worried.

Trade not only enriched Muslim Spain but introduced design ideas and crafts that transformed domestic life. Medieval Andalusians conceived stylistic touches that still grace houses throughout southern Spain, obvious in the many Arabic loan words that spice the Spanish-language vocabulary for architecture and the decorative arts. One need only recount the vocabulary to conjure images of the elegant advances these medieval architects and designers brought to domestic life: *azulejo* (ornamental tile), *alcoba* (bedroom), *alfombra* (carpet), *alféizar* (window sill), *baldosa* (flooring tile), and *azotea* (roof terrace).

Though Ziryab's Córboda was still a good century or more from the city's cultural apex, the trend was clear to the outside world. When ambassadors of the Byzantine Empire arrived from Constantinople in the 830s, they did not come to succor their beleaguered fellow Christians suffering the indignity of infidel Muslim rule. They came to honor Córdoba's emir and to pitch a Muslim-Christian military alliance against the Abbasid caliph. The Córdobans refused, ostensibly because Muslim loyalty extended even to the Abbasids, who had deposed their ancestors, but more likely after a hard-headed calculus that it wasn't worth jeopardizing al-Andalus's bright future for so risky a venture with uncertain prospects.

One can imagine the impression Córdoba made on the Byzantine ambassadors and others from the fragments of medieval Muslim commentaries that the seventeenth-century chronicler al-Makkari pieced into a mosaic depicting the Andalusian capital. Hyperbole abounds in his account, as does pained nostalgia for Islamic Spain's lost halcyon age; yet whatever liberties these chroniclers took with details, Córdoba's luxury and sophistication undoubtedly surpassed anything found elsewhere in Europe. Al-Makkari tells of pleasure gardens adorned with "all kinds of rare and exotic plants and fine trees from every country," irrigated by water channeled through an elaborate network of aqueducts and canals before spilling into "basins of different shapes, made of the purest gold, the finest silver." Centerpiece of the palace waterworks was an "astonishing water jet that raised the water to a considerable height."

More astonishing than this fountain powered by water pressure was a tenth-century caliph's aspirations toward even greater opulence. Abd al-Rahman III erected a yet more elaborate palace complex on Córdoba's outskirts, Madinat al-Zahra. Visitors to his reception hall were treated to some razzle-dazzle: a servant surreptitiously jostled a basin of mercury, igniting a dizzying dance of reflected sunlight all around the chamber's "pure gold and silver" ceiling tiles "sufficient to deprive the beholders of sight," like "flashes of lightning" that left visitors "trembl[ing], thinking the room was moving away."

The German ambassador John of Gorze was dazzled even before entering the hall of the caliphs. His biographer depicts John padding through the court's outer precincts, which were "carpeted with most costly rugs and coverings." The caliph's soldiers lined both sides of the road, "with spears held erect, beside them others brandishing javelin and staging demonstrations of aiming them at each other." The caliph's inner chamber brought the final touch of impeccable regal staging, as the appropriately awed John of Gorze found the caliph seated absolutely alone, "almost like a godhead accessible to none or to very few . . . reclined upon a most richly ornate couch."

Eulogius and fellow martyr-activists had been alarmed by Andalusia's cresting prosperity and distressed to see their fellow Christians' growing fascination with Islamic civilization. What they observed must have seemed portents of Christianity's utter demise: conversions to Islam were surging; Christians readily adopted Arabic culture and ways; Córdoba's bishops cozied up to al-Andalus's emirs; and Andalusian Christians eagerly served in the Muslim-run government and army.

How deeply would it have distressed Eulogius to know that even a future pope shared the widespread enthusiasm for the fruits of Islamic civilization?

5. The Pope Who Learned Math from Muslim Spain

Those who lived through the end of the Common Era's first millennium can be forgiven for anticipating it with fear verging on outright dread. Indeed, 999's crackpots were probably those who thought the world would *continue*. Farmers lay down their hoes and clambered to hilltops: what need to harvest food for a spring that would never arrive? Better to perch on high ground, prominently visible to the Redeemer who would descend from heaven to judge the living and the dead. Christians crammed the old basilica of St. Peter in Rome on New Year's Eve for what some presumed would be the final mass celebrated in human history. As Christians prepared to meet their maker, an added worry vexed a few: that Pope Sylvester II, who was shepherding humanity toward its imminent encounter with the Redeemer, might in fact be a black magician who had learned a bag of diabolic tricks in Spain.

Though the world didn't end on December 31, 999, Romans remained uncomfortable with Pope Sylvester. He was hounded from the Eternal City about a year later to end his papacy as an exile. Ultimately, however, his reputation for wizardry had not prompted Romans to expel him, but an even more odious offense: he was French.

The mental tricks that convinced Pope Sylvester's mystified contemporaries of his diabolical nature are by now so thoroughly *de*mystified that even thirteen-year-olds duplicate them effortlessly. His black art is today taught in every mathematics classroom in every corner of the world, but in the pope's own Europe such magical skills could be acquired only in Muslim Spain. The future pope's sojourn there changed his life and almost changed the world.

The scanty historical record suggests that Christendom's first French pope, Gerbert of Aurillac, later known as Pope Sylvester, was a genius of humble origins. Count Borrell of Barcelona encountered the prodigy at the Benedictine monastery at Aurillac and, astounded by his intellect, took him to Spain for further studies. Gerbert took up residence at a monastery tucked in the Spanish Pyrenees, straddling the fault line between Islamic and Christian Spain. Its scholars undoubtedly recognized the intellectual superiority of neighboring al-Andalus and did their best to gather its riches, turning their library into one of Christendom's finer centers of learning.

Gerbert's Spanish sojourn was well-timed. Spain's Escorial palace to this day preserves a rare manuscript known as the *Codex Vigilanus*. Dated 976, less than a decade after Gerbert's stay in Spain, the *Codex* provides the first documentation of an extraordinary technology then filtering from Islam to Christendom through Spain. The monk Vigila (hence Codex *Vigilanus*) notes in his manuscript that the Indian race "have a most subtle talent" when it comes to arithmetic and other mathematical arts, "and this is clear in the 9 figures with which they are able to designate each and every degree of each order of numbers." There follows a series of symbols hitherto all but unknown in European Christendom: 9, 8, 7 . . . Not, mind you, IX, VIII, VII . . .

The number system that found its way to Vigila's northern Spanish monastery in Albelda by 976 had found its way into Gerbert's hands at least a decade earlier. The intellectually agile Gerbert immediately grasped its advantages, which would elude his hidebound fellow Europeans for centuries. Roman numerals may look great on tombstones, but try using them for long division. What we today call the Hindu-Arabic numerals are not only a superior calculation tool but space-efficient. If three centuries from now our descendants are still pummel-ing each other up and down football fields, have no doubt that televi-sion producers will by then have tired of squeezing ungainly legends like "Super Bowl CCCXXXIV" onto TV screens. "Super Bowl 334" is vastly more economical, even if it suggests more pedestrian athletic combat than the epic struggle conveyed by Roman numbers.

There are other advantages. Each symbol in the cluster 334 an-nounces its value by its *position*. The digit 4 anchoring 334 *always* signi-fies 4 ones, just as its neighbor always signifies the number of tens. In contrast, the second digit in a Roman numeral could represent ones, tens, hundreds, or even thousands. Even the ancient Romans must have paused momentarily to decipher a numeral series like CCCXXXIV, whereas today's Roman youngsters lose not a moment unraveling 334.

Gerbert apparently unearthed other intellectual treasures in Spain. He was not only a mathematician, philosopher, and theologian, but, according to legend, an ingenious tinkerer: he's been credited with in-venting the pendulum clock and a pipe organ powered by water pres-sure. His outstanding intellect won notice from powerful supporters who paved his path to the papacy. He was retained as tutor for the prince who later became the Roman Emperor Otto II, and later tu-tored Otto's son, the future Otto III. When Otto III came into his im-perial own, he played an instrumental role in the machinations that installed his one-time mentor Gerbert upon the papal throne.

Still, even as pope, Gerbert could not impose Hindu-Arabic numer-als on his skeptical Christian flock. Europeans were stubbornly wedded to their primitive ways of doing things, and his modest attempts to dis-seminate the number system floundered. It was precisely Europeans' blindness to the obvious advantages of Hindu-Arabic numerals that led some to regard the pope as a black magician. Awestruck contempo-raries marveled as Gerbert performed impossibly complex (to the me-dieval mind) mathematical calculations in his head.

It's unknown what mental calculations so stunned and frightened Pope Sylvester's contemporaries. In backward tenth-century Europe, it may have been addition and subtraction of large sums, not even the more exotic realms of multiplication and division. Mental arithmetic is simpler with Hindu-Arabic numerals, but uncomprehending contemporaries resorted to darker explanations for Sylvester's rare skill. The pope died in 1003, but the reputation for sorcery dogged his legacy.

Centuries passed before Europe fully adopted the Hindu-Arabic system and the range of mathematical operations it simplified. As late as the sixteenth century, ambitious British parents could educate their children in the intricacies of multiplication and division only by packing them off to continental Europe for tutelage under Italian merchants. Why did it take Europeans so long to embrace such an obviously superior system? Prejudice against alien ideas played a part, of course. So did simple force of habit; today's U.S. citizens, for example, can't be weaned from their beloved feet, yards, and miles in favor of the vastly more efficient metric system.

There were also logical reasons why Hindu-Arabic numerals didn't catch on immediately. For one thing, the scant surviving records suggest that Gerbert learned the system without its most essential ingredient: the zero. Historians are unsure why. Gerbert may have been aware of the zero but discarded it as a superfluous extravagance because he had been raised with the zero-less Roman system. More likely, he was never even exposed to the zero. Vigila's 976 manuscript speaks of the "nine figures" used by the Indians to designate numbers. The usefulness of zero was little understood, nor was it introduced as the inseparable part of the numeral package it is today. Eleventh-century manuscripts often represented numbers such as 304 as 3.4, using a dot rather than a zero as a place saver. Whether Gerbert never grasped the significance of the zero or never even learned about it is moot; what's clear is that without this essential tool that supercharges the computational efficiency of Hindu-Arabic numerals, the whole system loses some luster.

There is a more obvious explanation for Europe's glacial conversion to the system: sad to say, it wasn't much needed. Though Hindu-Arabic numerals greatly simplify mathematical computation, Europeans did not have a whole lot of computing to do. Economies were moribund (outside of vibrant al-Andalus, that is). Urban life had collapsed with the Roman Empire. Feudal Europe puttered along, supported by subsistence agriculture rather than trade. There were no legions of busy shopkeepers, bankers, or merchants clamoring for advanced computational tools to track humming businesses.

Potential fraud was another problem. Those unwieldy, multidigit Roman numerals were a primitive encryption device for the precomputer age. A debt to a neighbor of $123 is one deft digit-change away from becoming a debt of $423; and a 1 can be fairly easily transformed to a 7. On the other hand, it takes a fair bit of work to transform CCCXXIII into CLXXIII without leaving traces, or even to change an X to a C. An even more obvious problem detracted from the numerals' practical usefulness. It may be far easier to scribble simple calculations on scrap paper using Hindu-Arabic numerals rather than the Roman variety, but that assumes one has paper! Medieval Europeans had vellum parchment, and considering the time and sweat required to transform sheepskin into parchment, no one was wasting the precious resource on something so inconsequential as toting up the medieval version of a grocery bill.

Al-Andalus actually had innovative solutions for some of these problems. A small Spanish town, Játiva, had pioneered in Europe a cutting-edge industry: paper manufacture. The explosive burst of conquest following the prophet Muhammad's death not only carried Islam's warriors to India and its sophisticated number notation system, but also to China's supremely advanced civilization. The Chinese had developed a rudimentary process for boiling down rags and pressing the pulp into paper, and by some accounts, Arabs learned the technology from Chinese prisoners captured in an eighth-century battle (specifically, a 751 battle near Talas, a remote region of present-day Turkestan not far from the Chinese border). The craft slowly filtered from central Asia to Islam's scholarly and administrative Near Eastern heartland before spreading across the Islamic world.

Within Europe, the process remained Muslim Spain's more or less proprietary craft, centered in the small enclave of Játiva, which fell into Christendom's orbit when thirteenth-century Crusaders overran Muslim Valencia. As the technology slowly crept across Europe, its dispersion boosted the utility and appeal of Gerbert's numbers. It became cheaper to produce paper than parchment and therefore more cost-efficient for merchants to use paper for calculating sums. What's more, paper provided lasting records of transactions, whereas prices calculated on an abacus were swept away forever with each new rearrangement of the counters.

Unfortunately, it also became cost-efficient to use paper for other purposes. Thank Spain, in a way, for that dreadful affliction plaguing modern civilization: paper-loving government bureaucracies. Spain was probably the first state to use paper on a broad basis for recording and preserving government records, setting humanity on its ineluctable course to those damnable paper mountains of triplicate application forms with their endlessly verbose, fine-print instructions.

Though paper didn't catch on for quite some centuries, another Spain-mediated technology took hold almost immediately, thanks in part to Gerbert. The future pope had learned his numbers in Spain and also learned how to construct a paperless device for manipulating them: an abacus. Gerbert most certainly didn't invent the abacus, nor did medieval Spaniards. Abaci had been used in Europe for centuries, including by the Greeks and Romans. But the device's popularity had waned until Gerbert's simplified version enhanced its efficiency and simplified its use.

A traditionally configured abacus was a crowded, cumbersome affair: nine ones were represented by slotting nine separate counters or pebbles into the ones column. Gerbert's improved version engineered an elegantly simple but conceptually important switch: instead of placing eight counters in the tens column to denote 80, for example, Gerbert instructed abacists to use only *one* counter with the numeral 8 etched or painted onto it. Thus, fewer beads were needed to manipulate the abacus, larger arithmetic problems could be solved more easily, and the abacus became an intuitively simpler device. While as many as thirty-two stones were needed to represent 8,789 on the traditional abacus, only four stones were needed to represent the same number on the new abacus.

What became known as Gerbert's abacus or the superabacus reinvigorated the tool's popularity. Still, in an unintended way, Gerbert the innovator may have actually slowed mathematical progress by inadvertently sowing the seeds of a later showdown between mathematical traditionalists and progressives. Merchants grew fond of Gerbert's abacus, and those adept at using it made a good living. As a result, the deeply entrenched abacists (or Gerbercists, as they were sometimes called in his honor) resisted the onslaught of the *algorists,* who by the thirteenth century were exploring more sophisticated uses of Hindu-Arabic numerals than pushing sums around an abacus with fewer stones.

The very words *al*gorithm and *al*gebra hint that these new-wave mathematicians had learned their tricks from Islamic civilization. One might also guess that al-Andalus played an important role in introducing the new capabilities to Europe. The ninth-century Arab mathematician al-Khwarizmi (the English word "algorithm" is a corruption of his name) was one of a long line of scholars who grasped the potential uses of the number system pioneered by Indian mathematicians. While Europeans were still unsure what the zero was or why it mattered, Arab scholars were cranking through quadratic equations and complex geometric proofs. Al-Khwarizmi wasn't the most gifted of these scholars, but his well-organized treatises lucidly explained how Hindu-Arabic numerals could be used in various operations, including in the field that most high school graduates surely wish he had kept to himself. Thank his *Al-jabr wal-Muqqabala (Completion and Balancing)* for introducing us to the torture we still call *al-jabr* (algebra). And thank al-Andalus for helping introduce Europeans to al-Khwarizmi. The Britons Adelard of Bath and Robert of Chester apparently learned their math in Spain, just as Pope Sylvester had. Adelard's output included excerpts of al-Khwarizmi's treatises, and Adelard's countryman Robert of Chester gave Europe its first definitive translation of the *Al-jabr.*

Even though Arab scholars had been solving advanced mathematical problems since at least the 800s, and even though Gerbert had grasped at least the superficial advantages of Hindu-Arabic numerals in the late 900s, Europe in the 1100s was still not prepared to digest the mathematical meal served up by Adelard and Robert. Hindu-Arabic numerals languished in a scholarly ghetto despite ever more accessible mathematical treatises published by Europeans (more by Italians than Spaniards, it should be noted). Ignorance stalled the new technology, as did some determined resistance. Those one-time wonder workers pushing counters around on Gerbert's once cutting-edge superabacus must have looked at new mathematical treatises the same way record manufacturers greeted compact discs, each fretting that their sunset industry was being eclipsed by new technology. In the end, Europe was finally shaken from its arithmetic slumber, not by its mathematicians, and certainly not by its abacists, but by merchants who found the Hindu-Arabic system too useful to ignore.

History is capricious in bestowing immortal renown. The early medieval Indian scholars who pushed mathematical science forward by leaps and bounds are largely unknown in the West. Talented ancient mathematicians like Euclid, Zeno, and Archimedes won some lasting name recognition. Gerbert the mathematician, suspected sorcerer, abacist, and first French pope is largely unknown, as is al-Khwarizmi, even though most high school students unknowingly honor him with every cringing utterance of the words algorithm or algebra.

Although Gerbert himself only barely understood the Hindu-Arabic numerals, much less that they would become part of a mathematical revolution, this precocious pope was in some small way a lonely sentinel heralding a dawning new age. Many of his contemporaries didn't see it that way, so obsessed with their own apocalyptic worries that they associated Pope Sylvester with the imminent end of the world.* Granted, as the first millennium staggered toward its close there did seem to be portents enough presaging a cataclysm in the offing. In 989, the comet that centuries later was named for Professor Halley cut its uniquely spectacular path through medieval skies, a pass that must have frightened many Europeans. Mt. Vesuvius belched forth one of its destructive, noxious eruptions in 993. A few years later, northern Spain suffered a far more frightening encounter.

6. Europe's Busiest Highway

In 997, a man-made cataclysm occurred in Santiago de Compostela that devout Christians might have interpreted as an omen of the end time, or at least the end of the civilization they knew. The cataclysm was the handiwork of Almanzor, one of the most powerful generals in Muslim Spain's history. Almanzor headed a well-disciplined army, drawn to northern Spain for far different reasons than the prayerful purpose that guided St. James's pilgrims. Unlike most visitors to Santiago, Almanzor had not come to revere the apostle, but, as a Muslim commentator put it, "to send down confusion and disappointment on the obdurate unbelievers."

Almanzor is an honorific, shortened from *Al Mansur billah* ("Victorious through Allah"). Victorious he most certainly was, whether through God's intercession or his own wits. The same chronicler boasted that he would never finish writing "were we to enumerate all the expeditions undertaken by Almansur to chastise the rebellious Christians of Andalus."

Santiago had thrived as a pilgrimage destination. Day after day, decade after decade, and century after century the pilgrims poured into the town. So did their money: votive offerings for the cathedral and payments to the townspeople who fed, housed, guided, and (sometimes) fleeced the visitors. The shrine exerted magnetic appeal for Europe's devout. But little besides plunder attracted a Muslim warrior to this inaccessible town of dubious military value. No great army was garrisoned there. The kingdom's capital lay many miles east in León. And for all its wealth, Santiago was a tiny town tucked in Iberia's underpopulated northwest. As al-Makkari put it, "None of the Moslem sovereigns had ever thought of penetrating as far as that city . . . owing to its inaccessible position, the strength of the spot on which it is situated, and the many dangers to be encountered on the road to it."

It was about as distant a conquest as Almanzor could have chosen within Iberia. His warriors departed Córdoba to trek four hundred miles through grueling, inhospitable, hilly terrain. Supply ships tacked north along the Portuguese coast, paralleling the army's progress until a resupply rendezvous at Oporto. Almanzor's engineers then lashed the empty vessels one to another as a makeshift bridge across the Duero River. From there, to the immense shame of the Christians, Almanzor swelled his ranks with Christian mercenaries familiar with the winding coastline of estuaries, hills, and ravines between Oporto and Santiago.

Reaching Santiago was the challenge, conquering it a mere formality. The populace fled before Almanzor's advance, as did the hapless pilgrims whose months-long, once-in-a-lifetime trek deposited them at St. James's shrine on the eve of its destruction. Almanzor briefly beheld an all but deserted city of grand churches and buildings before unleashing his destructive fury. Within hours, Santiago was so thoroughly sacked that, as one chronicler put it, "nobody could have imagined [what] had stood there only the day before."

With the town a smoldering wasteland, only one structure lay untouched: Santiago's tomb, surrounded by the rubbled remains of a once-mighty cathedral. While the orgy of destruction had unfolded, Almanzor's hand-picked sentries prevented any profanation of the holy site. The chronicler Ibn Hayyan depicts Almanzor picking his way through debris to find a wizened old monk perched atop the tomb, the only living Christian soul not to have abandoned Santiago. The bewildered old man declared himself "a familiar of St. James" and was left ummolested as Almanzor's armies began the long trek home after dividing up Compostela's booty.

Santiago's tenth-century pilgrims—and their twenty-first-century successors, for that matter—traditionally bear home a scallop shell as symbolic (and literal, and *littoral*) proof of completing the long journey. Just as Holy Land pilgrims clutched palm fronds redolent of semi-arid Jerusalem, St. James's pilgrims returned to landlocked hometowns in central France or Germany with scallop shells harvested from the Atlantic coast beyond Compostela. The distinctive shell remains St. James's characteristic symbol in medieval iconography. Distinguishing one apostle from another in an anonymous lineup of soberly visaged disciples arrayed across a church façade is as daunting a task for today's architecture scholars as it was for yesteryear's illiterate pilgrims. Medieval stonemasons helped where they could: St. Peter invariably brandishes the keys to the kingdom, while St. James sports a scallop shell affixed to his wide-brimmed pilgrim hat.

But nothing so chintzy as a mere scallop shell was a suitable souvenir for an Almanzor well attuned to spin control. While today's media-allergic militarists sometimes sequester prying journalists far away from the battle front, Almanzor pioneered "embedded" journalism by campaigning with three dozen poets and historians in tow. (Granted, none dared pursue a skeptical slant on his tactics.) Ever determined, in al-Makkari's words, to "send down confusion and disappointment" on Spain's Christians and eager to provide propaganda for his entourage, Almanzor chose a far showier memento of his Santiago sack. As dispirited Christians beheld the Muslim victory caravan slowly wending its way south, Compostela's cathedral bells glinted in the sunlight, shouldered by Christian war captives. The captured Christians were sold into slavery, and Santiago's cathedral bells were hung in Córdoba's great mosque for over two centuries.

No image better symbolizes the balance of power in turn-of-the-millennium Iberia: Santiago's wasted cathedral reduced to a quarry site, picked over by Almanzor applying finishing touches to Córdoba's mosque. Islam's grip on Iberia had never seemed as widespread or secure. It wouldn't last long. In little more than a generation, al-Andalus would collapse into a jumble of feuding fiefdoms as Muslim Spain succumbed to the same debilitating divisiveness that so long had hobbled the Christian north. Still, cathedral or no, Muslim Spain ascendant or Christian Spain resurgent, the pilgrims kept coming to Santiago.

This impulse to pilgrimage seems as ancient as religious history it-self. Medieval sermons count Adam and Eve the first pilgrims, exiled from paradise to wander the earth in atonement for their misdeeds. This is one strand of the pilgrim DNA: the penitential journey that amends for sinful wrongdoing. Yet this strand inextricably intertwines with another, more hopeful impulse. Adam's descendant Abraham forged a new covenant relationship with God, who outlined the terms of a more hopeful pilgrimage: "Go from your country and your kin-dred and your father's house to the land that I will show you. And I will make of you a great nation, and I will bless you, and make your name great." Accordingly, Abraham departed his native Ur (in present Iraq), wandered the Near East, and in the most unsettling episode of this pa-triarch's life pilgrimage, was famously spared at the very last moment from sacrificing his beloved son, Isaac.

In Muslim tradition, however, Abraham's older son, Ishmael, was the one spared. Father and son later honored God by worshipping at the Kaaba, a few miles removed from the near-sacrifice. They recon-structed the holy site that Muslims believe to have been established by Adam. Thus, the Kaaba, the world's most enduringly visible symbol of pilgrimage, symbolically links Adam the penitential pilgrim-exile to Abraham the hopeful pilgrim journeying to the promised land.

The world's three great monotheistic religions preserve the meta-phor Abraham embodied of life itself as pilgrimage. The New Tes-tament Epistle to the Hebrews recounts Abraham's journey before observing that we are all "strangers and exiles on the earth." Yet the exile's wanderings are not aimless, as Adam's were, for the life pilgrim is tracing a path blazed by Jesus that leads to eternal, blissful reunion with the Heavenly Father. The epistle's language evokes a fundamental human yearning for a brighter future, some innate conviction that pulls the religious and nonreligious alike ever forward along life's jour-ney: "If they had been thinking of that land from which they had gone out, they would have had opportunity to return. But as it is, they desire a better country."

It's no wonder all three Abrahamic religions customarily reenact rit-ual pilgrimage with its rich symbolic resonance. Islam does so most prominently. The pilgrimage to Mecca is incumbent on all Muslims at least once in a lifetime, health and resources permitting. Judaism enshrines ritual pilgrimage in the three great *hag* (pilgrim) festivals of Passover, Shabuoth (Weeks), and Succoth (Booths); as Deuteronomy instructs, "Three times a year all your males shall appear before the Lord your God at the place which he will choose." In observance of this ancient mandate, Jesus's parents "went to Jerusalem every year at the feast of the Passover," most famously when their twelve-year-old son became separated from them in the pilgrim-choked city and for three days dazzled the Temple scribes with his precocious wisdom.

Only Christianity lacks one universally observed pilgrimage feast: no journey to Mecca, no festival of Booths. Yet, ironically, perhaps precisely because the religion never grounded the pilgrimage impulse in any one formal outlet, Christianity has ceaselessly proliferated pilgrimage practices throughout the centuries. The Roman emperor Constantine and his mother, St. Helena, are somewhat arbitrarily regarded as Christianity's first pilgrims. The two journeyed to Jerusalem, where tradition credits Helena with discovering Christ's burial tomb.

The Holy Land understandably remained Christianity's pilgrimage destination par excellence with the unmatchable promise of tracing Jesus's own footsteps. But then, as now, it was not easily accessible. Modern technology may have whittled the time and financial resources needed for a Holy Land visit, but modern technology has also multiplied the threat of collateral damage from the religious strife that regularly seals off the Near East from all but the most intrepid pilgrims.

Europe offered closer, less costly, and safer alternatives to medieval European pilgrims. Foremost was Rome's rich Christian heritage dating to the martyrdom of the apostle and first pope, Peter. But at least a thousand other sites won pilgrims' attention through saintly relics or association with miraculous occurrences. Pilgrims traveled to Italy's Apulia, where the archangel Michael had appeared. Chaucer immortalized travelers to Canterbury Cathedral, where St. Thomas Beckett was slain. Paris was especially rich in relics: Jesus's crown of thorns, a sponge with his blood, a towel he had worn at the Last Supper, the point of the lance with which he had been pierced on the cross, and part of the head of John the Baptist, to name but a few.

But no site outside Rome, and by some estimates not even Rome itself, attracted as many pilgrims year after year as St. James's remains in Compostela. One Muslim traveler marveled that "so many people could be found in all Spain." Estimates ranged as high as 1 million and even 2 million pilgrim visitors a year at a time when Spain itself sheltered considerably fewer than 10 million people. Even if 1 million is almost certainly too high an estimate, for long stretches of the twelfth and thirteenth centuries the *camino de Santiago* was nontheless Europe's busiest long-distance highway. No mean feat for a road terminating not in a great commercial or political metropolis but in a tiny town of fewer than five thousand citizens.

Just as pilgrimage metaphorically embodied the life journey, so too was every human motive and instinct, base or elevated, manifest across the months and miles of a Compostela journey. Some traveled to search out a more meaningful life, others only to quit a meaningless one. Pilgrims journeyed to see the world, to find romance or adventure, or for want of anything else to do. Most hoped to better their lot in life, either through some favor bestowed by St. James or, taking matters into their own hands, by ripping off other travelers. Many sought healing or reparation for bodily ills, for some grievous transgression against neighbors or society, or for some sinful wrong that imperiled the soul.

Not all those seeking redemption traveled of their own volition. Catholics believe that sacramental confession erases sin and restores the contrite to a state of grace enabling future passage to paradise. But Catholic theology carefully distinguishes *forgiveness of* sin from *reparation for* sin. The priest's sacramental absolution may remove the soul-polluting stain of the murderer's grisly deed, but hardly remedies the worldly disorder he or she has caused. Hence, Christians must make earthly reparation ("to repair") for sins, and along with absolution a priest typically metes out a suitable penance.

Earthly penance notwithstanding, many face the prospect of yet further purification in purgatory as temporal punishment for earthly sins before entering the heavenly kingdom. Medieval Christians eagerly attended to whatever acts of reparation they could perform in this life to reduce their purgatorial sentence in the next. Where prayer and acts of charity occupied the mundane end of the reparative spectrum, pilgrimages to saintly relics were a more exotic, and in popular understanding more potent, way to atone for earthly misdeeds.

This complex theology of sin, forgiveness, and reparation unleashed a motley cast on Santiago. Roger da Bonito was sent there for murdering the bishop of Fricento; another pilgrim went for killing his neighbor's horse; and still others for arson. Confessors applied their own judgmental yardsticks to proportion the penance to the outrage. Bishop Hamo de Hethe of Rochester in England sent one adulterer to Canterbury "barefoot and naked but for breeches"; another adulterer, guilty of the more heinous offense of consorting with his own godmother, was sent all the way to Santiago de Compostela. Murderers bore not only the guilt of their sin but often its visible reminders: more than one penitent murderer traveled to Santiago shackled around the neck with irons cast from the murder weapon.

The sinners came, but so did the saints, the royals, and everyone in between. If the penitent common thief was a reluctant pilgrim exiled by his confessor, King (later Saint) Louis IX of France was admirably *self*-motivated. He prepared by dispatching messengers throughout France to catalogue grievances of any subjects who felt wronged by the sovereign. The pious and scrupulous monarch aspired to a more perfect peace with the Almighty by journeying to Santiago carrying this comprehensive national accounting of his perceived misdeeds with him. Murderers in chains shared the road with wealthy nobles accompanied by extensive entourages of servants and retainers. King Edward I of England journeyed to Santiago. Holy sightseers like Duke William V of Aquitaine went on pilgrimage annually, traveling to Compostela, Rome, and other holy shrines. One noble visitor made a particularly spectacular impression, consummating his long pilgrimage by keeling over and dying in front of Santiago's high altar.

With society's notables headlining the pilgrim parade, society's castoffs swelled the rear guard. Most Europeans were impoverished serfs bound to landed estates by feudalism's inviolable traditions; only with their lord's blessing could these virtual slaves down hoes and sally forth, even for purposes so laudable as religious pilgrimage. Those freed from feudal obligations were typically broken down, decrepit souls no

longer sturdy enough to earn their keep. Many feudal lords made a
hard-headed rather than spiritual calculus: better to release an unpro-
ductive old serf to fend for himself than support him in old age.

Many such pilgrims, infirm codgers already closing in on the advanced medieval age of forty, never even made it to Santiago. After securing their pastor's formal blessing, they were granted a passport of
sorts to certify their pilgrim status. They were counseled to put their
earthly affairs in order before departing. Not that it mattered: for most
who died en route there was no thought of returning the body home.
Nor was there even hope of notifying next of kin unless the deceased
traveled in a band of hometown companions lucky enough to survive
the pilgrimage and return safely home. The dead vanished, buried in
anonymous plots in crude cemeteries dotting the roadside. The law
stipulated that their pitiful few belongings were to be distributed
among the poor, but anything of worth just as often found its way onto
the backs and into the pockets of fellow pilgrims,

Those who survived discovered worlds they never knew existed. For
most it was their first time venturing further than a few miles from
home, seeing a mountain, hearing a foreign language, or beholding the
ocean. Each night brought new companionship in new towns, where
storytellers enthralled travelers with tales of saints and sinners who had
trod these very roads: Charlemagne, who battled the African giant
Aigolandus; Pelayo, who slew 187,000 Moors; and the other Pelayo,
who discovered Santiago's tomb (except in those accounts where Charlemagne discovered it).

Most pilgrims would have worried little about such logical inconsistencies, relishing the entertainment while ignoring the stories' political
undertones. Other stories did touch pilgrims directly, tapping the
deeper hopes that had prompted many of their journeys. For every
penitent on the road could be found another pilgrim seeking Santiago's
miraculous intercession for some particular cause. There was ample evidence that St. James heeded the pleadings of his devotees. The *Miracles
of St. James* gathered into one twelfth-century compilation twenty-two
of many hundreds of miracles attributed to Santiago. The miracles, so
varied in nature and benefiting so varied an ethnic swath, convinced a
pilgrim that *anything* was possible. No intervention seemed too great

and none too small for Santiago. A man struggling toward Compostela with his children miraculously received a strong donkey to ease his passage; a sailor named Frisonius fell overboard but was rescued by St. James; an Italian named Bernard was freed from unjust imprisonment, and another Italian was healed of an ailment by touching St. James's emblematic scallop shell.

The oddest and most harrowing of the *Miracles of St. James* features an unfortunate young bachelor named Gerald, an annual visitor to the shrine. Though Gerald "could contain himself for a very long time . . . [he] was overcome by the voluptuousness of the flesh" and succumbed to an amorous liaison with an attractive maiden. He rushed toward Compostela to beg forgiveness but was intercepted by the devil masquerading as St. James. Satan induced the gullible Gerald to chop off the offending organ that landed him in such trouble. Gerald did so and promptly died (whether of blood loss, shock, or dismay we don't know), but was soon after restored to life, if not completely to masculine vitality, through St. James's miraculous intervention. Gerald's notoriety spread, and to bolster confidence in his unusual tale, Gerald often "showed his scars and even showed what had been in his most private place to the many people wanting to see it."

The exact moral of this complicated tale is not easily unraveled, but some listeners might have concluded that chastity during the journey was a safer bet than counting on St. James's rehabilitative intervention. Still, such admonitions to good behavior would have vied with a host of temptations. After a grueling day's trek the alcohol flowed freely when each pilgrim band settled into an inn for the night. One twelfth-century sermon, still preserved in the Santiago cathedral treasury, droned on at great length about drunken pilgrims "oblivious, raging, idiotic, silly, insane, lustful, and given over to sleep."

Medieval inns offered primitive accommodation. When bedtime came the besotted band of pilgrims typically flopped down as one on a large straw mat spread across an inn's upper room. The same sermon condemned the serving staff at such inns who, "for the sake of ravishing and of stealing money, are accustomed to go to the bed of any pilgrim." Nor were such temptations limited to the nighttime hours; prostitutes loitered along the route to lure passing pilgrims into the woods. The pilgrim demographic may have melded Europe's wealthy and poor, but the motley collection was in one respect homogeneous: other than some wives accompanying husbands, the large majority of pilgrims were men. Freed once in a lifetime from the watchful gaze of wife and fellow villagers, more than a few weak-willed pilgrims were distracted from their holy purpose and succumbed to the minefield of lurking temptations, giving rise to the Spanish proverb, *Ir romero, volver ramera* ("Go a pilgrim, return a whore").

The same medieval preacher who excoriated such disgraceful behavior nonetheless celebrated the multinational parade that year after year tromped toward Santiago: "French, Normans, Scots, Irish, Welsh, Germans . . . Norwegians, Russians, Prussians, Nubians, Parthians . . . Cyprians, Hungarians, Bulgarians, Slovenians . . ." The list drags on, comprising some seventy ethnicities before the preacher finishes with the caveat that his list is not exhaustive. Continental European pilgrims trickled out of hamlets and villages, eventually streaming into four main pilgrim tributaries that snaked through France before cascading over the Pyrenees into one great river of humanity coursing across northern Spain.

Religion, commerce, and geology each shaped the route's meandering course through France. One route welled up in Paris, where pilgrims started by begging favor at the Virgin's majestic cathedral (Notre Dame) and commenced along the Paris street that still commemorates its famed destination: Rue St. Jacques (St. James's Street).

Italians and southern Europeans, on the other hand, hewed to a route tracking the Mediterranean coastline and detoured to the French shrine of St. Giles in Arles. With Santiago still many months distant, sanctuaries like St. Giles, a famous destination in its own right, afforded travelers opportunities for rest, prayer, and diversion. Civic and religious leaders coveted the pilgrim traffic that primed their local economies, even though their resources were sometimes swamped by swollen pilgrim bands unable to restrain their excitement on reaching some saintly miracle worker's shrine. One abbot of St. Giles pleaded for papal assistance to maintain order in his church precincts. Pope Innocent IV's reply offered plenty of sympathy but not much material support. "Since a multitude of pilgrims flows from different parts of the world to your church," the pope wrote, "because of quarrels and fights, which very frequently arise, the church itself is violated by the spilling of both blood and seed. Wherefore you have humbly requested that we come mercifully to your aid."

While entrepreneurial abbots and wily town fathers diverted pilgrim routes through France's preeminent shrines, geology eventually steered the religious travelers toward a more accessible course. Three main pilgrimage routes converged for a punishing climb through the Pyrenees to the nearly five-thousand-foot-high pass of Roncesvalles. The rocky path was prone to freak snowstorms even in May, but it was the pilgrim's best alternative to the nearly uninterrupted curtain of Pyrenees peaks topping out over eleven thousand feet.

Today's pilgrim crosses the Pyrenees and transits northern Spain to reach Compostela, but medieval pilgrims passed through an array of smaller kingdoms. First came Navarre, nestled snugly against the French border and guarding its independence from Spain and France until the early 1500s. Navarre gave way to Castile's ever shifting border with neighbor León. Finally, pilgrims entered Galicia, home province of the treasured shrine of Compostela. Navarre's Basques greeted the pilgrim in Basque, Castilians in the language that became known as Spanish, and Galicians in Galician.

Although these northerners were linguistically and ethnically diverse, they were often united by their determination to part pious pilgrims from their meager financial resources. The famous twelfth-century sermon commemorating the *Veneranda Dies,* or "honored day," of St. James laments the varied shenanigans occurring along the pilgrim route. Its author unleashes a dyspeptic rant against the endless array of rip-off schemes perpetrated by merchants, innkeepers, and other miscellaneous hucksters. Innkeepers along the route "show [pilgrims] the best wine for sampling, and sell them inferior wine if they can." Merchants portion out measures of grain with specially rigged measuring scoops, "very large on the outside but narrow, scant, and not fully hollowed on the inside." Hostel managers steal the belongings of their drunken guests, sell goods at inflated prices, and hide drinking water to force parched guests to buy wine to slake their thirst.

Impostors garbed in priestly robes marketed "walk-by" confessions along the pilgrimage route. After hearing the pilgrim's sins and mumbling some mangled absolution in what they hoped passed for Latin, they would instruct the penitent to have masses said as a penance and then conveniently offer to say those masses in exchange for a cash offering. Other hucksters squatted by the roadside feigning dreadful deformities, "their legs and arms, dipped in rabbit blood or ashes . . . so that they might extort alms." Business was good enough that many scam artists could afford to be discriminating consumers of their ill-gotten gains: "They do not want to accept bread or modest alms, but do take coins."

Long before the publishing industry discovered the eager market for travel guides, a twelfth-century Frenchman scratched out a primitive Baedeker for other would-be pilgrims. It outlines perils of the expedition, from struggling through vertical Pyrenees climbs to warding off temptations to coping with corrupt merchants. The author coaches prospective travelers through the journey's mundane challenges, like finding potable water in an era centuries before indoor plumbing debuted. He warns pilgrims away from the River Salado, noting that two Navarrese opportunists are every day "seated on its banks and sharpening their knives," waiting for any donkey to sip its water and keel over, providing fresh raw material for their animal hide business.

Could a free-flowing stream be so noxious? Maybe not, but the guide's author spares no opportunity to slander the Navarrese. He depicts them slopping the courses of their evening meal into a single bowl, followed by an unruly scrum as everyone from lowly servant to master of the house digs in with unwashed hands: "If you saw them eating, you would take them for dogs." Navarrese eating habits, however, are far less shocking than their unconventional sexual proclivities: "The Navarrese also make use of animals for incestuous fornication. It is told that the Navarrese affixes a lock to the behind of his mule or horse, so that no one else but he may have access to them."

Against all odds, most pilgrims actually survived the Navarrese, the innkeepers, the River Salado, and other assorted calamities to enter Santiago, their safe arrival itself perhaps no small miracle on St. James's part. Christian Europe left behind family, friends, homes, and kingdoms to venture to a tiny town numbering fewer than five thousand citizens in its heyday. Pilgrims had to be housed and fed; there were trinkets and souvenirs to be purchased; offerings to the cathedral re-dounded to the general prosperity once recycled into construction projects or payments for upkeep. Santiago's crafty citizens grew "fat as pigs and slothful at that," according to one disgusted late medieval chronicler. Still, after all they endured during long, unfamiliar, danger-ous, and exhilarating journeys, or perhaps precisely because of all they endured, many pilgrims were swept up on arrival by the same emotion reported by a visitor to the tomb of St. Catherine of Sinai: "For great joy and devotion everyone began to weep, like people who had found what they had longed for; and for a long time we had longed to come to that blessed body."

The pilgrim class of 998 could still find Santiago's remains at the end of their grueling expedition, even if Almanzor's sack had reduced to rubble the cathedral that once sheltered that tomb. The resilient town soon rebounded. Within a few decades, one of Europe's finest Romanesque cathedrals was rising on the spot. Improbably, while the ransacked Santiago de Compostela was in the process of rebuilding, tri-umphant Muslim Spain was collapsing—and even more improbably, entrusting a Jew with extraordinary military and political power. Samuel ha-Nagid was to wield his power so effectively that modern his-torians would hail his successes as "the highest achievement of a Jew in Medieval Muslim Spain."

7. A Jewish General
in a Muslim Kingdom

"I Am the David of My Age"

As Almanzor's armies wended their way south from Santiago de Compostela in 997, Christian captives shouldering its cathedral bells, the general was lord of all he surveyed. Neither Muslim Spain nor Almanzor himself had ever been more powerful. But his ambitions transcended military glory. While the strong-willed general paid lip service to a puppet caliph squirreled away in a Córdoba palace, he gathered and hoarded the power to rule al-Andalus. Almanzor ordered the construction of a grand new palace complex a few kilometers from Córdoba—not for the caliph, but for himself. When pious Muslims gathered for Friday worship in Córdoba's grand mosque they now added Almanzor's name when reciting the customary prayers for the caliph.

A wiser Almanzor might have foreseen that he was hastening the demise of the Andalus he had made so mighty. Almanzor was no Umayyad prince; in a dangerous precedent, he was exercising authority and assuming privilege reserved to the caliph alone. Almanzor's power grab seeded revolutionary ideas among Muslim Spain's myriad clan and ethnic leaders, descendants of those schemers who once subjected pre-Umayyad al-Andalus to backstabbing, revolt, and instability. Those genies that Abd al-Rahman and his Umayyad successors had stuffed into a bottle through enlightened yet heavy-fisted rule now seeped out. Factional chiefs beheld Almanzor's power grab and dared to wonder: If Almanzor, why not us?

Umayyad power ultimately rested not on overwhelming force but on the same subtle alchemy of fear, tradition, and trust that has supported so many other dynasties throughout history. Almanzor had stripped the veil of permanence from Umayyad rule, and after his death in 1002 the dynasty began crumbling. Within a decade al-Andalus was plunged into a political maelstrom. Its Hispano-Arab elite tussled among themselves and with the North African Berbers who steeled the state's military backbone; even southeast and central Europeans imported to Andalusia as mercenary fighters and slaves, *the Saqaliba* or Slavs, waded into the succession free-for-all. (The English-language word "slave" traces its origin to these Slavic-speaking peoples of southeastern and eastern Europe, captured and sold into servitude across western Europe and especially into affluent al-Andalus throughout the Middle Ages.) Within a generation of Almanzor's death, al-Andalus had splintered into more than two dozen petty Muslim kingdoms vying for dominance or, at a minimum, to preserve newly won independence.

Muslim Spain's fragmentation presaged slow-motion disaster for its military and political power. Almanzor had unleashed the fury of a united state against Christian Spain; henceforth, Christian Spain would face off against a galaxy of weakened mini-states.

But not every outcome of al-Andalus's political implosion was regrettable. Just as wealthy Italian merchants and princes would one day patronize Renaissance artists in the hope of turning Florence or Siena into the envy of all peers, so, too, petty Muslim princes scrambled to burnish their reputation for decorousness and refinement. Andalusian culture flourished. Muslim city-states lavished patronage on leading artists. Where Córdoba once exerted an irresistible gravitational pull on Muslim Spain's finest artisans and craftsmen, now Seville, Granada, and other Andalusian cities competed successfully for their talents.

The mini-states also competed for political and military talent to head the multiple armies and bureaucracies that replaced the one government of Umayyad Spain. As opportunities multiplied, Samuel ha-

Nagid (or Samuel ibn Nagrela) seized his. The courtier and poet called the David of his Age may well have been the most extraordinarily accomplished Jew not only in Spain but anywhere in medieval Christendom, and one of the most accomplished of any era in European history. One historian ventures the generous assessment that "Spanish Jews were the greatest luminaries of Hebrew civilization since Biblical times," and Samuel was among the very brightest luminaries of this most creative, prosperous Jewish civilization.

No one knows exactly when or why Jewish believers first made their way to Iberia, though Jews arrived long before Muslims or Arian Visigoths. Jews may even have lived and worshipped in Spain before Christians did. Scholars date the earliest Jewish settlers to the first two centuries of the Common Era. Medieval Jewish scribes preserved the tradition that the Roman emperor Titus (c. 80 C.E.) dispatched a handful of "Jerusalem's nobles" to Spain at the request of Mérida's governor. The dubious story is unsupported by any surviving documents, but it served the interests of some medieval Jews who perpetuated it mainly to bolster their own pedigrees by claiming descent from these first-century nobles.

Among the earliest rock-solid evidence of Spanish Judaism is a third-century tombstone inscription from the southern coastal town now known as Adra. Perched on the Mediterranean, tiny Adra would have been spiced by the cosmopolitan flavor common to trading ports the world over. One imagines a largely pagan Iberian town tolerating the unfamiliar religious observances practiced by small pockets of Jewish traders.

Fourth-century Spain's Jewish population, impossible to estimate accurately, was certainly tiny by modern standards. But it was nonetheless sizable enough to alarm Spanish bishops convening in Elvira in 305. The prelates took a dim view of interfaith relations, forbidding Christians from living in any house that also sheltered Jews or even from eating in their company. (One presumes that the bishops would not have proscribed practices that weren't actually occurring.) Within another two centuries, Elvira's discriminatory pronouncements had yielded to the Visigoths' full-throated anti-Semitism, culminating in outright prohibition of Jewish worship.

Jewish fortunes abruptly reversed with Islam's uninvited 711 arrival. Córdoba's Jews must have been more stunned than delighted when its Muslim conqueror gathered their community leaders and "left them in charge . . . trusting them in preference to the Christians, on account of their hatred and animosity toward the latter." This was no isolated occurrence, as is clear later in the chronicler al-Makkari's report: "This practice became almost general in the succeeding years; for whenever the Moslems conquered a town, it was left in custody of the Jews, with only a few Moslems, the rest of the army proceeding to new conquests."

The unlikely gesture fit the general pattern of Muslim conquest. Whether in the Near East or Spain, Islam's military machine remained unencumbered and focused on fresh conquest by entrusting governance to locals. Spain's Jews were both blessed and cursed to constitute a small minority of Iberia's population. Conquering Muslims feared Christian uprisings; the smaller Jewish population presented no such threat. Muslim military commanders quite sensibly delegated temporary authority to Jews rather than entrusting Christians with the levers of power.

Yet the same minority status rendered Jews vulnerable and ever dependent on the whimsical forbearance of Iberia's Muslim (or Christian) masters. Though religious tolerance was woven into the Quran's fabric, it hung by a slender, uncertain thread. Nothing better exemplifies how tenuously the Jews clung to this thread than the extraordinary rise and fall of Samuel ha-Nagid's family.

Samuel's great opportunity unfolded—though he hardly recognized the opportunity at the time—when rampaging Berber Muslims ransacked the Umayyad capital of Córdoba in 1013, hastening the dynasty's disintegration into a constellation of factional or ethnic principalities. Córdoba's Jews had prospered under the Umayyads. Prospects under Berber rule seemed less certain. The Berber sack of Córdoba was hardly an encouraging omen. Many Jews fled, including Samuel.

That he settled in Granada seems a lucky rather than studied choice. According to unlikely legend, Samuel's eloquence brought him to the attention of Granada's King Hubbus, one of myriad petty Muslim potentates fancying himself a king in the fragmented mishmash of rival states that replaced the unified Umayyad Spain. Samuel had become an important court official when King Hubbus's death ignited a succession struggle between his sons Badis and Bullugin. Samuel backed the right contender and was duly rewarded. As Badis's chief vizier and military commander, he attained power unmatched by any other medieval Jew. An embittered Muslim courtier, Abu Ishaq, angrily denounced such prominent Jews: "Turn your eyes to other countries and you will find the Jews are outcast dogs. Why should you alone [Granada] be different."

Nor was Samuel himself modest in assessing his talent, status, and achievements, proclaiming himself "the David of my age." In many respects he was. If loyalty to Badis at a desperate hour boosted Samuel's career, extraordinary talent secured his grasp on power. The Muslim chronicler Ibn Hayyan conceded Samuel's greatness even while begrudging his faith: "This cursed man was a superior man, although God did not inform him of the right religion." For nearly twenty years Samuel captained Granada's army, no mere honorific trifle in the early years of Muslim Spain's petty kingdoms. Strife was constant as newly spawned Muslim mini-states tested neighboring kingdoms in constant bids to expand territory and influence. Granada's forces waged campaigns in all but two years of Samuel's generalship. Granada successfully defended its borders and even won unexpected dominance by defeating the powerful state of Seville.

It rankled rival Muslim states and a good many Granadans that the kingdom's military might answered to a Jew, not to mention a Jew who counted himself Badis's most powerful courtier. But the David of his age acutely understood how tenuous was any Jew's grasp on power in Muslim Spain. One of Samuel's poems offered this sober assessment:

A monarch will not favor you unless he hopes to be
at ease while you labor and exert yourself in his service.
You are caught in his tongs: with one hand he brings you into
The flames,—while protecting you from the fire which with
     both hands he sets against you.

In other words, Badis's loyalty extended no further than Samuel's continued success. Military authority was a double-edged sword.

Samuel's victories cut his path to power, wealth, and influence, but failure could at any time expose him to a fickle Badis's wrath. Samuel was, as he says, dangling above "the flames," hanging by the thread of a Muslim king's whims.

Samuel's grasp on power may have been tentative, but his military leadership was bold. Granada surged to victories over rival Muslim states. After crushing his enemies, Samuel the poet exulted, "And the fire of death consumed them and they were annihilated like wood in a hot stove and cooking oven."

After battle he rejoiced; before battle he prayed. This devout Jew attributed his success to divine favor rather than to a Muslim monarch's patronage: "And the Lord heard my prayer when I called like a woman in labor, like one who brings forth her first child in anguish." Samuel called on the God of Hebrew Scripture and discerned in his victories direct parallels to the biblical Yahweh's providential support of his chosen people. Recounting his enemies' utter collapse at the Battle of Alfuente, Samuel recalled the God who smote Egyptian soldiers pursuing Moses and the Jews across the Red Sea: "And He blew upon them as on the day of the Sea of Reeds and they were destroyed by his storm."

Here was something without precedent among Europe's diaspora Jews: war poetry composed by a Jewish commander. Samuel's wide-ranging talents did indeed summon recollections of the biblical David. Like ancient Israel's archetypal king, warrior, and psalmist, Samuel's gifts spanned war, poetry, civil governance, and scriptural commentary. Yet, unlike biblical David, Samuel uncomfortably straddled two worlds. His poetry adopted Arabic forms and style while incorporating biblical imagery and ideas. He waged war in the service of a Muslim state. He spoke Arabic and socialized with Granada's Muslim elite. But he also understood himself, like biblical David, as a protector of fellow Jews. Spain's small, ever vulnerable Jewish communities survived and succeeded partially through well-tended relationships with the Muslim or Christian powers that be. Samuel's military success cloaked him in wealth, prestige, and glory, but also unfurled a protective mantle over Granada's Jews.

Not every Jew saw it that way. That a Jew served a Muslim government and led its army against other Muslim states didn't please all Samuel's coreligionists. Class distinctions often tore rifts through medieval Spain's Jewish communities. A gulf gaped between the wealthy elite and the cobblers, tailors, and other menial laborers constituting the majority of any town's Jews. Class differences were sometimes exacerbated by profound disagreement over the identity of the Jewish nation in exile. Instead of showering Samuel or other well-placed Jewish protectors with gratitude, some Jews condemned them for serving Muslim and Christian governments and indulging in banquets, social life, and the other trappings of high office.

The Jews' treasure was their religious law alone, the dissenters argued, more ancient than Christian or Muslim law and richer than any material wealth proffered by these societies. It was scandal for Jews to surrender even to the appearance of bowing to another law; better to suffer as outsiders distinguished by faithful and total witness to the Jewish law while exiled from the Jewish homeland. But pragmatism prevailed. In addition to his military roles, Samuel served as *nagid,* the official appointed by Muslim governors as civic leader of the Jewish community. Jewish Granadans understood how critical Samuel's influence was to their security.

But Samuel construed his life mission in more personal terms than serving the state or even protecting his coreligionists. The eve of Granada's crucial battle against Almería found Samuel not plotting strategy but cherishing what could be a last opportunity to impart fatherly wisdom to his beloved son, Joseph. Any parent would recognize Samuel's sentiment, even if few parents ever face the battle-ready soldier's stark prospect of imminent death:

> Joseph, all that I endured and the anguish I suffered,—was for
>   your sake.
> . . . If it is decreed, my son, that you not see me again, nor I you
> Give heed to my letter.

There follows a remarkable document, steeped in Jewish tradition but resonant with ideals cherished by all religious believers:

With your life and possessions and in all ways fear your Creator
  and Rock.
. . . Be beloved by all creatures, and before you gain wealth,
  —acquire a good name in your community.
Joseph, give alms to each who asks according to his request, and
  if you have not,—speak gently to him.

Samuel survived the battle of Almería, and a good many more, to mold Joseph into a courtier worthy to succeed him as Granada's vizier. That opportunity came sooner than either father or son would have hoped. Samuel died not during leisurely old age but in the midst of a military campaign; his son succeeded him at age twenty-one.

Joseph's career rapidly took a different turn from his father's, exemplifying the ever precarious fortunes of Spain's Jews. Bad luck that Granada's crown prince died after a feast at Joseph's house, a misfortune pounced on by enemies, who circulated rumors of plots and poisons. Plenty of Granadan Muslims had silently seethed over Samuel's success but dared not challenge the powerful Jew. Samuel's death afforded an opportunity to vent grievances against an inexperienced young Joseph still scrambling to find his political footing. The Muslim courtier Abu Ishaq gave voice to their anger:

He [Granada's king] has chosen an infidel [a Jew] as his secretary
when he could, had he wished, have chosen a [Muslim] Believer.
Through him the Jews have become great and proud
And arrogant—they, who were among the most abject . . .
And how many a worthy Muslim humbly obeys
The vilest ape among these miscreants.

Abu Ishaq's plaint coincided with a tipping point in Granadan society. Joseph was soon after murdered. Long-nursed outrage at the prosperity of Samuel, Joseph, and other Jewish courtiers exploded in a murderous Muslim riot through the town's Jewish quarter. Though Granada continued to prosper among al-Andalus's petty kingdoms, the short-lived "Jewish dynasty" that helped secure its prominence was extinguished. As Samuel had so perceptively observed, "You are caught in his tongs: with one hand he brings you into/The flames,—while protecting you from the fire which with both hands he sets against you."

Samuel's and Joseph's bittersweet careers crystallize the painful dilemma confronting Spain's Jews under Muslim or Christian rule. Ever a minority, Jews lacked the natural resources to defend their lives, secure their livelihoods, and safeguard their children's future. All medieval Spain's Jews, whether rich or poor, influential or powerless, suffered wildly gyrating fortunes, where persecution could suddenly yield to prosperity that might at any time be dashed by a new crisis.

Nonetheless, much recommended them as able additions to any Christian or Muslim ruler's court. The Jewish community spawned talented merchants and administrators, adept go-betweens who assimilated the cultural and language skills needed to thrive in the dominant Muslim or Christian society. Steeped in their law's mandate to study Torah, devout Jewish families educated their children to fulfill this holy duty and in the process blessed Spain's broader society with a disproportionate share of literate citizens. As Spain's nonthreatening minority, well-educated Jews were valuable and safe additions to the civil service.

And so the Jews' precarious bargain. Secular power entailed unique privilege that redounded to the benefit of the wider Jewish community. But position and privilege were never secure, as Joseph ha-Nagid's brief, unhappy tenure so clearly illustrates. The prominent presence of Jews at Muslim and Christian courts inevitably embroiled the wider Jewish community in broader cultural struggles to define their place in "nonbelieving" society. Was it appropriate—was it even *possible*—for a Jew to accommodate alien laws and the new ways of thinking that came with assimilation to Muslim or Christian society?

There was, of course, one way to avoid the dilemma entirely: leave Spain. Ferdinand and Isabella's counselors were to impose this solution on Jews in 1492. Throughout the centuries leading up to the great expulsion, some Jews made the same choice for themselves. Others, attuned to the political winds in Iberia's seesawing struggle between Muslim and Christian Spain, migrated to whichever kingdom seemed more hospitable to the Jewish minority in any given era.

Muslim Spain's early eleventh-century fragmentation ushered in a period of instability. Late in that same century, in 1085, Christian Spain would make a dramatic thrust to reclaim Muslim territory, and Muslim Spain would turn in desperation to a North African Muslim dynasty for support. The momentum was slowly, tentatively, yet almost inexorably shifting to the Christian side, but the balance of power remained uncertain, and violent religious rhetoric intensified as both sides called coreligionists to holy war.

8. The Frontier

Jihad, Crusades, Cowboys, and Sheep

Muslim Spain's fragmention into petty kingdoms boded disaster for Muslim power. While Muslim Spain was fraying, Christian Spain was coalescing. Christian kingdoms long accustomed to forking over humiliating tribute payments to buy off the threat of Muslim invasion now turned the tables. Christian princes extorted annual levies from their Muslim brethren, a practice that would continue off and on for centuries. Reconquest rhetoric may have portrayed Christian Spain's monarchs as undyingly committed to clawing back the Peninsula for Christendom, but they frequently found it better business to leave economically vibrant Muslim mini-states intact and rake in the tribute.

No Christian kingdom was better situated to benefit from Muslim Spain's sudden vulnerability than Castile. The successor state to Asturias-León traced proud roots to the legendary eighth-century guerrilla fighter Pelayo, who had resisted the Muslim onslaught from his mountain redoubt in the far north. Now Pelayo's heirs took the fight to Islam. Castile's long border with Muslim Spain, once a curse, became a blessing. The long frontier exposed Castile to the brunt of Muslim attacks, but as Muslim Spain dissolved into petty fiefdoms, that same long border ideally positioned the Christian kingdom to snatch great chunks of the frontier *meseta*. As its rulers enlarged their kingdom, they typically crowned each newly won slice of frontier with a defensive *castillo* (castle). Thus, Castile, so often at the vanguard of Christian Spain's southward push, became identified with its warlike symbol.

In 1085, Christian Castile took advantage of divided al-Andalus to besiege and seize Toledo. The shocking, deeply symbolic loss for Muslim Spain was a setback no Christian or Muslim would have dared predict decades earlier, when Almanzor reduced Santiago de Compostela to a smoldering ruin. Toledo was one of al-Andalus's finest cities and Visigoth Spain's former capital. Its capture blared a wake-up siren at Muslim Spain's petty emirs. But unable to summon the political will to unite themselves against Christian Spain, they bowed to the distasteful necessity of petitioning military support from North Africa's Muslim Almoravid dynasty.

None of Spain's petty Muslim monarchs looked forward to inviting the Almoravids into their midst. Hispano-Arab emirs had vied to outdo one another in turning their principalities into refined, luxuriant cultural oases; the austere Almoravids hailed from different stock and prized different values. Their religious and political movement had galvanized nomadic Berber tribesmen of the Sahara desert expanses straddling today's Niger and Mali. Where Ziryab once coaxed Córdobans into seasonal fashions bleached dazzlingly white by his patented laundry agents, the Almoravids instead sported a distinctly unfashionable, even chilling visage. With veils muffling their faces against windwhipped sandstorms, they swarmed from the desert in the early eleventh century to dominate much of North Africa.

The Almoravids succeeded through a volatile mix of militancy, asceticism, and unwavering religious zeal, a formula that has so often energized explosive political movements in the Islamic world. Their name itself attests to their vision and tenacity: Almoravid, *al-Murabitun,* the "ones bound (to religious duty)." Almoravid further conveys the image of the *ribat* (or fort) famously associated with their history. Huddled within ribats guarding Islam's North African desert frontiers, the Almoravids wed strict religious observance to military struggle. Chroniclers record well-disciplined Almoravid fighters subjected to the lash for daring to forgo communal prayer.

Muslim Spain's princes may have been loath to entrust their fortunes to Almoravids they considered uncouth, primitive fanatics, but faced with the prospect of Muslim Spain's imminent collapse, they held their noses, made a pact, and hoped for the best. There seemed no alternative. Alfonso VI's siege and capture of Toledo had been a stunning reversal. Even if the Andalusian princes had managed to pull themselves into alliance, they lacked the consolidated military punch to hold off a surging Christian Spain. As Seville's emir al-Mutamid put it, "Better be a mule driver than a driver of pigs." Faced with two bad options, al-Mutamid preferred to tend the Almoravids' desert livestock than "become the captive of Alfonso, and keep his swine in Castile."

Even so, al-Mutamid confessed himself torn between doubt and certainty before throwing his lot in with the Almoravids. It says much about Andalusia's distinctive Hispano-Arab culture that this Muslim ruler would even hesitate before allying with Muslim coreligionists who might defend him against a Christian army. Al-Mutamid eventually chose religion, reasoning that a pact with fellow Muslims would be an act "agreeable to God," whether or not it would serve him personally.

Al-Mutamid and his fellow emirs did in fact become little more than mule drivers serving the Almoravids. Muslim Spain's princes invited the Almoravids to Spain the year after Toledo's fall, securing their pledge to wreak retribution on Alfonso VI's Castilian armies and promptly disappear back to the North Africa hinterlands from whence they came. The Almoravids routed Alfonso VI's armies at the 1086 battle of Zallaqa. The Christian side was overwhelmed by the Almoravids' ferocity and intimidated by their startling appearance: banging on drums of elephant hide and brandishing shields of hippopotamus skin, the Almoravids surged forward, their cavalry including fighters astride camels. The victorious Almoravids withdrew to North Africa as promised, but the prosperity of al-Andalus and, in Almoravid eyes, the dissolute lifestyle of Andalusian Muslims guaranteed their eventual return.

Muslim Spain's sophisticated princes didn't think much of the Almoravids, and the distaste was distinctly mutual. The austere North Africans were appalled at the Hispano-Arabs, tracing Muslim Spain's near downfall to their religious and moral laxity. Muslim Spain's elite defied the Quran by besotting themselves on Spanish wines, from grapes grown in Muslim-owned vineyards, no less. They insulted fellow Muslims by awarding Christians and Jews positions of authority in government. The Almoravids returned in 1089, asserted authority across Muslim Spain, and temporarily stopped the unravelling of Muslim power by stitching the patchwork petty kingdoms into the semblance of a united al-Andalus. Still, while holding Christendom at bay, they lacked the resources to roll back its steadily encroaching tide.

Al-Mutamid of Seville soon enough regretted inviting the Almoravid storm upon Iberia. Desperate to save his throne, he offered his widowed daughter-in-law, Zaida, to his one-time enemy Alfonso VI as seal of a Muslim-Christian alliance against the Almoravid invaders. Zaida bore Alfonso his only son, Sancho, who himself died in battle against the Almoravids. Muslim Almoravid armies, for their part, were regularly swelled by large contingents of Christian mercenaries. What was labeled religious war often enough pitted coreligionists against one another, as those pursuing power or wealth pursued it expediently, overlooking religious allegiance when convenient to do so.

History hasn't been kind to the Almoravids, sometimes portraying them as the barefoot country cousins stupefied by the tall buildings after wandering in from the farmlands. Illiterate tribesmen a generation or so removed from the lifeless Sahara, the Almoravids found themselves stewards of medieval Europe's most splendid palaces and cities. But they differed in at least one critical respect from the stereotypical country yokel: they were steeled by the unflinching zeal of the reformer and brandished the military fury to implement their will. Yet, before they got around to reforming spiritually lax al-Andalus, they themselves succumbed to its pleasures, cultivating the same refined Andalusian lifestyle that once disgusted them. As their reforming zeal waned, so did Muslim hopes of reversing the Christian tide lapping at Muslim Spain's ever receding border.

The Almoravid movement was rooted in religion rather than politics. These revivalists first pursued political power to impose their vision of Islam; they hadn't cynically cloaked political ambition in religious rhetoric to curry mass appeal. They urged a more literal embrace of what they deemed Islam's core values. They bestowed on al-

Andalus an intensified religious sensibility that the modern era might call fundamentalist. Their disapproval of Muslim Spain's culture is faintly but distinctly echoed today in Muslim groups that seek, by violence if necessary, to bend various Islamic states toward their own particular interpretation of a more authentic practice of Islam.

The heightened religious consciousness in Almoravid Spain intensified alienation from Spain's Christians and Jews. To be sure, relations among adherents of the three religions were uneasy even in the best of times, as Eulogius's story so vividly illustrates. But in the Andalusia of the Umayyads and the petty kings, Christians and Jews could enjoy economic opportunity and remain true to their faith. Neither rulers nor ruled went far out of their way to accentuate religious differences.

The Almoravids did underscore those differences, digging an ideological trench between Islam and those considered unbelievers. A veteran of the 1147 Christian reconquest of Almoravid-held Lisbon depicted Muslim warriors atop its town walls taunting Christian besiegers: "They displayed the symbol of the cross before us with mockery; and spitting upon it and wiping the filth from their posteriors with it, and finally making water upon it as something vile, they threw it at us." Whether the shocking gesture actually occurred or was invented by an imaginative Christian chronicler, the anecdote evinces the profound antagonism the North African Almoravids harbored toward Christian Spaniards.

Exactly the same antagonistic spirit was seizing Christendom. Not only was menacing rhetoric about Islam intensifying, so was the determination to act. A decade after the Almoravid arrival in Spain, Pope Urban II exhorted Christian princes at the Council of Clermont in France to liberate the Holy Land from Islam. Those brave enough to enlist in the cause were promised complete remission of all penance due for their sins.

Thus began the Crusades, a chaotic, ruthless, rarely edifying, and ultimately pointless wave of at least nine campaigns over two centuries. The First Crusade captured Jerusalem in 1099, establishing the West's military foothold across the Levant; the fall of Crusader-held Edessa in 1144 occasioned the second; the 1187 surrender of Jerusalem to Muslim armies whipped up the third; and so the campaigns lurched along spasmodically until Muslim dynasties reasserted near total domination of the Mideast by the late 1290s. So resented were the Crusades that even today radical Muslim groups successfully rally sympathy for terrorist acts by proclaiming them vengeance on the Crusaders.

The early Crusaders carved out four Crusader kingdoms along a narrow coastal stretch of today's Turkey, Syria, Lebanon, Israel, and Jordan. In truth, "Crusader carbuncles" might better describe the reality of these enclaves. Handfuls of knights remained bottled up in picturesque castles strung out along the Levant's six-hundred-mile coastline. Isolated from other Crusader outposts and from the surrounding populace, the Crusaders projected little influence beyond their own fortified cities. Commerce and Muslim worship continued around them, much as scar tissue eventually seals off an offending boil.

The Crusades' ultimate impacts were many, varied, and mostly the opposite of Pope Urban's original hopes. Jerusalem was not restored to Christian rule. Indeed, instead of securing the Holy Land for European pilgrims, the Crusaders left the region far less hospitable to Western visitors, whether they bore swords or prayer books. The Crusaders kindled undying suspicion and prejudice against indigenous Mideast Christians who had been enjoying relative tolerance as near majority populations in Egypt, Syria, and elsewhere.

But the Crusades' greatest impact may be the bitter, lingering aftertaste that made them the freighted symbol of Muslim mistrust of the Christian West. Knights Templar once tramped through the al-Aqsa mosque and proclaimed it their military headquarters, desecrating what many consider Islam's holiest site outside Saudi Arabia. The offense still grates on Muslim consciousness. So does the Crusaders' legacy of brutality. King Richard I the Lion Hearted in 1191 massacred some three thousand Muslim prisoners of war, hoping to intimidate his enemy into a speedy surrender; instead, he stirred up anger that engulfed his own armies and still seethes today.

The First Crusade illustrates the outrages that characterized the others at their worst. Itinerant preachers like the barefoot, avowed nonbather Peter the Hermit wandered Europe inducing the unarmed but faithful into campaigns that brought certain death on first encounter with battle-hardened opponents. Better-armed Crusaders like Count

Emich of Leisingen, galvanizing followers by claiming that a cross had been miraculously seared onto his flesh, couldn't contain his destructive itch long enough to depart his German homeland. His band of knights zigzagged through the Rhineland, robbing and massacring Jews in Worms, Mainz, and Cologne as a warmup for their Holy Land showdown with Islam.

Three years passed before the Crusader vanguard reached Jerusalem in spring of 1099. Some sixty thousand noble knights, bedraggled peasants, and miscellaneous opportunists had made it as far as Constantinople, gateway to the Islamic East; a mere ten thousand straggled into Jerusalem, the army shriveled en route by disease, starvation, and military engagements. Still, ten thousand Crusaders were more than enough Christians for the job at hand. Raymond of Toulouse soon exultantly informed the pope that mounted Crusaders had sloshed through Solomon's Temple with "the blood of the Saracens up to the knees of their horses."

Oddly, no one really knows exactly what Urban II said to ignite such militant fervor among those knights gathered at Clermont. The purported firsthand accounts contradict one another. This much is clear: the one thing Urban *didn't* do was announce a "Crusade." That term was a much later invention, referring to the cross (Latin *crux*) with which knights marked themselves after pledging their vows. Instead, early Crusader generations typically referred to their journey as a *peregrinatio* (pilgrimage). They were warrior-pilgrims, bound to liberate the Holy Sepulcher in order to worship there. They journeyed to a holy place just as Santiago's pilgrims did, seeking the very same remission of purgatorial penance bestowed on his devout visitors. But there was a difference: knights on pilgrimage to Santiago traditionally foreswore violence and left behind their military armor; Urban's new pilgrim code stood this long-standing tradition on its head.

While Urban's successors continued to preach the liberation of Jerusalem, they became equally preoccupied with the Muslim presence in their own backyard. The birthplace of Jesus resonated with special meaning, but Muslim Spain, a few weeks' forced march from Rome, radiated its own compelling urgency. The indulgences doled out to Jerusalem Crusaders were extended to knights warring in Spain. Indeed, Spain's knights were ultimately *forbidden* from enlisting in romantic Holy Land jaunts, enjoined instead to stay home and support their native Spain's Reconquest. In 1101, a perturbed Pope Paschal II reproached Spain's warrior-pilgrims, "We wrote to you previously that you should not abandon your country because of the expedition to Jerusalem . . . For we are not a little fearful of the tyranny [of the Muslims] . . . We command you to stay in your country; fight with all your strength against the Moabites and the Moors."

Spain's knights responded, most exotically by joining the military orders that sprang up in the First Crusade's wake. Just as Urban had engineered the illogical feat of transforming warfare into pilgrimage, the crusading movement now turned forts into monasteries and warriors into monks. The image of the knight-crusader has since become so familiar that it's easily forgotten just how alien the notion once was: the warrior's violent occupation grafted onto the monk's serene life.

Yet the roots of this quintessential icon of militant Christendom may not even be entirely Christian. The Crusaders who sallied forth from their castles to battle Islam mirrored in part those Almoravid warriors who charged from the ribats earlier in the eleventh century. The Almoravids, too, were devout warriors; they, too, lived an ascetic, prayerful common life; they, too, engaged in religious wars, inspired by the promise of a reward in paradise. No Christian churchman studied the Almoravid model and adapted it to militant Christendom, but ideas emerge within a historical context, and the Christian Crusader model intriguingly resembles that of Islam's perfect warrior-ascetic. Historians debate whether the parallels are anything more than coincidence.

The first bloom of the warrior-religious confraternity was the twelfth-century Order of the Temple (or Knights Templar). Founded to protect pilgrims traveling to the Holy Land, the Order fortified a string of "Crusader castles" along the land route to Jerusalem. A flurry of copycat orders proliferated, seven in the twelfth century alone—fully four of the seven launched expressly for Spain's domestic Crusade. The wealthiest and most prominent of these Spanish orders naturally looked to draft Spain's own patron as its guardian: the Order of Santiago.

St. James had passed earlier centuries simply as Santiago Peregrino, Santiago the Pilgrim, humble patron of the hundreds of thousands of pilgrims who streamed to his shrine to do penance, offer thanks, seek miraculous intercession, beg cures, or attain enlightenment. But a new type of pilgrimage was emerging, and the new pilgrims bore not walking staff but sword. These won entry to heaven not through lives of penance and good works, but through victory, or death, in a holy war against Christendom's enemies. Pilgrimage became war, and James the Pilgrim became James the Muslim Killer. The world now turned perfectly upside down: pilgrimage turned to war, cleric to warrior, and St. James himself to archwarrior patron.

The Order's motto was straightforward: *Rubet ensis sanguine Arabum* (The sword runs red with the blood of the Arab—i.e., Muslim). They settled frontier outposts where few other Spaniards dared venture, barricading themselves in castle-monasteries. They were in one respect monks like any others. They pronounced the same religious vows of poverty, chastity, and obedience to superiors. They lived simply, fasted, and communally prayed the same Divine Office chanted by Benedictine and Augustinian friars.

But there were differences. The Order of Santiago was the first military order to admit married men. Accordingly, their rule spoke to concerns irrelevant to the chaste members of traditional monastic orders: "The brethren should not approach their wives when they are fasting, nor on the feast days of St. Mary, St. John the Baptist . . . for an impetuous lover of his own wife is an adulterer." Religious vows notwithstanding, these religious warriors were harder-bitten specimens than typical monks, more like foreign legionnaires of the spiritual life. Their rule contemplated transgressions atypical of the pacific environment of most monasteries. St. Benedict's sixth-century monastic rule dictated penances for such grave offenses as mispronouncing the words of sacred Scripture during communal prayer. In contrast, the Order of Santiago's rule stipulated penances for killing innocent civilians, wounding fellow monk-warriors, lying, fomenting conspiracies, or "beat[ing] [one's] wife with a stick or with any other kind of weapon with which the bones may be broken."

Such offenses merited a year of harsh penance. Stripped of his arms, the penitential monk contented himself with the servants' food. While brother knights dined at table, he squatted on the floor, forbidden to shoo away cats or dogs that wandered by to lap up his ration. He was flogged regularly, reduced to bread and water rations once weekly, and endured a host of other privations.

But there was a strange irony in all this. The modern mind may regard these monk-warriors quizzically: by embracing not only monastic asceticism but also war's mortal peril, they deprived themselves of the looting and whoring that is popularly (if wrongly) assumed to have been the very point of much premodern warfare. Yet, however straitened each individual monk's lifestyle may have been, the Order as a whole was massing unimaginable wealth. Grateful rulers lavished land grants on the Order encompassing vast tracts of the Iberian meseta and estates as far away as France and England. The Order was the law in its meseta territories, subject to no religious authority other than the pope himself and administering justice in territories otherwise devoid of civil authorities. True, the Order was typically granted territories in Spain's most undesirable frontier neighborhoods, but it helped transform those lands by creating a sense of security and mixing in a dash of entrepreneurial instinct.

Much of the Order's frontier land had been nearly worthless, sparsely settled no-man's land even before Muslim and Christian armies began trading it back and forth. Frigid winters and furnace-like summers made for an uninviting climate. If the first challenge confronting Castilian and Muslim rulers was driving the enemy off some slice of meseta, the second, often greater challenge was convincing anyone to settle their godforsaken fresh conquest. Those who did were often motivated by religious duty, the misanthrope's love of the wilderness, or lack of better prospects anywhere else. Two distinctive frontier icons emerged. The Crusader survives only in memory; the other icon has taken on larger-than-life dimensions, a distinctly Spanish legacy yet so universal an archetype that from Argentina's pampas to the Texas panhandle to Canada's Great Plains, each of many nations celebrates it as a cherished expression of national culture: the cowboy.

Traditional farming made little sense on this remote, underpopulated, infertile terrain: too few farmers, fields that yielded too meager produce, and the ever looming threat that enemy raiders would seize the land and end the lives of those foolish enough to till it. Land no good for farming wasn't generally good for much else in medieval Europe. But Spain's frontiersmen pioneered a business ideally suited to this finicky landscape. The ideal frontier crop would not remain rooted in the earth when danger threatened but would walk away on its own four feet; it wouldn't demand fertile, well-watered soil but contentedly root out wild grasses while grazing hilly terrain under the watch of intrepid herders. Sheep and cattle ranching became more important in Spain than anywhere else in the medieval world.

It would be no great exaggeration to credit these frontier Spaniards with inventing much of what became the modern ranching tradition. Spring's first shoots cued the roundup (*rodeo* in Spanish) of vast flocks wintering in the southern meseta that warrior-knights had reclaimed for Christianity. Ranchers drove flocks north to summer pasture as far north as León on Santiago's pilgrimage route. Seasonally hired camp hands drove and shepherded the great flocks and herds, spurring their mounts to chase down straying livestock.

As years stretched into decades and then centuries, the swelling herds trod seasonal migration trails into well-established grooves tracking the land's contours. Royal charters ensured the herder's right to unmolested passage and confirmed the crown's lucrative right to tax each herd. Sheep and cattle tramped out the north-south passages that Roman engineers or Muslim emirs never bothered to construct; some *cañadas* ("sheep walks") stretched four hundred miles. If the motley animal processions were less disciplined than one of Almanzor's armies foraying north to sack hapless Christian towns, they were probably better organized than most ragtag pilgrim bands straggling toward Compostela.

Disagreements inevitably arose as flocks owned by the military orders became intermingled with those of monasteries or wealthy independent *caballeros*. Petty ranching disputes were resolved no differently in the thirteenth century than in the twenty-first: by consulting the distinctive brand burned into an animal's hindquarter by its rightful owner. Larger disputes found their way before magistrates, whose records convey the enormous scale of this business. One legal quarrel settled ownership of a single flock numbering some forty thousand sheep. By the late fifteenth century, as many as 3 million sheep were roaming the meseta.

Once Columbus opened the New World, many conquistadors who followed hailed not from Spain's coastal provinces but from landlocked meseta regions like Extremadura and La Mancha. The same gene that spurred their ancestors to leave northern Spain and settle the barren meseta prompted the adventurers who sought fortune on Spain's New World frontier. The conquistador settlers transferred their well-honed ranching skills to sparsely settled, rolling scrub plains in the Americas that must have vaguely recalled their own meseta.

Indeed, the American plains even came preequipped with cattle, though Spaniards soon enough realized that the bison, despite superficial similarities to the docile cow, was not about to be ranch-broken. Just as the first cowboys were imported from Spain, so was another characteristic ingredient of the ranching recipe: horses had roamed the Americas ten thousand years before any Spaniard did, but the animal had become extinct and was reintroduced by the early conquistadors.

As ranching took root across the American frontier, so did its Spanish-language vocabulary. If there is no more American English word than cowboy, much of what he does all day relies on Spanish. The rodeo (*rodear* = to round up) celebrates his skill at lassoing (*lazo* = knot or snare) a mustang (*mesteño* = wild) or a bronco (*bronco* = rough or crude) with a lariat (*la reata* = tethering rope). However well-honed his skills, no cowboy stands much chance of stopping a stampede (*estampida* = a crash or uproar).

The ranchers, crusaders, and petty farmers who ventured onto Spain's frontier faced peril even greater than loneliness, harsh climate, and infertile terrain. Ranching became big business on Spain's frontier, but so did raiding. In addition to cattle raids, *human* raids regularly spurred armies and freebooters across the ever shifting frontier separating Muslim from Christian Spain. Those captured were usually destined for slavery, trafficked for sale as a fresh crop of infidel labor.

Slave raiding in turn spawned the equally lucrative, brisk business of slave redemption. Christian and Muslim agents criss-crossed enemy lines ransoming enslaved coreligionists. Jewish intermediaries some-times specialized in trading and redeeming slaves, capitalizing on their status as the neutral minority trusted by both sides. Ransomers bore safe-conduct passports honored by Muslim and Christian authorities alike, as both sides benefited from the smooth operation of an enter-prise that could command hefty ransoms equivalent to two full years of a laborer's pay.

The religious Order of Merced was a quintessentially Spanish adap-tation to the unsavory reality of slave raiding. More exotically known as the Brothers of Ransom, these clerics and lay brothers sallied forth from Catalonian strongholds armed not with swords and armor but with bags of money to redeem captives. So zealous was their dedication that the Ransomers eventually supplemented the standard religious vows of poverty, chastity, and obedience with their own special fourth promise, to "remain, held as a pledge, in the power of the Saracens [i.e., Muslims] if this be necessary for the redemption of Christ's faithful."

Time and technology eventually transformed Spain's vast meseta. Agri-culture supplanted ranching by exploiting the one resource Spain's high plains supplied in abundance: wind. Windmills pumped from under La Mancha's plains the water that too seldom fell from its skies, the meseta became arable, and the fictional Don Quixote had something to tilt at.

Quixote had leisure to tilt at idealistic causes because the Muslim threat had faded from Spain's plains by the time the sixteenth-century Miguel de Cervantes imagined his knight-errant. Freelancing do-gooders like Don Quixote and warrior-knights of the Order of Santi-ago had essentially worked themselves out of jobs by the late fifteenth century, when all vestiges of Muslim rule were extinguished from Spain.

But this homogeneous, united Spain was still centuries distant when Muslims and Christians battled each other across the length and breadth of Spain's frontier. During those embattled centuries, Spain seemed to have settled into the inexorable cyclical rhythm of her climate and geography. Winter frost yielded to summer heat before autumn's chill signaled another turn of the inevitable cycle. The sheep went south, and the sheep returned north. So, too, Muslim and Christian monarchs sallied forth to seize chunks of meseta, then relinquished them before the onslaughts of stronger enemies, who enjoyed their own short-lived grasp over the same conquered territory. The great Muslim general Almanzor, for example, carted Compostela's cathedral bells southward as a gaudy souvenir of his late tenth-century sack of Santiago; those same bells would one day find their way back north, hoisted by a victorious Christian army.

Christian Spain's dead heroes sometimes mimicked the same back-and-forth rhythm. After his death in Córdoba, the remains of martyr-activist Eulogius were eventually translated from Muslim Spain to the north's Cathedral of Oviedo. Isidore of Seville, too, made the journey north, accorded a revered resting place alongside kings and queens in the Leonese church renamed to honor him. San Isidro de León remains a treasured stopover for Santiago-bound pilgrims. The church has a less happy association with medieval Spain's inexorable north-and-south, back-and-forth rhythm: Almanzor had also visited this place, razing a predecessor church during one of many raids into the Christian north.

The north-south journeys of the living were unfortunately more poignant than the posthumous travels of Eulogius or Isidore. The Christian captives bearing Santiago's bells to Córdoba were destined to end their lives as slaves, as did countless Christians and Muslims captured or banished in seesaw military struggles that characterized these centuries. Christians, Jews, and Muslims traveled north and traveled south, as warriors, slaves, opportunists, or exiles, the timing of their ultimately pointless migrations less predictable and less sensible than the regular comings and goings of Spain's sheep.

The ancient Greek sages had imagined history as a great cyclical wheel, endlessly turning and repeating itself from the beginning of time into a future that would continue eternally. Aristotle mused, "Probably each art and science has often been developed as far as possible and has again perished" as human civilization made its great march through time. Some three centuries later, the Latin poet Virgil somberly opined, "New wars again shall arise, and a mighty Achilles be sent to Troy." So it seemed in Spain. The soldiers and saints went forth; the captives, exiles, and bodies came back. The bells were stolen; the bells were returned. To what end?

Isidore of Seville died convinced that history was no meaningless circle but a passage forward, one might say a pilgrimage, toward a more promising future. In one way, much of what transpired during these centuries proved Isidore wrong. Instead of moving forward, Spain seemed stuck on a treadmill of hatred and violence. With Toledo's capture, that treadmill began spinning at a faster pace. Muslim revivalist Almoravids faced off against Crusader knights. Both sides ratcheted up the religious rhetoric to accompany the more hostile tempo of their encounter.

Christendom's heroic King Charlemagne had been comfortably enjoying his eternal reward for almost three centuries as this Reconquest struggle to dominate Spain escalated. Europe's epic poets found in the many legends surrounding this venerable king one that seemed particularly apt to Christian Spain's crusade. And so, in the late eleventh century, the long-dead king was pressed into service as mythic spokesperson for Christendom's emerging Crusade. Yet, by the end of the great epic *Song of Roland,* one wonders whether Charlemagne was eager to have stepped onto that treadmill of violence gripping Iberia.

9. Charlemagne

"God, How Wearisome My Life Is"

They make odd bedfellows. The one, medieval Europe's greatest emperor and its enduring archetype of Christian kingship. The other, an outlaw.

Such are the heroes central to Europe's two great medieval epics. The *Song of Roland* revolves around Charlemagne; the *Poem of El Cid* celebrates Rodrigo Díaz de Vivar, better known as El Cid. It's symbolically rich that Christian Spain's paramount epic hero is better known by his Arabic honorific name: El Cid, from *al-sayyid,* "the lord." It's equally revealing of the age that the confrontation between Christianity and Islam forms an overriding preoccupation of both these semilegendary tales.

As literary heroes, the sober Charlemagne and buoyant Cid anchor opposite ends of Spain's tumultuous twelfth century. Most scholars date the written *Chanson de Roland* (*Song of Roland*) to approximately 1100 and the *Poema de Mio Cid* (*Poem of My Cid*) between 1201 and 1207. *Roland*'s bard wrote on the heels of military triumphs that presaged vast opportunity for Christendom. King Alfonso VI had seized Muslim Toledo in 1085; Muslim rulers were vanquished from Sicily in 1091, after a two-century hegemony. In 1094, El Cid engineered the astonishing feat of capturing Muslim Valencia on Spain's Mediterranean

119

coast, a victory that would be immortalized one century later in the epic poem that honors him.

The victories in Sicily, Toledo, and Valencia dangled the tantalizing prospect that Christian Europe might finally surmount Islam. Pope Urban II had accordingly summoned heroic Christian knights in 1095 to seize the moment by liberating the Holy Land. *Roland*'s author sculpted his King Charlemagne fully aware that the monarch and his brave nephew Roland represented the arch role models for Christian knights, the Crusades' recruiting poster par excellence.

Beyond rallying Christian knights, the two epics depicted the sort of Spain that should emerge from the Reconquest. Just as Santiago's schizophrenic image (pilgrim and Moor killer) mirrored two strains of Christian Spain, so too did these two epics offer competing visions struggling for its soul. How would Christian Spaniards deal with the Muslims and Jews falling under their dominance? The *Song of Roland* embodies one solution to Spain's dilemma: a homogeneous Christian Spain where those who worship differently face the unappealing choice of conversion or death—it doesn't much matter which, so long as Islam's menace is exterminated. Charlemagne journeys from his Christian France to invade Spain's swirl of Muslim, Christian, and Jew. This alien, disordered world seems to frighten him, and he wants nothing more than to set it right and be done with it.

As will be seen in the following chapter, however, *El Cid* champions a very different Reconquest vision. Where Charlemagne recoils from Spain, the Cid will revel in it. The Cid's companions will hail him throughout the epic as a man "born in a fortunate hour." Unlike Charlemagne the outsider, who presumes to "fix" another country and then leave, the Spanish Cid's perspective is that of a man who will continue to live alongside those he conquers and knows he must reap the consequences of how he treats them.

The action of the French epic *Song of Roland* transpires almost entirely in Spain. Here is a showdown between right and wrong, and Spain alone offered a vast enough stage for such a mythic struggle. The epic is simply plotted, as if to boil off extraneous detail to stage a starkly spotlit confrontation between Christian Good and Muslim Evil.

There were also practical, nonartistic reasons for the sparse plots of these medieval French epics, called *chansons de geste* (songs of brave deeds). They were not published works to be read; few Europeans could read, and producing hand-crafted books was expensive. Instead, chansons de geste were typically sung at banquets, fairs, and wherever itinerant *jongleurs* might find appreciative, and paying, audiences. Jongleurs were entertainers, not scholars, and the related English word "juggler" hints at the deep bag of tricks they typically plied. It served both jongleur and listener to keep the story simple. Jongleurs didn't have to master elaborate plot lines, and late-arriving audience members who missed the last installment could easily catch up.

A definitive manuscript of the *Song of Roland* bears the signature of Turoldus. Some scholars credit this putative composer with significantly shaping older oral legends and written chronicles into the epic we read today. Others fancy Turoldus as a mere copyist of an epic that acquired near-final shape decades earlier. Until academicians finish plowing this fertile field of scholarly debate, the name Turoldus can serve as proxy for whatever wider cast of poets, historians, and itinerant entertainers polished and amplified the raw material that ultimately became the *Song of Roland*.

Medieval audiences would have been familiar with the legend surrounding eighth-century Charlemagne and his nephew Roland, so the epic accordingly devotes a mere nine lines to background before plunging listeners into the midst of a crucial deliberation. Charlemagne's forces have ravaged Spain for seven years: "There is no castle which can resist him/No wall or city left to be destroyed." His punishing siege is now tightening the noose around Saragossa, the only Muslim principality to have eluded his grasp. Its desperate overlords duplicitously propose a deal, never intending to honor it: if Charlemagne relieves his siege and returns to France, King Marsile of Saragossa will follow and convert to Christianity; hostages from Saragossa will accompany Charlemagne's armies to guarantee Marsile's later arrival.

Charlemagne accepts the proposed deal, though key advisors, including his beloved nephew, suspect deceit. Events vindicate their fears, through even more abominable treachery than they imagined: Roland's own stepfather, Ganelon, harboring some unexplained hatred, has surreptitiously plotted with Saragossa's Muslims, "To try to bring about the death of Roland."

Charlemagne decamps for what should be a joy-filled homeward journey. Saragossa's surrender has crowned his Spanish campaign's success; his soldiers will soon reunite with lovers and families after war's harsh deprivations. Yet grim foreboding settles on the soldiers winding through narrow, twisting Pyrenees passes:

> High are the hills and the valleys dark.
> The rocks are dull-hued, the defiles filled with horror.
> The Franks spent the day in great sorrow.

The audience knows what Charlemagne's soldiers vaguely dread. As the army picks its way through the Pyrenees' labyrinthine defiles toward France, Roland's contingent falls far behind Charlemagne's vanguard. Distant trumpets announce the Muslim ambush that ignites a desperate French struggle for survival. Roland might better the odds by sounding his battle horn to summon reinforcement but refuses to do so, fatally determined to die in Charlemagne's service rather than draw his lord into harm's way:

> It is our duty to be here for our king:
> for his lord a vassal must suffer hardships
> and he must lose both hair and hide.

Roland's grossly outnumbered band acquit themselves heroically in a battle scene offering all the technicolor goriness of today's violent action films. Roland strikes one attacker, "splits his breast and shatters all his bones/Severing from his back his entire spine." His colleague Oliver slays another: "He smites both his eyes out of his head/His brains come spilling out over his feet."

Although the Muslims pay dearly for each Frankish life, their superior numbers carry the day; the battle's ultimate outcome seems never in doubt. Roland's unit is slaughtered. Only brave (if fatally headstrong) Roland is spared death at Muslim hands. Exhausted and wounded, he finally takes up his battle horn "and gave a feeble blow." He is summoning Charles, not to wage battle but to bury his dead. Roland expends his final energies dragging his companions' lifeless bodies to receive their chaplain's absolution, then confesses his own sins and breathes his last; his lonely death heightens the poignant nobility of his heroic last stand. Angels immediately descend and "bear the count's soul to Paradise."

Though the poem's emotional apex passes with Roland's death, nearly half its action remains. After the heightened intensity of Roland's struggle, readers may have trouble shaking the unsatisfactory feeling of anticlimax as the remaining scenes unfold. Charlemagne's armies wreak vengeance on King Marsile's Muslim army. A final battle pits Charlemagne against a Muslim contingent drawn from all corners of the globe. After emerging victorious, Charlemagne finally returns to France for the epic's last piece of unfinished business: the trial and execution of the traitorous Ganelon, who betrayed Roland.

Though much of the epic's action is poetic invention, the *Song of Roland* is rooted in historical events. Every tower demands sturdy foundations, and Charlemagne is the sure historical bedrock on which this epic rises. Charles the Great unified France and subdued swaths of modern-day Italy, Germany, and Spain. Indubitably medieval Europe's greatest monarch, his life and legend defined the ideal of Christian kingship for centuries.

Charlemagne did indeed besiege Saragossa, but the circumstances differed considerably from Turoldus's depiction. *Roland*'s Charlemagne is primarily motivated to recapture Saragossa for Christianity. Turoldus never says so explicitly because he doesn't need to: Charlemagne's motives become self-evident as the epic's opening stanza reveals that Saragossa's King Marsile "does not love God;/He serves Muhammad and calls upon Apollo." But the historical Charles was motivated by more practical concerns than Saragossa's dominant religion. Surely the restoration of Christianity to Spain figured among this devout king's aspirations, but his Spanish foray was not a missionary venture, nor had the pope or Charlemagne's court chaplains urged a proto-crusade against Muslim Spain.

Rather, Barcelona's Muslim governor enticed Charlemagne into

Iberia, proposing an alliance against Saragossa's emir. Hence, Charle-magne invaded Spain as an ally of Islam as much as its enemy. Above all, he was driven by hard-headed national interest. The feud between two Muslim governors presented Charlemagne's opportunity to scoop up Spanish territory as a buffer zone insulating France from future Muslim attacks. The 711 Islamic invasion that overwhelmed the Visi-goth King Roderic and swept through Iberia one generation later spilled over the Pyrenees to imperil France. Muslim armies drew within two hundred miles of Paris before Charlemagne's grandfather, the aptly named Charles Martellus (i.e., Charles "the Hammer"), repulsed Islam in 732. Two generations later, grandson Charlemagne strove to ensure that France would never again suffer such an incursion.

So Turoldus simplified Charlemagne's motives to distill a more pris-tine icon of the good Christian knight as Europe geared up for the Cru-sades. Why begrudge a poet his poetic license? Yet another poetic invention soon follows in Turoldus's account of the Muslim sneak at-tack on Roland's rear guard. Here, too, the epic tracks historical events before veering sharply into invented territory, the facts be damned.

Charlemagne's army did in fact withdraw hastily from Saragossa, not because of any false promise of conversion by its emir but to quell a reported uprising in faraway Saxony. Saragossa was abandoned as un-finished business; Charlemagne's army undertook a forced march to-ward what is today Germany. Despite the urgency of reaching restless Saxony before its uprising spiraled out of control, Charlemagne's armies nonetheless lingered long enough en route to pillage the Basque stronghold of Pamplona. Basque raiders exacted revenge in an ambush recounted by Charlemagne's court historian Einhard: "Rushing down on the last part of the [French] baggage train . . . [the Basques] killed them to the last man. They then snatched up the baggage, and . . . scat-tered in all directions without losing a moment." Thus, Charlemagne's army was ambushed in the Pyrenees by vengeful Basque raiders, not by the Muslims so roundly vilified in the epic. (The epic's false accusation of Islam for a Basque attack would be eerily, and tragically, mirrored nearly a millennium later, when Basques were wrongly suspected of the deadly March 2004 Madrid train bombings perpetrated by Muslim terrorists.)

Einhard's facts are milled into *Roland*'s showdown between noble Christianity and perfidious Islam. By conveniently slipping a Muslim army into the Basque raiders' historical shoes, Turoldus creates the climactic event around which to structure *Roland*'s struggle between good and evil. His considerable skill at denigrating Islam is matched by his ignorance (perhaps cultivated?) of its teachings. Saragossa's Muslims "hoist Muhammad on high in the tallest tower . . . No pagan fails to pray to him and adore him." Europe, gripped with Crusading fever, hardly spared time to absorb Islam's core tenets; safe to say that few to none of Turoldus's Christian audience would have known or cared that worshipping Muhammad is the *last* thing a devout Muslim would do, respecting Muhammad's admonition against "associating" the merely human with the divine.

Turoldus stretches yet further. Monotheistic Muslims are mangled into polytheist pagans. One of them prays, "May Muhammad, who has us in his power, and Tervagant and Apollo, our lord, Save the king." Roland reminds his comrades why they fight, boiling the confrontation down to conveniently simple terms: "The pagans are wrong and the Christians are right." This unambiguous struggle between Muslim black and Christian white is metaphorically (and literally) depicted in the enemy forces bearing down on Roland and his Christian compatriots:

> Out in front rides a Saracen [i.e., a Muslim], Abisme
> . . . A man of evil traits and mighty treachery
> He does not believe in God, the son of the Virgin Mary
> And is as black as molten pitch.

The French chaplain Archbishop Turpin rallies Roland's forces to Holy War by outlining the terms of their Christian jihad:

> Help us now to sustain the Christian faith
> . . . you will be blessed martyrs
> And take your place in Paradise on high.

After Turpin absolves their sins, "As penance he orders them to strike [the Muslim side]."

After Roland's death, the struggle between Saragossa and France assumes cosmic dimensions. Islam's worldwide leader enters the fray to support Spain's flagging Muslims. Baligant approaches Spain with recruits drawn from forty kingdoms: "Vast are the forces of this infidel race." His pagan warriors seem more animal than human:

> They are a race which does not serve the Lord God
> . . . Their skins are as hard as iron
> for this reason they scorn helmets and hauberks [i.e., body
> armor].

The poet rounds out his depiction of incarnate evil by situating Baligant's capital in Babylon, that ancient Mesopotamian city synonymous with all things godless in the Old Testament—never mind that the fabled Babylon had been long abandoned before Islam ever reached the Near East. Charlemagne's troops make short work of Baligant's vast Babylonian legions, notwithstanding their ironlike skins.

By the last of its 298 stanzas, Charlemagne has restored order to this disordered world of Christian right pitted against Muslim wrong. Though he mourns the loss of Roland and countless valiant knights, he has ultimately triumphed. Muslim Spain has bowed to his authority, with 100,000 Saragossans submitting to Christian baptism. Even Saragossa's Muslim Queen Bramimonde has embraced Christianity.

Yet, despite Charlemagne's righteous cause and his mission's success, the epic closes on a sorrowful, discomfiting note. The angel Gabriel appears to exhort Charlemagne once again into battle against Islam: "Charles, summon your imperial armies . . . The Christians call upon you and cry out for you." Surely the poet has set the stage for a vigorous, enthusiastic response to this heavenly summons. Charlemagne's victory over Baligant has thrown Islam into backfooted disarray. The saintly Roland's tragic death cries out for further vengeance. Christian audiences have vicariously fought, died, and triumphed alongside Roland and Charlemagne; the long epic wind-up has poised them for Charlemagne's pitch that a few good Christian knights join the real-life Crusade to Jerusalem.

Yet, against all expectations, audiences are instead left pondering a puzzling, unforgettable final image. Charlemagne, awakened by Gabriel's call to duty, lies alone, weeping in his chambers. We are told that the battle-weary emperor "had no wish to go" [back to war]. His final words are a stunningly disconsolate lament: "God . . . how wearisome my life is."

No medieval Christian would doubt Charlemagne's ultimate response. The pious emperor will rise to Christendom's defense and not shirk his Christian duty. Yet *Roland* has ended on a chord more ambiguous than rousing. Charlemagne's existence seems a mirthless one, no less foreboding than when his armies scaled Pyrenees passes on the eve of the fateful ambush: "The rocks are dull-hued, the defiles filled with horror./The Franks spent the day in great sorrow."

The *Song of Roland* leaves us pondering an odd paradox. There is clarity in this world: "The pagans are wrong and the Christians are right." As simple as that. Yet sureness of purpose neither comforts nor encourages Charlemagne, not even when the divine messenger Gabriel reinforces the call. Triumph has not relieved the gloom that afflicts the king. "God, how wearisome my life is."

Why isn't the emperor happier? Turoldus never tells us. There are some obvious possible explanations. His victory notwithstanding, he has endured the grievous loss of soldiers and, most painfully, of his nephew Roland. But Charlemagne's words suggest a more straightforward explanation for his world-weariness. Called yet again into battle, "he had no wish to go." Who would? Charlemagne will essentially be refighting the battle he has just finished. And so will it be, endlessly. He's become mired in an endless cycle that can be broken only by the total annihilation of Islam. *Roland* brooks no possibility of living alongside this enemy in peace or tolerating Muslim beliefs; there is no common ground between Muslim and Christian in this world. No wonder, called again to step onto this unrelentingly hateful and pessimistic treadmill, the reluctant emperor "had no wish to go." Ironically, Charlemagne, who embodies Christianity with its vision of a history that moves ever forward, has instead become trapped in an endless circular wheel of history where violence ever begets violence.

Predictably, the back-and-forth wars to which Charlemagne "had no wish to go" were still being waged a good century after the *Song of*

Roland was finalized. In the meantime, a new epic hero emerged for the Reconquest. But this new Crusader hero, El Cid, was native to Spanish soil, not a French import like Charlemagne. The Cid's epic status was backed by unimpeachable Crusader credentials: he not only fought on Spain's Muslim-Christian frontier but had conquered his way through Muslim territory right to the Mediterranean.

Yet, there would be something unexpected in the epic Cid. In the poet's hands, Charlemagne had been transformed into a more aggressive Crusader than the Charlemagne of history, promoting an uncompromising vision of a homogeneous Christian Spain. But the *Poem of El Cid* would give Spaniards a different model to contemplate. Where Charlemagne saw only black and white, El Cid gallops through a decidedly more multihued Spain. Where Roland was unshakably convinced that the "pagans are wrong and the Christians are right," El Cid seems less certain where goodness and nobility lie as he observes the Christians and Muslims around him. Spain's new Reconquest hero seems little bothered by such ambiguity. Indeed, he seems a good deal happier.

10. El Cid

"Born in a Fortunate Hour"

The *Song of Roland* closed with King Charlemagne weeping. So begins the *Poema de mio Cid*: "Tears streamed from his eyes." The Cid has just been banished from his native Castile by King Alfonso VI. Yet, while the victorious Charlemagne lamented his destiny, the unjustly exiled Cid embraces his: "I give Thee thanks, O God, our Father in Heaven. My wicked enemies have contrived this plot against me."

It is the first of many contrasts between these two epic figures. Charlemagne, the storied king, boasts exactly the pedigree expected of a medieval hero. El Cid boasts only the dubious distinction of being banished by the storied Spanish king who conquered Muslim Toledo in 1085. With Alfonso undeniably one of Christian Spain's "good guys," surely whoever he banished must be a bad guy.

Except El Cid. No medieval Spaniard needed the *Poema de mio Cid* to learn its protagonist's exploits. The Cid's legend began blossoming almost immediately after his death (1099); a subsequent century of burgeoning oral tradition and historical chronicle was eventually filtered through the poet's imaginative lens to create the epic Cid. That a man banished by so storied a monarch as Alfonso VI could be regarded a hero speaks for El Cid's iconic status. Indeed, well before the epic poem was finalized, the Cid's life story had already been documented in a historical chronicle (the *Historia Roderici*), a distinction rarely accorded during the medieval era other than to saints or royals.

As with *Roland*'s Turoldus, the exact identity of *El Cid*'s author is unknown. Though the authoritative manuscript's closing lines seem to leave no doubt, "Per Abbat wrote it [this book] down in . . . 1207," scholars debate this phrase's exact meaning. A medieval copyist, for example, could have used the same word *escrivió* ("wrote") in describing his craft. Per Abbat may have merely copied an earlier original work or transcribed a well-known oral epic.

Whoever shaped the poem was almost certainly influenced by the *Song of Roland. El Cid*, structured as a typical "song of brave deeds," echoes some of *Roland*'s plot devices. *El Cid* stands out not as a new form of epic storytelling, but for its strikingly original protagonist, who all but breaks the familiar heroic mold.

Though nearly equal to *Roland* in length, *El Cid* narrates a much more involved story. *Roland*'s plot revolves around Charlemagne's siege of Saragossa and the ambush suffered by the French; both historical events transpired in the single year of 778. In contrast, *El Cid*'s skeletal episodes sprawl over a decade, from El Cid's second banishment (1089) by King Alfonso to his capture of Muslim Valencia (1094) and death (1099). *Roland*'s spare plot unfurls systematically: Saragossa's surrender yields logically to the Muslim ambush and Charlemagne's revenge. In contrast, *El Cid*'s action rambles along almost haphazardly. After entrusting his wife and daughters to a monastery's care, the banished Cid departs Castile. A contingent of knights eagerly follows, captivated by his charisma and eager to win fortune beside him.

The Cid's men are essentially outlaws scavenging a living on Spain's frontier, though Per Abbat never stoops to label them as such. Forced by the terms of banishment to leave behind his wealth, the Cid finds prosperity anew by raiding frontier towns and making them his tributaries. Unlike Charlemagne's overtly religious purpose in besieging Saragossa, the Cid's marauding swing can hardly be called a crusade. No mass conversion scenes accompany his victories, and though the Cid typically conquers Muslim principalities, Christian princes also feel his sting.

The Cid piles up victories along a vaguely southeastward arc of conquest that begins near his native Burgos and ends in Valencia on the Mediterranean coast. While *Roland* leaves Spain strewn with France's valiant dead, none of the Cid's key lieutenants and precious few of his rank-and-file soldiers perish. The Cid wins every battle he joins. With good reason did his followers in real life (like his followers in the epic) hail him with vibrant pride as *Campeador,* "the battlefield hero."

Everybody loves a winner. Muslim-ruled states capitulate, and the victorious Cid claws back his lost status. King Alfonso's estimate of his banished subject warms considerably as the Cid apportions the monarch a share of booty from each new conquest. The Cid's growing prosperity also attracts the envious interest of the two noble *infantes** of Carrión. They propose marriage to the Cid's daughters, coveting his wealth in exchange for the stepped-up status that will accrue to the daughters by marrying noble infantes. At the King's bidding, El Cid agrees to the match.

It proves disastrous, for the infantes are everything the Cid is not: cowardly, selfish, cruel, and dishonest. After making themselves laughingstocks by shrinking from danger and fleeing in battle, the infantes resort to the time-honored outlet for impotent male rage: venting their anger and shame on the women. Showing the Cid's daughters "signs of tender love" one night, the next morning they strip and abandon their wives in a wild forest after "beat[ing] them with their buckled straps and hack[ing] their flesh cruelly with their sharp spurs . . . The two young men struck till they were weary, trying to see which of them could deal the hardest blows."

Though the Cid is more than capable of the vengeance these scoundrels deserve, he instead sues for justice before the King. Credit the infantes with consistency: they stick to their caddish credo throughout the ensuing trial, vigorously defending their reprehensible behavior by blaming their victims. As nobles, they are fit to marry "the daughters of kings and emperors" rather than the Cid's lesser-born children. And by deserting the Cid's daughters, they argue, "we are raised, not lowered, in the esteem of the world." One can imagine how well

---

*An *infante* here refers to a son of a king or high noble who is not the presumed heir to the throne; over time, the term was reserved for offspring of the king alone.

this line of argument played with countless peasant audiences enjoying performances of the epic during stopovers en route to Santiago.

As it turns out, the Cid's daughters *are* worthy of marriage to kings and emperors, for just as the infantes wind up their pathetic self-defense, two messengers unexpectedly arrive to request the Cid's spurned daughters as marriage partners for the princes of Navarre and Aragon. (Granted, the timing is a bit too convenient, but such things happen in epic poetry's compressed time frame.) The marriage proposal rebuffs the infantes and provides sturdy epic thread to help sew together Christian Spain's ever feuding kingdoms. With the marriage of his daughters, El Cid's native Castile will be symbolically wedded to Navarre and Aragon. (Though their betrothal to the Carrión infantes is pure poetic invention, El Cid's daughters did marry into the noble houses of Navarre and Barcelona.) Thus, three of Spain's great constituent kingdoms—Castile, Navarre, and Aragon (i.e., the region including Barcelona)—could claim some stake in the epic hero's legacy.

After the interlude in royal matchmaking, one knight refocuses the discussion on the despicable infantes: "Because you [infantes] deserted them, the Cid's daughters are superior to you in every respect." Another voices what readers have already concluded: "It was an honor for you [infantes] to be connected with the Campeador." Still, though there is little doubt where justice lies, the dispute is resolved not by royal pronouncement but by a joust pitting the infantes' side against the Cid's knights. After all, this is epic entertainment. Why deprive the audience of one last taste of knightly derring-do? (Medieval audiences would also recognize the outcome of a joust as symbolically representing God's judgment in the dispute.) The infantes are soundly thrashed by the Cid's warriors and slink back to Carrión in disgrace. And the poet rightfully wishes, "May such a fate or worse befall anyone who treats a noble lady shamefully and then abandons her." El Cid and his daughters presumably live happily ever after, as does Spain, for "Today the Kings of Spain are related to him and all gain lustre from the fame of the fortunate Campeador."

El Cid's core themes shine forth even before exploring the saga's historical underpinnings. Glory can be won on Spain's frontier, won by men like the Cid: brave, honest, adventurous, and devoted to family, faith, and companions. Yet, as with *Roland,* it's illuminating to examine where *El Cid* tracks history and where it invents it.

Rodrigo Díaz, the Cid, was born near Burgos into a family of lesser nobility and raised in court circles. As a favored lieutenant of León-Castile's Prince Sancho, he distinguished himself in a military engagement that reduced Muslim-ruled Saragossa to tributary status. With the death of Sancho's father (King Fernando I), Christian Spain endured another of those crippling partitions that deflected aggressive energy from Muslim Spain and channeled it into a feud among Christian states. Fernando's kingdom was parceled out among three sons, who succeeded him as Sancho II of Castile, Alfonso VI of León, and García of Galicia. Given medieval Spain's history, it would have been surprising had these three *not* turned on each other. As one twelfth-century chronicle put it, "The Spanish kings are reputed to be of such bellicosity that when any prince of their line has reached manhood . . . he prepares to contend by force, against his brothers . . . or his parents, so that he alone may exercise royal authority."

Though Sancho seized the upper hand in the internecine squabbles, his premature, childless, and unnatural death left Alfonso VI the uncontested ruler of León and Castile. Sancho's prized lieutenant, Rodrigo Díaz (El Cid), suddenly found himself in a precarious position. Still, talented warriors were not cast aside lightly, and a marriage was hastily arranged between El Cid and one of Alfonso VI's nieces. But the headstrong, ambitious Cid, determined to forge his own destiny rather than yoke it to Alfonso's star, led an unauthorized military raid against a frontier province allied to King Alfonso and was subsequently banished.

He resurfaced as a mercenary serving Saragossa's Muslim emir, the very same Muslim Saragossa that the Cid had besieged a decade earlier in the service of the Christian Prince Sancho. The ensuing decade demonstrated the Cid's military prowess and genius, but above all proved that he was his own man, bound by allegiance to himself against all others. Throughout his campaigns, the religious affiliations of his enemies and allies mattered less than the opportunity for personal gain. He besieged Muslim Saragossa; he defended Muslim

Saragossa. He later joined King Alfonso VI's campaign against the Muslim Almoravid dynasty; he deserted that campaign, suffering the banishment that remained in force until his death.

During this banishment, the Cid engineered the stunning conquest of Muslim Valencia (1094) that crowned his career. Lush Valencia was an Andalusian jewel, later idealized by one Muslim poet as "the dwelling of all beauty/This they say both in the East and in the West." Its surrender was a shattering blow for Muslim Spain, though the humiliation was not long endured. El Cid died a half-dozen years later, and Valencia, deep in Muslim territory, was soon after abandoned as indefensible. His remains were later borne to the monastery of San Pedro de Cardeña and attained cult status as his legend flourished. (There is an unlikely legend that the Cid's favorite horse is buried in the monastery courtyard; if it was, that's unfortunately all the monks now have, as the powerful bishop of Burgos eventually wrestled away the Cid's remains in the early twentieth century for reburial in Burgos's Cathedral.)

The epic poem frames El Cid as a hero of fathomless mythic appeal, its author(s) masterfully cropping away whatever facts mar the desired portrait. The historical Cid's misadventures gave Alfonso VI and any other right-thinking monarch good reason to keep him at arm's length, yet the epic sidesteps the Cid's miscues to portray his banishment as a wholly unwarranted scheme engineered by a jealous court enemy. Within the poem's first few verses, a Greek chorus of townspeople lament the Cid's plight: "What a good vassal. If only he had a good lord."

A not-so-subtle—and not-so-accurate—portrait emerges of the Cid as self-made everyman. That the Cid is a noble raised in court circles is downplayed. The epic Cid evinces a *personal* nobility won through deeds, not inherited through birth. Any enterprising Spaniard can emulate the epic Cid. The noble-born but shiftless infantes of Carrión are the opposite, as underscored by their overweening obsession with status: "The Cid comes from the village of Vivar and we are of the noble house of Carrión."

As the finishing touches were being applied to El Cid's epic, Christian Spain sorely needed men daring enough to follow his adventurous lead. While the epic Cid never lost a battle, real-life events had not unfolded so rosily for Christian Spain in the century after the Crusades were launched and the *Song of Roland* finalized. The Cid's Valencia had fallen back into Muslim hands almost immediately after his death. So too Jerusalem: the First Crusade's hard-won trophy had been recaptured by the Muslim warrior Saladin in 1187. In 1195, a Muslim army decimated a Christian army in the battle of Alarcos. Such setbacks hardly coaxed would-be Crusaders and settlers onto the frontier.

The mythic Cid righted the uncertain impression left by real life. He was the Campeador who never lost a battle, the knight who conquered his way to the Mediterranean coast (never mind, as Per Abbat conveniently forgot to remind his audience, that the Cid's Valencia conquest proved ephemeral). El Cid's conquests showered him in wealth, undoubtedly inspiring some intrepid souls to risk their lives pursuing similarly outsized rewards.

Equally inspiring was the epic's portrayal of the Cid as a flesh-and-blood character accessible to the common man. The banished Cid endures setbacks, just as his audience members did in their own lives. He doesn't sponge off inherited wealth but earns his living, just as normal people must (granted, his marauding livelihood is not quite a normal trade). Whereas *Roland* offers scant clue that Charlemagne is married and a parent, the Cid champions tenderness and family loyalty as virtues no less vital than bravery. Facing banishment, he agonizes not over the danger and uncertainty ahead but over the wife and daughters he must leave behind. The prospect of departing "pains as when the finger-nail is torn from the flesh." As the Cid rides into banishment, he turns back to steal a few final glances at his family, until a companion finally chides him to look forward with optimism.

The Cid was hewn from the multilayered rock of Spain's reality rather than the pure white marble of its Reconquest mythology. The Cid served Islam as well as Christendom during his military career, and primarily served *himself.* His allegiance to Spanish royal authorities, and their embrace of him, was ever tenuous and wary. One would have expected these wrinkles to be ironed away when time came to tailor the mythic El Cid of epic poetry. Yet *El Cid* casts aside traditional heroic garb to shape a fresh vision of heroism and honor that rings true to the complex reality spawning it. Yes, the Cid's epic handlers airbrush away his more wayward exploits to present an ever loyal vassal of King Alfonso, a credible recruiter to pitch the Reconquest and resettlement of Spain's frontier. But the epic elevates the Cid on his own merits; he shines brightly enough on his own, so that the epic's author doesn't resort to tarring Spain's Muslims with a blackened brush to create contrast.

To be sure, the epic incorporates stereotypical Crusades imagery, as when a bishop leads El Cid's forces into one battle: "[I] came here to join you for the desire I felt to kill a Moor or two." Similarly, one trusted lieutenant refuses any share of war spoils "until, on my good horse, fighting Moors in the field, I use my lance and my sword till the blood drips down to my elbow." But unlike *Roland,* this is no set piece of Christian good against Muslim evil. Neither the Cid nor his companions mock Islam or turn its warriors into ghouls. There are no mass conversions; the Cid's conquests are not about religion but, well, *conquest.* The Cid reaps war plunder but allows vanquished Muslim townspeople to resume their lives (including, presumably, their customary worship). Relations between Moors and Christians don't lapse into *Roland*'s unthinking creed that "the pagans are wrong and the Christians are right." Indeed, *El Cid*'s battles sometimes pit Muslim against Muslim and Christian against Christian as mixed-religion armies square off at either end of the battlefield—just as happened in real-life Spain.

Early in the epic, Alcocer's Muslims, subjugated by the Cid, remain neutral while an army of Muslim coreligionists battles to liberate the town from the Christian Cid's rule. Why had the townspeople not turned on the Cid during the battle? The answer becomes self-evident as the Cid departs for new conquest: "When the Cid decided to leave the fortress all the Moors were sorry to see him go. 'You are going, Cid,' they said. 'May our prayers go before you! We are well satisfied with the way you have treated us.' When at last he took his departure from Alcocer, the Moors wept." The despoiled inhabitants of any violated frontier town, Christian or Muslim, would hardly have wept to see the backs of their invaders. But the unlikely vignette nonetheless sketches a wholly different ethic than does *Roland*: namely, that a Christian conqueror might somehow accommodate a vanquished Muslim population and establish grounds for future coexistence based on trust rather than terror. The Cid's heroism lies not only in his conquests but in fair treatment of his tributaries.

Roland painted a global struggle between Christian right and Muslim wrong as Charlemagne squared off against Baligant, emir of Babylon. *Roland*'s *universal* struggle between good and evil contrasts with *El Cid*'s *personalized* study of the noble person. What makes the Cid, or anyone, honorable is neither station in life nor religious beliefs but *deeds*. The epic lionizes El Cid as a brave, optimistic knight and loyal family man. When the Crusading rhetoric evaporates after each battle, the spotlight lingers on contrasts between honor and dishonor. The Cid's counterpoint is not a Muslim archvillain patterned after *Roland*'s "black as pitch" soldiers but the infantes of Carrión: *Christians,* and *nobles* no less.

In *Roland,* honor includes religious creed. Some of *Roland*'s Christian characters may fail the standards expected of honorable men, but all Muslims fail the same standard simply by virtue of their pagan beliefs. More than once *Roland*'s poet observes of some otherwise admirable Muslim knight, "Had he been a Christian, he would have been a worthy baron." *El Cid*'s very different outlook is personified in the Muslim Abengalbón, El Cid's vassal and friend. In a remarkable gesture, the Cid confides his daughters to this Muslim's care as they journey through Spain's frontier. Abengalbón serves the Cid's family "for the love he bore to the Campeador." In the Cid's world, so profound a bond as love can even bind Muslim to Christian.

Why such different outlooks in *Roland* and *El Cid,* the one obsessed with evil Islam, the other more nuanced? A simple difference of circumstance may offer partial explanation: the Cid, the Spanish poets who immortalized him, and the Spaniards who heard his saga remained neighbors of those they conquered. They lived, worked, and did business with Spain's Muslims. Unlike *Roland*'s French knights, these were no invaders intent on righting Spain and returning home. Spain *was* their home, its Muslims their neighbors. The first Spanish Crusaders inherited cities and cultures far wealthier and more sophisticated than those in their native north. Though they would have preferred a Toledo populated entirely by Christians, they were often savvy enough to understand that wholesale banishment or mass forced conversions would have destroyed the very sources of the wealth they coveted.

Roland's uncompromising vision contemplates the annihilation of pagan Islam as the only acceptable solution for Spain's future. Charlemagne looses his Saragossa siege only with its emir's (falsely) promised conversion. Though the false promise leads to the strife that spills precious French blood, the sacrifice is not vain. Before the epic closes, 100,000 Saragossans have converted. That these pagans convert is vastly more important than how or why they convert. The Muslim King Marsile's widowed queen is the exception proving the rule. Charlemagne takes her a captive to "fair France," wishing her "to become a convert through love." No such consideration is extended ordinary Muslims as Charlemagne's knights rampage through a moonlit Saragossa's synagogues and mosques, smashing statues "with iron hammers and hatchets." They round up non-Christians:

> They take the pagans up to the baptistery
> If there is anyone who withstands Charles
> He has him hanged or burned or put to death
> More than a hundred thousand are baptized.

The scene almost mirrors harsh reality. In 1064 Pope Alexander II had urged French knights to liberate Muslim-held Barbastro in the kingdom of Saragossa, the first major foray of French knights in support of a Reconquest expedition. The engagement is frequently deemed the precursor of the Crusades, as the pope extended a plenary indulgence to participants. Barbastro's exhausted Muslim defenders endured a forty-day siege, their situation rendered dire once a malfunctioning aqueduct choked off their water supply. The parched town capitulated after its negotiators secured a safe conduct from the French-led besiegers.

The victorious Christians entered a Barbastro far more populous than they had imagined, and as depicted by the Muslim chronicler Ibn Hayyan, the jittery captain of the outnumbered French reconsidered his pledge to spare so many Muslims: "[He] therefore decided on exter-

minating them all, if he could, and ordered a general slaughter." Six
thousand were slain before "it was announced by the public crier that
the slaughter had ended, and that every citizen might return in safety to
his dwelling." Not exactly. As families emerged from hiding, many
were taken captive to be sold as slaves. Ibn Hayyan adds, "It was an invariable custom with the Christians, whenever they took a town by
force of arms, to ravish the daughters in the presence of their fathers,
and the women before the eyes of their husbands and families." This
Muslim account betrays the exaggerated strokes of an aggrieved narra-
tor, but even Christian chroniclers agreed that horrific abuses punctuated the conquest, even as they groped to extenuate their compatriots'
atrocities: "The devil . . . out of envy of this happy progress by the
Christian faith . . . put lustful thoughts into the minds of the Christian
knights."

The knight liberators of Barbastro mostly hailed from beyond the
Pyrenees; Spanish Crusaders often practiced greater restraint on their
native soil. Contrast Barbastro with King Alfonso VI of Castile's conquest of Muslim Toledo some twenty years later. Its defeated Muslims
were neither expelled nor forced to convert; Muslims continued to
worship in Toledo's great mosque and Alfonso appointed an Arabic-
speaking Christian governor to oversee civil authority. Muslim chronicles portray Alfonso presenting himself as "the Emperor of the Two
Religions." If Alfonso did use the appellation, it was remarkable less for
sheer audacity than for the plain recognition that there were two religions, a revolutionary, even heretical notion at the time.

Like too many episodes in medieval Spain's often sorry history,
Christian Toledo's early promise tarnished, starting with the appointment of the French-born Bernard de Sauvetot as its archbishop (it may
not be entirely coincidence that the land of *Roland* would once again
produce a *Roland*-like approach). In Alfonso's absence, the archbishop
seized and converted Toledo's grand mosque to a church. An enraged
Alfonso threatened sanctions on the archbishop, only to be dissuaded
(so the chronicles report) by Toledo's own Muslims, who believed that
capitulation would spare them later reprisals.

In medieval Spain, just as in today's troubled world, Muslims and
Christians sometimes misinterpreted even genuine gestures of recon-

ciliation as part of some sinister agenda. Muslim chroniclers discerned craftier motives underlying Alfonso's benign treatment of Toledo: "Alfonso began to govern the people with justice and moderation, hoping to gain them over to polytheism, and make them embrace his abominable religion." Therein lies an irony more sad than delicious. The Muslim chronicler, steeped in his monotheist creed that there is no god but God, despaired that the Christian conquerors were polytheists: how else to understand the Christian dogma of the Trinity but as worship of *three* gods? (Pagan Irish wrestled with the same conundrum until an inspired St. Patrick legendarily plucked a shamrock to elucidate the Trinitarian concept of "three in one.") Toledo's Muslims abhorred Alfonso's polytheism, exactly what the equally misguided Christian conquerors despised about Islam. (Recall *Roland's* polytheist Muslims bowing before Muhammad, Apollo, and other unnamed idols.)

For the twelfth-century Muslim chronicler Ibn Bassam, disposed to interpret Alfonso's moderation as a ploy to manipulate Muslims into embracing Christian "polytheism," what followed was cruel retribution on devout people unwilling to renounce sacred beliefs: "Seeing that he [Alfonso] could not accomplish this [i.e., convert the Muslims], he set about polluting the principal mosque and turning it into a church for the celebration of detestable rites." The account ends with Christian soldiers tramping through the mosque and tearing down all insignia of Islam, leaving unmolested one wizened Muslim who continued to pray as the noisy desecration unfolded around him.

How reconcile Barbastro's atrocities with Alfonso's tentative overtures toward tolerance in Toledo? In one respect, these are merely two isolated incidents in a centuries-long Reconquest that witnessed shameful barbarity, enlightened leadership, and everything in between. Yet such examples can't merely be waved aside with the facile explanation that "such things happen" in war. Barbastro and Toledo reflected the respective mind-sets of their conquerors. Toledo had been Alfonso's client state for a decade before his military conquest; he had protected Muslim Toledo from its enemies in exchange for annual tribute payments. He understood that Toledo's commercial and cultural sophistication far outstripped his own León-Castile. He captured Toledo to enlarge, enrich, and enhance his domain, not to transform a vibrant city into an empty museum. Retaining its skilled, commercially savvy Muslim populace figured prominently in his priorities. If all of the above inclined Alfonso to tolerance, no such considerations motivated the outsiders, opportunists, and (occasionally) devout believers who besieged Barbastro with interests that sometimes extended no further than whatever spoil they could extract and lug home.

It is gross oversimplification to pluck Barbastro and Toledo from the Reconquest's long history as Exhibit A demonstrating that *El Cid* offers a more enlightened vision of a multifaith Spain because its authors hailed from Spain, whereas *Roland* reflects the outsider's harsher viewpoint. A century separates the epics and three centuries the historical events on which they are based; both bear many authorial fingerprints, from chroniclers determined to advance particular religious or political views to entertainers determined only to tell a good story.

But *El Cid*'s deep Spanish roots and *Roland*'s lack of them are not irrelevant. *El Cid*'s epic world and Alfonso VI's real-life Toledo are home to those who have to rub shoulders daily with those of different faiths, beliefs, and outlooks and who will continue to rub shoulders with them for centuries to come. *El Cid* is as rooted in reality as in Spanish soil. Like it or no, Muslims, Christians, and Jews are here to stay. El Cid wants wealth and power, but the pragmatic Cid also seems to pick his way toward workable accommodation among those who share the Iberian Peninsula.

Charlemagne's perspective differs: as an outsider, whatever the consequences of his intervention, he can simply go home and leave it behind. *Roland*'s fanciful notion of making them all into Christians and then returning home to France is an elegantly simple worldview. But no twelfth- or thirteenth-century Spanish monarch seemed to embrace that worldview as practical, or even, perhaps, desirable. That would change in time. Ferdinand and Isabella's counselors would goad them into just such a policy and devise ways to make it eminently (if tragically) practical by banishing Jews and Muslims who refused to embrace Christianity. Under their leadership, Spain "returned home" to the idealized, homogeneous Christian Spain of the distant Visigoth past.

Charlemagne's world no longer exists. In a world made small by modern transport, media, and weaponry, no community can "go home to France" and isolate itself from the religious other. Nor can one forcibly reorder another community's lives and affairs, then assume, as Charlemagne did, that it will be possible to separate oneself from the consequences and repercussions. To assume the posture of the outsider is as naïve as to imagine that Muslims, Christians, and Jews can today carve out completely separate futures in a world that will continue to grow smaller with each passing generation.

El Cid and *Roland* close with starkly different images. *Roland*'s audiences are left contemplating Christendom's mightiest emperor alone and weeping in the black of night, bewailing "how wearisome my life is." In *El Cid*'s last stanza, the storyteller simply reminds the audience that the Cid is "el que en buen ora nació" ("he who was born in a good hour," or more simply, "the fortunate Cid"). The weeping Charlemagne is trapped on a treadmill to nowhere; the Cid glimpses a way forward.

As the Crusading vanguard seized territory and booty, the scholarly rear guard were to gingerly wander into more prosperous towns and better-stocked libraries than any in Christendom. While the Reconquest lurched along around them, medieval Spaniards thought about the human body and how to heal it, learned new ways of manipulating numbers, reflected on whether their religious faith could ever be reconciled with what science and reason taught them. They learned or recovered knowledge the West had never known or had long forgotten, some of the lost wisdom that Bishop Braulio had so lamented and his friend Isidore had tried to recover.

Some of what Europe learned or rediscovered was mediated by the perpetual minority in this ever changing Spain: its Jewish population.

11. The Second Moses
and Medieval Medicine

 King Alfonso VI, who in 1085 conquered Muslim Toledo (and who banished the Cid in 1089), once proclaimed himself Spain's Emperor of the Two Religions, or so an anonymous Muslim chronicle tells us.

Spain's *third* religion was unworthy of his recognition, it would seem.

But Spain's Jews were sometimes best off when least noted. It rarely benefited them to occupy the forefront of public or royal consciousness. Indeed, it usually redounded to their catastrophic detriment, most tragically in 1492, when tens of thousands of Jews boarded leaky, overcrowded ships and sailed into uncertain exile just as Christopher Columbus struck out for the brighter promise of a New World. Granted a scant four months by Ferdinand and Isabella to embrace Christianity or flee Spain forever, many Jews remained and converted—at least nominally. Large numbers of forced converts surreptitiously honored their ancestral Jewish faith while hoping to escape the potentially fatal gaze of Inquisition authorities determined to round up every last crypto-Jew. Suspected false converts were paraded through Spain's towns and villages in gaudily horrific *autos da fe* (demonstrations of faith), then roasted alive at the stake, the fiery complement to watery exile.

These sorry events were a good many centuries in the future when the heroic Cid romped across Spain's frontier. He died in 1094; his epic poem is dated 1207; the Spanish Inquisition was inaugurated in 1481; and Spain's Jews were expelled in 1492. Yet El Cid's epic dropped its own vague hints of trouble ahead. The Cid's honor code exalted bravery, religious devotion, and fair dealings with others. Well, not completely. One community was conspicuously exempt from the Cid's honorable treatment.

Before venturing into banishment, the Cid coped with what modern entrepreneurs would call a cash flow squeeze. Forbidden from transporting his wealth into exile, the Cid lacked "startup capital" to tide his knights over until they garnered booty from frontier raids. He tricked two Jewish moneylenders, Rachel and Vidas, into advancing 600 gold dinars. Suddenly flush with the gold he needed, the Cid rode off to frontier glory. As he begged divine favor for the adventures ahead, he fashioned a prayer that twisted Christianity's central symbol of love into a mangled emblem of contempt: "Thou [Jesus] didst allow Thyself to be taken by the Jews, and on Mount Calvary in the place called Golgotha they put Thee on the cross."

Rachel and Vidas briefly resurfaced to nag the Cid's lieutenant for repayment of their loan. They were bundled off with blithe reassurances, leaving the audience doubting that the now fabulously wealthy Cid would ever honor his obligation. The same question lingered as the epic closed, not that many audience members enjoying the Cid's heroics would have spared much thought for two swindled Jewish moneylenders. The bit players Rachel and Vidas are hastily sketched stick figures, prefiguring a stock caricature of the Jew in later literature and rhetoric. The canny financiers, a bit too clever for their own good and too eager to profit from a hard-pressed Christian, succumb to the greed that occasions their downfall. No need for the Cid to regret swindling these two. After all, to paraphrase his prayer, the Jews crucified Christ.

Though *El Cid*'s portrait of Spanish Judaism fills a mere twenty of the epic's 3,700 verses, those twenty lines tell enough of a story. One finds in them the roots of a weed that was nursed rather than uprooted, blossoming into the overgrowth of religious enmity that choked off Spain's Jewish civilization.

But *El Cid*'s brittle caricatures belie the far richer reality of medieval Spanish Jewry in the centuries before the ugly thistle of anti-Judaism attained full bloom. Spain's legacy includes the most creative, prosperous Jewish civilization of the medieval era, and only against this magnificent legacy do Spain's stake burnings, expulsions, and forced conversions emerge in their most horrific poignancy. Spain's Jews created and nurtured what dazzled scholars have called a Jewish Golden Age. Their legacy still enlightens Jewish and world thought, long after the living flame of that Golden Age was swamped in watery exile or snuffed out at the charred stake.

Prominent among Spain's Golden Age heroes is Moses Maimonides, whom the soberly objective *Encyclopedia Judaica* deems "the most illustrious figure in Judaism in the post-Talmudic era." Another modern scholar seconds the judgment in simpler terms, calling Maimonides "the outstanding representative of Jewish rationalism for all time"; chapter 12 will explore Maimonides' enduring intellectual contributions to Judaism. This chapter will focus on Maimonides the physician and on other profoundly influential thinkers and translators who helped rouse European medical science from a centuries-long torpor. This Jewish physician's improbable story begins with the fanatical North African Muslim dynasty that spurred his odyssey from Spain to greatness in the Near East at a Muslim royal court.

Moses Maimonides was thirteen when North African invaders touched down in Córdoba in 1148, like other religiously inspired warriors who had battered Iberia since Tariq ibn Ziyad's 711 invasion. Ascetic Almohad fighters had surged from their Atlas Mountain base (in present Morocco) and dominated much of North Africa before launching their jihad into Spain. Like the eleventh century Muslim Almoravid dynasty they displaced, the Almohads aimed to both shore up a faltering Muslim Spain and restore it to greater religious fervor.

The name Almohad reflects the dynasty's fervent embrace of Islam's core belief: they were the *al-Muwahiddun,* those "who affirm the Oneness of God." In their reforming zeal, these Almohads had no room in their Spain for Jews and Christians equally committed to the same dogma of God's absolute unity. Judaism and Christianity were proscribed; synagogues were closed. An Almohad commentator was affronted that Jews "had become so bold as to wear Muslim clothing and . . . mingl[e] with the Muslims in external affairs." That outrage was soon remedied. Jews were forced to don distinctive costumes, and both Christians and Jews were pressured to convert. Some did, often in name only. By day they marched to the cadence of new religious practices; locked away at home they recited older, familiar prayers, undoubtedly with greater fervor, and undoubtedly plagued by doubt over the choice they had made. Others fled, and Spain's exilic "sheep walk" began anew as Christians and Jews streamed from Almohad al-Andalus in search of more tolerant spiritual pasture.

Rabbi Maimon ben Joseph, Moses's father, wandered Spain with his three children for nearly a dozen years seeking a hospitable religious climate. In 1159 the family quit Spain for exile further afield. Historical perspective makes it easy to second-guess his choice: What sense to flee Almohad fanaticism by retreating to the sect's North African base? Predictably, a few years later, the family was again on the move, by some accounts escaping an increasingly hostile Morocco only through the compassionate intervention of a Muslim friend.

Nearly twenty years after fleeing Córdoba, Maimonides' family settled in Fostat (old Cairo) in Egypt, where Moses would live, work, worship, raise his son, and die. If exile, persecution, and refugee life hadn't yet sufficiently tested this family's endurance, other grief would. Moses's father died a year after arriving in Egypt. His younger brother David drowned not long after, during a business expedition; he nearly pulled the whole family under with him, for his trading income had supported the extended family. Suddenly, David's life, livelihood, family assets, and precious jewels consigned by customers were all swept away. Moses found himself liable for the lost wealth and sole guardian of his brother's wife and child. The toll nearly crushed Moses's spirit. He seldom rose from his bed through the course of the succeeding year.

What happened next epitomizes the profound resilience of the human spirit and the wonder of an era when a Jew's fortunes could swing wildly with a changing dynasty, a brother's drowning, luck, determination, talent, and often some mix of all these. Moses tapped inner reservoirs of strength that spurred intense creativity and profound religious devotion while bringing him material success. Within two years of his brother's death, Maimonides the Jew, a religious exile from Almohad discrimination, had won appointment as personal physician and advisor to the Muslim al-Fadil, vizier to the famed warrior-sultan Saladin, who had wrested control of the Holy Land from the Crusaders.

Saladin's 1193 death brought Maimonides yet a further step forward. He was named court physician to Saladin's eldest son and successor, al-Afdal Nur al-Din Ali. With the prestigious post came personal sacrifice: "I am obliged to visit him [the Sultan] every day, early in the morning, and when he or any of his children or concubines are indisposed, I cannot leave." The sultan's priorities were Maimonides' priorities. "Office hours" for others began only *after* Maimonides returned from court. He recounts receiving patients at his home until all hours, "even while lying down from sheer fatigue. When night falls, I am so exhausted I can hardly speak."

Though the sultan's entourage undoubtedly considered their health concerns urgent, such concerns would not strike dispassionate observers as crises. While father Saladin devoted himself to recovering Islam's lost territories, son al-Afdal and his cohort indulged in sybaritic pleasures closer to home. Dr. Maimonides' *Treatise on Cohabitation* responded to one courtier's request for a "regimen that is helpful in increasing sexual potential, because he said that he has a weakness in this regard." Such attenuated virility may seem unbecoming in a powerful royal, but consider the prince's extenuating circumstances. He complained—if "complained" is the right word—that the "multitude of young maidens" available to him were sapping his energies.

Maimonides' home-concocted virility aid wouldn't lure most modern males away from the more expensive potency aids now marketed by major drug companies. Indeed, one wonders whether an exasperated, exhausted Maimonides wasn't merely toying mischievously with the dissolute royal when he prescribed "a wondrous secret which no person has (heretofore) described: take one liter each of carrot oil, and radish oil, one quarter liter of mustard oil, combine it all and place therein one half liter of live saffron-colored ants placed in the sun for a week, then massaged on the member." One hopes for the prince's sake that the ants died before the ointment was applied.

Most of Maimonides' medical secrets were not in fact original. Though one of medieval Europe's outstanding medical minds and a prolific author, he pioneered few new approaches to diagnosis and treatment. Instead, he digested and synthesized medical wisdom inherited from ancient authorities like Galen and Hippocrates, wisdom long lost in the West but revived in the Islamic East. Maimonides' diagnostic indicators of incipient pneumonia seem as if they could be drawn from a modern medical text: "acute fever, sticking pain in the side, short rapid breaths, serrated pulse and cough, mostly with sputum." But Maimonides had merely embellished the insightful diagnosis outlined a millennium earlier by Galen.

Even more striking, however, is the contrast between the Greek and Islamic wisdom synthesized by Maimonides and medicine's primitive state in the Latin West. Christian Europe's so-called doctors were mired in a swamp of ignorance and sinking deeper each passing generation. Sixth-century John of Beverly had castigated nurses who were foolish enough to bleed patients while the moon was in its unpropitious waxing phase. Well, no great surprise: he was writing in the darkest days of Europe's Dark Ages. Yet, seven centuries later, Europeans remained bogged down in the same murky morass. No less an authority than the Aragon royal court decreed in 1312 that barbers should bleed their patients only when the astrological signs were favorable.

Granted, many of the practices that now seem so patently superstitious had also been inherited from those same wise ancients. The great Galen, not some illiterate medieval sorcerer, had linked the efficacy of a bloodletting to the moon's phases. The Greeks had championed the "science" of bloodletting, convinced that the ill suffered an imbalance of the four "humors" constituting the human body: yellow bile, black bile, phlegm, and blood. What better than a therapeutic bloodletting to restore the bodily humors to equilibrium? Although the ancient Greeks and Romans had occasionally endorsed some (in retrospect) bizarre practices, at least they were thinking, debating, and writing. In contrast, the medieval West had descended into an intellectual funk

This tenth-century ivory perfume jar exemplifies the superb craftsmanship and refined sensibilities of Muslim Córdoba. The inscription explains the artisan's inspiration: "The sight I offer [i.e., the jar's shape] is of the fairest, the firm breast of a delicate maiden . . ."

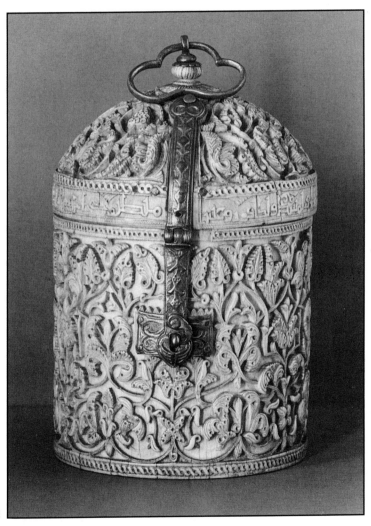

1

Pilgrims reaching Santiago de Compostela after months-long treks bought souvenirs just as modern tourists do. This sixteenth-century jet carving depicts a benevolent St. James bearing a walking staff and the scallop shell emblem characteristic of Santiago pilgrims.

The pilgrim St. James's alter ego was Santiago Matamoros (St. James the Muslim Killer), patron of the Christian Crusade against Muslim Spain. Here the saint wields his sword in holy war against the Muslims.

Pilgrims to Santiago were treated to an architectural feast en route. *Below:* The thirteenth-century Burgos Cathedral, a UNESCO World Heritage site, soars skyward in the Gothic tradition; El Cid is entombed here. *Opposite page, top:* The austere eleventh-century Romanesque Church of San Martín in Frómista. *Opposite page bottom:* San Tirso in Sahagún, engineered by Muslim or Muslim-trained builders who traveled north as captives or hired craftsmen; the patterned brickwork betrays the Muslim influence.

5

6

7

This Hispano-Moresque plateware from the Valencia region combines Muslim styling with Christian themes: one bowl features a Jesus monogram *(above)*, an Ave Maria inscription rims the other *(below)*. Valencia's Muslim craftsmen also introduced Christian Europe to the then revolutionary process of manufacturing paper.

8

Ávila's eleventh-century town walls, forty feet high and buttressed by eighty watch towers, are among many fortified remains dotting Spain's one-time frontier no-man's land, where Muslim and Christian raiders battled for supremacy. Ávila is also associated with Spanish mystics, including the Christian St. Teresa and the Jewish Moses de León, who shaped kabbalah's most important treatise.

Seville's cathedral stands where its great mosque once did. The church tower is the former mosque's minaret, transformed for Christianity when crowned with a bell housing.

The columns of the Prayer Hall of the Great Mosque of Córdoba were quarried from Roman Empire ruins and Visigoth churches; the mosque was later adorned with Santiago de Compostela's captured cathedral bells. Today, Córdoba's cathedral rises above the former mosque.

Granada's picturesque, sprawling Alhambra *(opposite page and below)* is one of the world's most extensive examples of medieval Islamic architecture. Its palaces, baths, gardens, and fortifications include elaborately carved wood and stucco and polychromatic glazed tiles. Water piped from the Sierra Nevada mountains once fed gravity-powered fountains that enlivened its courtyards.

This elaborately illuminated Hebrew Bible was completed c. 1492, when Spain's Jews were given four months to convert to Christianity or depart Spain forever. Medieval Spain may have housed as many Jews as all other European nations combined. Today their Sephardic descendants, scattered throughout the world, may account for as much as 20 percent of world Jewry.

oledo's El Tránsito reflects the glories and agonies of Spain's mixed religious culture. The Jewish financier Samuel Halevi constructed it as a synagogue in 1357, employing Muslim artisans who incorporated Moorish design touches. The synagogue was made into a church after the expulsion of Spain's Jews.

Spain's Inquisition is the subject of Pedro Berruguete's *Auto-da-fe,* composed in the early 1490s. Two alleged heretics are at the stake, yet their guardsmen seem bored or amused—Berruguete's social commentary on human callousness in the face of the Inquisition's horrors?

A portrait of Queen Isabella the Catholic, attributed to Jan Sallaert (also known as Juan de Flandes). In the momentous year of 1492, Ferdinand and Isabella dispatched Columbus to the New World, eliminated Muslim rule in Spain, and forced Spain's Jews to convert or flee.

17

Pedro Berruguete's *St. Dominic Burning Books* depicts the saint's Christian text miraculously leaping from the flames while heretical books are consumed. Not long after this work was painted, Archbishop Cisneros was organizing bonfires of Muslim holy books in Granada.

from which no medical writer of note emerged for nearly a millennium after Galen; worse yet, most volumes of classical authors had been lost in barbarian rampages. Absent any stimulus to progress, European medicine regressed. Baseless practices like bloodletting became further encrusted with layers of folk medicine and superstition as so-called physicians stumbled around a dark medical alley.

A little light was shed onto these archaic practices from the Islamic East, often enough mediated by Spain. A decade or so before Maimonides' family fled Spain, the Italian Gerard of Cremona arrived in Toledo, destined to unlock a treasure trove of Greco-Arabic medical knowledge for fellow Europeans. Gerard was one of a long procession of European scholars drawn by Spain's intellectual riches. Gerbert of Aurillac, the French mathematician and future pope, had been one of Spain's first intellecutal pilgrims in the tenth century. A polyglot, multinational scholarly parade followed. The Slav Hermann the Dalmatian settled in Spain's northeast and completed the first translation of the Quran into a European language in the early 1140s. The Italian Plato of Tivoli labored over astronomical and mathematical texts from his base near Barcelona. The Briton Daniel of Morley first headed to Paris, but distressed at its intellectual aridness, journeyed to Toledo and found the libraries and intellectual stimulus he sought.

Toledo, most sophisticated of Spain's scholarly centers, boasted one of Europe's most diverse ethnic and cultural mixes even before these scholar-immigrants arrived. It was a thriving Muslim city when Alfonso VI conquered it and proclaimed himself Emperor of the Two Religions. Many Muslims had remained, despite Christian rule. Three generations later, the Almohad invasions had chased Jews and Christians from Spain's southern coast. While some, like Maimonides, fled Spain completely, others headed for Christian Toledo, its architecture and customs evoking the Andalusian culture with which they were so comfortable.

So a scholar like Gerard of Cremona entered a Toledo already crawling with every conceivable ethnic and religious permutation. Christian immigrants from Spain's north had trailed the Reconquest armies; Muslim Toledans were pursuing livelihoods under Christian rule; Arabic-speaking Christians and Jewish refugees arrived from al-Andalus after the Almohad invasions. There was no shortage of language coaches to help new arrivals master alien Arabic texts. Nor did creed or ethnicity stifle academic partnerships, as, for example, Archdeacon Dominic Gundisalvi of Toledo teamed with the Jewish scholar Avendauth.

One final ingredient was needed to ignite the cultural explosion. Twelfth-century academics plied an even less lucrative trade than their modern counterparts (if that's possible). There were no universities to speak of; a steady teaching post, a paid sabbatical, and academic leave are all inventions of a much later age. Medieval scholars often relied on the Church's patronage. To humanity's good fortune, an early wave of scholar-translators arrived just as the enlightened Archbishop Raymond of Toledo resolved to sponsor the *re*translation into Latin of Arabic translations of Greek classics by Aristotle, Galen, and others.

Gerard of Cremona emerged as the most prolific translator-scholar of the whole medieval era. One medieval chronicler reported that Gerard was staggered by what he discovered in Toledo, and, "seeing the abundance of books in Arabic on every subject, and regretting the poverty of the Latins in these things, he learned the Arabic language." The indefatigable Italian ferreted through Toledo's libraries, churning out translations of at least seventy major works previously unavailable in the Latin-speaking West.

Translators like Gerard didn't follow a predefined road map. After all, there was no master list of ancient manuscripts and no way of knowing which would be most enlightening. Translators gravitated toward whatever struck them as most interesting. As Gerard's colleagues put it in a rather frivolous remembrance, their mentor worked like a "wise man who, wandering through a green field, links up a crown of flowers, made from not just any, but from the prettiest."

Medicine was one of the fields that struck Gerard as, well, "prettiest." He provided Europe's first translation of the *Canon of Medicine,* an exhaustive treatise on health and medicine by the eleventh-century Persian philosopher-doctor Ibn Sina (Avicenna in the West). As Gerard plowed through the *Canon*'s million words, he could not possibly have predicted Avicenna's long-lasting impact on Western medicine. The *Canon* is the most famous text in medical history, and Gerard's transla-

tion was the first of at least thirty editions prepared over the succeeding
five centuries. Spain's medical school at Salamanca was still using Avicenna's text in 1650, probably an all-time record for a scientific text-
book—a record that unfortunately speaks less to Avicenna's undoubted
genius than to the abysmal pace of progress in Western science. However advanced the medical science of our own age, one dearly hopes
that fledgling neurosurgeons in 2650 will not still be consulting the
same textbooks as did the class of 2004.

Though medical science did (fortunately) eclipse Avicenna eventually, the so-called Prince of Physicians fully anticipated modern practice in at least one field. Medieval pharmacology was a vibrant business
with unregulated apothecaries and quacks peddling every conceivable
potion for every conceivable ailment. The physician to tenth-century
Córdoban Abd al-Rahman III sought to cure a caliphal earache by
pouring a dove's blood into the ear of his imperial patient. Maimonides' premodern virility recipe was no more outlandish than this medieval Celtic concoction for combating baldness: "Let calcine [i.e.,
burn] a raven, his ashes boil in sheep's suet, and rub to the head, it
cures." Humanity's health concerns haven't much changed in a millennium: preening, insecure males still guarantee a booming market for
impotence and baldness remedies.

But if health concerns have changed little, the regimen for testing
prospective cures fortunately has. Government agencies review extensive clinical trial results before approving drugs for sale—almost exactly
what Avicenna proposed a millennium ago. He advocated group trials
to ensure statistical validity, recommended human trials as a late stage
of drug testing, and stressed the need to monitor each drug's long-term
impact and potential complications.

Unfortunately, not all of Avicenna's ideas were thoroughly grounded
in the scientific values of observation and experiment. It's no coincidence that medieval medicine's great authorities all seemed to be
philosopher-doctors: Avicenna, Maimonides, and another brilliant
Spanish Muslim named Averroes. No tormented appendicitis sufferer
today would relish an appendectomy inflicted by some stereotypically
tweedy, pipe-smoking philosopher ever prone to distracted absorption
in deep thought. But educated medieval Europeans saw nothing odd in

the joint profession of philosopher-doctor. Indeed, quite the opposite. Those falling under the sway of ancient Greek wisdom revered philosophy as the highest science, uncovering logically demonstrable and therefore unquestionable truths. Study of the human body was only one part, and most definitely a subsidiary part, of the broader intellectual quest for timeless certainties. Ancient and medieval Europeans understood the term "philosophy" much more broadly than moderns do, as encompassing the sciences and all other fields that pursued truth via rational speculation.

Scholars like Avicenna arrived at truth by *deduction* from basic principles, not by the *inductive* process of scientific method, where hypotheses are tested by observation and experiment. The medical pioneer Galen was convinced of the (in retrospect) wacky theory that the body was constituted of four humors not because of detailed *observation,* but because the theory elegantly paralleled Aristotle's *theory* that the whole material universe was constituted of four elements (fire, earth, water, and air). The same reverence for philosophical truth (and for Aristotle) infected medieval thinkers like Avicenna, who summarily dismissed apparent facts that happened to contradict Aristotle's theories: "Although their [the physicians'] view appears to be superficially more plausible," he once wrote about a disputed point, "the philosopher's [Aristotle's] view is really the correct one." Why? Because Aristotle said it.

Nor were medieval philosopher-doctors particularly interested in *verifying* the so-called truths that reason uncovered. Avicenna boldly parroted Aristotle's conjecture that there were three heart ventricles furiously pumping away inside us, never attempting to investigate the claim. Thus, even as Avicenna and others liberated Christendom from numerous medical fallacies, they also misdirected medicine by emphasizing theory over experimentation. Avicenna and contemporaries belittled surgery, for example, as little better than manual labor to be performed by hacks.

On the one hand, Avicenna's systematic compendium pushed European medicine forward. His medical texts exposed Europeans to the valid insights of ancient Greek physicians, as updated by Muslim scholars in the Near East. More important, he helped rescue medicine from dominance by amateur folklore and transformed it into a professional discipline. But Avicenna's approach was not thoroughly scientific. And because he held Europeans in his thrall for centuries by dint of his sheer genius, Europe long lacked the confidence to identify his shortcomings and steer medicine onto more solid scientific grounds.

The quest for greater professionalism faced another stumbling block. All well and good that translators like Gerard of Cremona gamely exposed Europe to Avicenna's wisdom. Unfortunately, Gerard preached science to a society more interested in faith. At about the same time Gerard labored to translate Avicenna's massive *Canon*, the French monk (and saint-to-be) Bernard of Clairvaux was advising his fellow Christians, "To consult physicians and take medicines befits not religion and is contrary to purity." A full century later, the Fourth Lateran Council of bishops in 1215 seconded Bernard's sentiment: "[We] order and strictly command physicians of the body, when they are called to the sick, to warn and persuade [the sick] first of all to call in physicians of the soul." In one respect, these churchmen were giving sage advice: one undoubtedly increased one's chances of reaching old age by steering clear of the barbers, surgeons, village healers, and assorted charlatans passing themselves off as the medieval equivalent of doctors.

But Bernard was not protesting medieval medicine's deficient quality. Rather, he feared that medicine was violating the fundamental Christian disposition to lodge trust in God rather than man. With the Roman Empire's collapse, the sparse medical care available to the public had fallen disproportionately into the laps of cathedrals and monasteries, much as the Church had similarly served as illiterate Europe's educator of last resort. The Church's involvement in health care worthily honored the legacy of Jesus, who spectacularly healed the blind, deaf, and lame during his short life.

But these gospel accounts could be read two ways. Every Christian agreed that Jesus challenged followers to minister to the sick, but not all commentators interpreted that challenge as encouragement to understand the science of medicine. Some drew exactly the opposite conclusion: Jesus's miraculous healings demonstrated that only God held power over illness and health, and that humans should trust divine rather than human intervention. As a result, a large dollop of faith was often stirred into medieval pharmaceutical compounds. A tenth-century manuscript prescribed, "Against dysentery, a bramble of which both ends are in the earth, take the nether root, delve it up, cut nine chips with the left hand and sing three times the Miserere Mei Deus and nine times the Pater Noster [i.e., the Our Father]."

Other medieval Spaniards could have steered European medicine onto the right track. Among Gerard's many translation projects were excerpts of a treatise by the Spanish Muslim Abu-l-Qasim, also known as Abulcasis (936–1013). Whereas our blunter age offers up books with titles like *Medicine for Dummies,* the more considerate Abulcasis christened his masterwork *The Recourse of Him Who Cannot Compose (a Medical Treatise on His Own).* Unlike Avicenna, who sniffed at medicine's messy practicalities, and Christian theologians, who shunned it on theological grounds, Abulcasis seems to have gotten his hands quite dirty in the everyday travails of yanking decayed teeth, delivering squalling infants, setting fractures, and cauterizing wounds.

Seems to have gotten his hands dirty. Though scholars are unsure to what extent Abulcasis actually practiced surgery, his writings on surgery, translated by Gerard of Cremona, became the practical companion to Avicenna's theoretical *Canon.* Abulcasis baby-stepped readers through the basics of repairing hernias, amputating limbs, treating abdominal wounds, removing bladder stones, and even fashioning artificial teeth from beef bone. He not only provided instructions for common surgeries but illustrated the tools of the trade. His encyclopedia depicted more than two hundred dental and surgical instruments, many of them apparently designed by Abulcasis himself and some of them previously unknown in the West: a tonsil guillotine, the syringe, a prototype of the plaster cast, and the use of animal gut for sutures. No medieval surgeon could ring up a local medical supplier for a new forceps. Forced either to engineer one's own tools or coach some blacksmith to do so, Abulcasis's sketched prototypes were invaluable to medieval physicians. Unfortunately, copyists embellished each new edition with their own exotic renderings of Abulcasis's tools, treating the surgical instruments as decorative doodles that prettied up the manuscript rather than as life-saving equipment.

Abulcasis and Avicenna accounted for only a tiny share of the flourishing Arabic-language medical literature. Historians have catalogued medical writings authored by some seventy Muslim scholars during the period from 800 to 1300. In contrast, the full medical school library at Europe's showcase University of Paris shelved a grand total of nine volumes at the end of the fourteenth century.

What did Maimonides add to this mix other than his dubious formula for rejuvenating a libidinous sultan? He made few groundbreaking contributions to diagnosis or treatment, but there was something original in his medical work: a holistic vision that a healthy life paid equal attention to body, environment, and spirit alike. Maimonides was not the first to advocate a "healthy mind in a healthy body," an idea already promoted by his classical sources. But he articulated a further-reaching, more integrated notion of human health than either his ancient sources or even most moderns. As a Spanish Jew, he straddled a fault line of medieval civilizations. His viewpoint was unique: the Islamic East exposed him to the most developed medical knowledge of his day; as a rabbi's son, he filtered that knowledge through a religious vision of the human person.

In our modern specialist culture, the doctor tends to the body, public health specialists to the environment, psychologists to the mind, and preachers to the soul. Maimonides would have balked at rigid demarcations among medicine, public health, psychology, and spirituality. The human person is a whole being, not divided into slices. Body, mind, and soul are interrelated. What sense does it make to segregate health practitioners into arbitrarily narrow, rigid boxes of expertise? Maimonides instead treated the continuum of body, soul, spirit, and environment. Long before public health researchers documented the correlation between asthma incidence and inner-city pollution, an intuitive Maimonides warned against the health risks endemic to city living: "Comparing the air of cities to the air of deserts and forests is like comparing thick and turbid waters to pure and light waters . . . And if you . . . cannot emigrate from the city, at least try to live on the outskirts."

Maimonides staked out even more adventurous arguments by exploring the nexus between psychological and physical well-being. Modern research linking positive patient attitudes to speedier recovery from serious illness wins only grudging acknowledgment from many medical professionals who are accustomed to treating only the body's physical machinery. Yet Maimonides pressed doctors to consider their patients' emotional state and not just their bodily parts: "One must pay attention and constantly consider emotional activities . . . In all these the physician should not give precedence to anything before improving the state of the psyche by removing all these (extreme) emotions."

Maimonides' final step along the body-environment-spirit continuum was his boldest, suggesting that the *soul's* health could impact the *body's,* that religion and medicine are complementary and related disciplines, utilizing different tools but ultimately linked. Body and spirit are inseparable, and physical health and happiness entail proper attention to spirituality. Worldview, values, and religious practices do not merely concern the afterlife but this bodily life as well. Illness could be caused or exacerbated by what might be called "moral unhealth." In such cases, treating the body as a machine was useless; rather, said Maimonides, "These situations can (only) be obtained through speculative philosophy and from moral admonitions of the [religious] Law."

In fact, speculative philosophy and religious law absorbed the greater part of Maimonides' mental energies. Though Maimonides the physician complained that his labors left him so exhausted he could hardly sleep, he was not too drained to focus his incisive intellect on his religious faith. If his contributions to medicine are limited, his contributions to Jewish thought were revolutionary. The same Greek wisdom that buttressed his medical knowledge spurred daring analyses of Jewish law and Scripture. His approach would alternately invigorate and terrify his Jewish contemporaries.

12. Rethinking Religion

"To Long with an Exceeding Longing"

Imagine the mind-set of Maimonides, who championed this advice for a healthy night's sleep: "A person should not sleep on his face or on his back but on his side; at the beginning of the night on the left side and at the end of the night on the right side." Forget entirely whether the odd regimen actually benefits health. Who would bother to wake up in the middle of the night and calculate whether it's time to flip over?

Well, Maimonides apparently. Now imagine the same disciplined mind-set applied to Judaism's sacred tradition, anchored by its Torah ("Law"). Narrowly understood, the Torah comprises the Hebrew Bible's first five books (Genesis, Exodus, Leviticus, Numbers, and Deuteronomy). Orthodox Jews understand this Written Law as God's direct revelation to Moses atop Mt. Sinai, immortalized in the Exodus episodes that culminate in Moses's presentation of God's Ten Commandments to a Jewish nation forlornly wandering the desert in search of their Promised Land.

The Mt. Sinai revelations also included a body of Oral Law, so Jewish tradition holds. More fragile than hand-copied parchments, the precious Oral Law was inscribed not on stone tablets but on Moses's heart and mind, then passed from one generation to another of Jewish religious leaders and eventually compiled as Talmud (Hebrew for "teaching" or "learning") in the fifth and sixth centuries.

We often perceive law with a negative connotation: certain behaviors are proscribed to prevent civilized societies from disintegrating into chaos. But Jewish tradition celebrates law's equally rich positive dimensions. Proscriptions declaring certain foods unclean sanctify the totality of human existence, reminding pious Jews to reverence God even in the minutest details of daily life's most mundane chores. When the gospel Jesus famously rails at the Pharisees' punctilious observance of their seemingly arcane laws, the Pharisees never get to tell their side of the story: that the treasure of Jewish law was a divine gift enabling Jews to heed Scripture's injunction to keep the Lord's word ever on their hearts, minds, and lips.

Like any compilation of ancient religious wisdom collected over centuries, the Torah and Talmud are messily organized, to say the least. Inconsistencies abound, starting with two contradictory Creation accounts that tumble unapologetically from Genesis: in its first chapter, the human person *finishes* God's creative activity; yet a chapter later, Adam is molded from clay *early* in God's creative endeavors, even before vegetation is introduced to Eden. Similarly confused is the beloved tale of Noah's ark. In Genesis 6:19, "two [animals] of every sort . . . male and female" waddle, slither, hop, or gallop up the ark's gangway. Yet a few verses later, Noah's embarkation orders are inexplicably different: "Seven pairs of all clean animals . . . and a pair of the animals that are not clean."

Apparent contradictions are equally rife throughout the Talmud's often-dueling interpretations of scriptural texts and expansive, freewheeling digressions. Competing or contradictory scriptural interpretations are never reconciled, nor does a workable index enumerate competing interpretations. A devout Jew hoping to reap Talmud and Torah wisdom relating to Sabbath practices, for example, undertakes an exasperating harvest of countless scattered citations.

The disciplined, well-ordered Maimonides sought to rescue the devout Jew who lacked Talmud texts or the education to decipher them, or who simply wanted to understand his or her Sabbath duties clearly. Maimonides' *Mishneh Torah* (*Repetition of the Law*) eschewed encyclopedic compilation of competing rabbinical viewpoints to offer instead his judgment of the "correct" interpretation of Jewish law wherever possible. Maimonides inherited over a thousand years of learned rabbinical commentary, yet was bold enough to assert that "a man who first reads the Written Law and after that reads this [*Mishneh Torah*], will know from it the entire Oral Law and will have no need to read any other book besides them." True to his word, he painstakingly parsed Jewish law on marriage rituals, sabbath practices, clean and unclean foods, prayer, and countless other matters. The *Mishneh Torah* closes by imagining Jewish history's longed-for end time: "In that era there will be no famine, no war, no envy, no strife." Wisdom and knowledge, rather than unbridled pursuit of earthly delights, will characterize this halcyon age: "The things that are now vague and deeply hidden will be revealed . . . and the land shall be full of the knowledge of the Lord, as the waters cover the sea."

The vision epitomized Maimonides' conviction that God had created a rational world, blessed the Jews with a rational law, and gifted humans with the intellectual prowess to decipher God's ordered design of nature. Accordingly, the *Mishneh Torah* did not merely elaborate *what* the Law taught but *why* one interpretation was demonstrably superior to another, or *why* a certain Genesis passage should be understood metaphorically, not literally. Maimonides believed that revelation was reasonable and would not contradict what logic or science could discover independently.

Maimonides explored these ideas in the *Guide for the Perplexed,* a follow-up to the *Mishneh Torah* for educated Jews whose faith had been shaken by exposure to philosophy and its reasoned dissection of assumptions about ethics, religion, and the human person. The Islamic world had rediscovered long-forgotten works of Plato, Aristotle, and the other ancients. Maimonides sought to teach fellow Jews that philosophy—and by extension, all science and rational inquiry—was not only compatible with their beliefs but would enhance faith and deepen understanding of Jewish law.

More to the point, practicing philosophy—*thinking*—was distinctly divine behavior that embodied one's *most* God-like trait. Maimonides analyzed a beloved Scripture passage to prove his point. What did God mean on that sixth biblical day of creation by declaring, "Let us make man in our image, after our likeness"? Surely not that human beings physically resemble God. Faces and internal organs are common to all earthly creatures, and however superior the human may consider his snout to the manatee's, the difference between physical attributes is relative rather than absolute. Rather, God's "image and likeness" had to refer to some quality uniquely differentiating humans from other animals, "which no other creature on earth possesses . . . [therefore] on account of the *Divine intellect* with which man has been endowed he is said to have been made in the form and likeness of the Almighty." Applying one's divine intellect to interpret religious law and Scripture was, therefore, God-like, prayerful activity. Or, as Maimonides put it elsewhere, humans must strive to "harmonize the law with what is intelligible."

Maimonides may not have feared unfettered rational inquiry to harmonize faith and reason, but not all his contemporaries were so sanguine. Some Jews feared he had pried open a Pandora's box. Who should decide, for example, which passages of Scripture and which articles of faith were open to rational scrutiny, and whose reinterpretation was valid?

Maimonides scandalized some by applying his logical scalpel even to the beloved Genesis passages portraying the God of creation. Genesis depicted an unmistakably fleshy, potter God who, after a misty rain softened the earth, "formed man of dust from the ground, and breathed into his nostrils the breath of life." Many generations later, the God of Exodus chiseled out Ten Commandments, "and the writing was the writing of God, graven upon the tables." How else to mold the human or hammer out commandments but with Divine Hands? But literal interpretation of such passages made no sense to Maimonides. However extraordinary a pair of Divine Hands one might imagine, the fingertips would mark the *finite limit* of their reach. Yet God was an *infinite* being and therefore a purely *spiritual* entity. Moreover, physical bodies have *parts,* yet Deuteronomy assured Jews that God is One.

Maimonides understood the Creation story as anthropomorphic metaphor that helped simple minds grasp the harder to fathom concept of a spiritual Deity creating a material world out of nothing. He railed against rabbis who clung to literal interpretation of such stories: "Most ignorant of human beings and more erring than the beasts, their

brains being filled with the superstitions of old women." His theological musings betrayed a deep debt to the ancient thinkers he studied in
Spain and in the Islamic East. Plato and Aristotle, for example, had glorified the intellect as seat of the human soul. Maimonides likewise portrayed the intellectual soul as "God's image and likeness" and shook
many Jewish contemporaries by asserting that this soul, freed of the
meddlesome body after death, might live eternally with God.

One medieval rabbi wrote of devout Jews deeply dismayed by Maimonides' teaching about this purely spiritual afterlife, "Their hope had
turned to despair and their longing had been in vain." For as they
understood Maimonides, their bodies would perish, and "Only their
souls will hover about the world and fly in the air like angels."

Maimonides' death-defying spiritual soul, though perfectly compatible with Greek wisdom, was alien to his own Jewish tradition. Deuteronomy's authors would have fumbled futilely for a suitable Hebrew
word to express so alien a concept. Even later books of the Hebrew
Bible, which explicitly begin to broach a concept of afterlife, contemplate bodily resurrection rather than some disembodied spiritual paradise. The prophet Daniel assured (and warned) Jews, "And many of
those who sleep in the dust of the earth shall awake, some to everlasting
life, and some to shame and everlasting contempt." One medieval
rabbi accordingly attacked Maimonides' Greek-inspired notion that
glorified the intellectual soul over the body: "In what way is the soul of
the righeous man superior to his body . . . ? . . . both . . . [body and
soul] have an equal hand in their righteousness as well as their wicked-
ness."

Maimonides' ideas about God and afterlife were not all new; some
had even won fairly wide acceptance among well-educated Jews. But
never had a Jewish thinker, and rarely a philosopher in any of the three
monotheistic traditions, so comprehensively pondered questions that
many modern believers never seriously grapple with: What is God like?
What does it mean to be a human person? Should I accept Scripture,
law, and revelation as written, or are they open to interpretation?

Maimonides' incisive intellect and unflinching embrace of philosophical method prompted a crisis in Judaism. What was later dubbed
the Maimonidean Controversy swept Spain and southern France as

rabbis debated Maimonides' opinions. Passionate letters traded charges and excommunications. The controversy featured the unlikely spectacle of Jews denouncing Maimonides to Christian inquisition authorities. Not that Jewish rabbis regarded inquisitors as authorities on anything Jewish, but some derived satisfaction from seeing Maimonides' works in flames, even in Christian-kindled bonfires.

Still, however ingenious his effort to reconcile reason and faith, Maimonides' most profound gift to modern generations may be his simple piety and humility before God. The brilliant archrationalist who saw so much farther than his contemporaries also saw and accepted the human mind's inability to fathom God's infinite majesty, power, and goodness. "Our knowledge," he wrote, consists in knowing nothing more than that "we are unable truly to comprehend Him." Even our "endeavor to extol Him in words, all our efforts in speech are mere weakness and failure." Because our finite minds cannot plumb the infinite, we can only accurately proclaim what God *is not,* never what God *is.* A devout Maimonides finally falls silent in awe, urging believers to heed the fourth Psalm's admonition: "Commune with your own heart upon your bed, and be still." Or, as Maimonidies expressed it in the words of another psalm, "Silence is praise to Thee" (Psalm 65:2).

The depth of Maimonides' devotion belies the stereotype of a remote intellectual sterilely divorced from emotional engagement with his God. Rather, as Maimonides exclaimed, "When a person contemplates His great and wondrous works and creatures, and from them obtains a glimpse of His wisdom which is incomparable and infinite, he will straightway love Him, praise Him, glorify Him, and long with an exceeding longing to know His great Name."

Maimonides' twelfth-century analysis of sacred texts and religious belief foreshadowed an approach that discomfits many twenty-first-century believers committed to literal interpretation of Scripture: God said what God meant, and humans should not question but simply obey. The Maimonidean Controversy prefigured a struggle that became only more challenging across centuries as scientific method, literary deconstruction, archaeology, and historical criticism developed and evolved. It was one thing for Maimonides to suggest that God didn't literally mold Adam with divine hands; many of his contemporaries had already relinquished literal interpretation of this passage. But where draw the line? It became quite another thing some four centuries later when Galileo argued from natural reason that the earth revolved around the sun, defying a scriptural worldview stubbornly defended by Catholic churchmen. Or when modern Muslims reject coreligionists who entice would-be suicide bombers with the promise of literally passing to a place populated by "Companions with beautiful, big, and lustrous eyes" (much less whether anyone will get there by taking his or her own life and that of innocent humans).

Maimonides encourages us to believe that faith need not fear reason. Applying God's extraordinary gift of intellect to dearly held beliefs does not affront the Creator, but praises God. Yet, at the same time, he teaches the limits of our intellectual capabilities. The genius Maimonides who ultimately falls silent before the Creator God gives pause to all who would make man the measure of all things.

The struggle to marry faith and reason gripped not only twelfth- and thirteenth-century Judaism, but Islam and Christianity as well. Two ingenious Spanish Muslims were to ignite in Islam the same intense intellectual friction that the Maimonidean Controversy sparked in Judaism. Indeed, in the course of a century, Judaism, Islam, and Christianity would each be wracked—and forever changed—by the struggle to reconcile faith and reason, philosophy and theology, and, in a sense, modernism and orthodoxy. One Spanish Muslim, Averroes, would distinguish himself as his era's foremost thinker, surpassing even Maimonides and out-thinking any contemporary philosopher in Christendom. Utterly rejected by his own Muslim community, he would inspire the most creative generation of Christian thinkers in a millennium.

Averroes would be brought to prominence by a friend and mentor, Ibn Tufayl, whose only surviving complete work, a slender allegorical tale, challenged his Muslim coreligionists and warns of the awesome responsibility humans inherit as stewards of God's creation.

13. A Muslim Commentator Enlightens Christendom

"You Who Have Eyes to See, Reflect!"

In 1719, Daniel Defoe published *Robinson Crusoe,* the archetypal tale of the desert island castaway. Modern readers ensconced in comfortable domestic cocoons typically focus on Crusoe's material struggle for food and shelter, but Defoe himself was just as preoccupied with Crusoe's *spiritual* struggle. When not scrounging edible berries and gathering firewood, Crusoe ponders more sublime matters, relying on his reasoning powers to work out "God's commands, and this without any teacher or instructor."

But Robinson Crusoe was neither the first nor the most enlightened fictional character stranded on a remote island. A decade before *Robinson Crusoe's* debut, an English-language translation of *Hayy Ibn Yaqzan* was published. This unusual tale by a twelfth-century Spanish Muslim, Ibn Tufayl, recounts one stranded man's battle for survival and spiritual enlightenment. Some scholars have wondered whether Defoe borrowed his premise from this medieval Muslim author. But Ibn Tufayl's ultimate purpose was far more daring than the eighteenth-century Defoe could have sensed: so controversial a critique of Muslim society that its author may have chosen the camouflage of a fairy tale to ensure his own safety.

Raised from birth on an island inhabited only by wild animals, the tale's protagonist, Hayy ibn Yaqzan, learns to forage, hunt, and imitate animal cries. Donning eagle feathers to mask his nakedness and intimidate enemies, Hayy reaches adulthood blissfully ignorant of his bizarre upbringing. When self-reflection dawns, it spurs an intellectual journey remarkable for one who has never encountered another human. A relentlessly curious Hayy surveys the broad sweep of material creation and concludes that the contingent, material world can make sense only if an immaterial, eternal Necessarily Existent Being (God) sustains it. Hayy further reasons that human happiness must entail contemplation of this God. The metaphysical musings are, to say the least, impressive for a man with feathers strapped around his privates who imitates animal squawks.

When a new character, Absal, arrives from a nearby inhabited island, Hayy becomes the sharp point of author Ibn Tufayl's thrust to vindicate human reason and question his era's Muslim practices. After Absal recovers from his first frightful encounter with the feathered Hayy, the two become friends. Hayy learns that the formal religion of Absal's island is entirely compatible with Hayy's own natural form of worship, though they eventually agree that Hayy's contemplative worship is a purer form of Absal's ritual-based religion. They journey to Absal's island to spread its practice.

Though Absal's religion is never named, its identity becomes unmistakable as its core practices are enumerated: fasting, pilgrimage, alms to the poor, and a daily regimen of prayer. Hayy is gratified that these rituals mirror his own devotional practices but is alarmed by much else he finds. The island's believers express their faith only through symbolic and anthropomorphic language, "allowing mankind to fall into the grave error of conceiving the Truth corporeally and ascribing to Him [i.e., the Divine] things which He transcends and is totally free of." More worrisome, the faithful are obsessed with the outward show of religious rituals yet persist in "amassing of wealth and overindulgence in eating, leaving men idle to busy themselves with inane pastimes and neglect the Truth." Their religious practice is entirely preoccupied with the letter of the religious law while missing its spirit. Hayy, hoping to sway the island's inhabitants to his own contemplation-based worship, arrived expecting to find persons of "outstanding character, brilliant minds and resolute spirits." Instead, he and Absal quit the island, concluding that "most men are no better than unreasoning animals, and . . . all that could possibly help them was contained already in the words of the prophets and the religious traditions."

At one level, Ibn Tufayl is simply defending Islam as compatible with natural reason, much as Maimonides did for Judaism. The castaway Hayy has never been taught the tenets of revealed religion, yet he more or less deduces them logically. But Ibn Tufayl's message is more cutting, whether in his own twelfth-century society or today's. He seems to suggest that one can attain religious enlightenment outside organized Islam and further asserts that this natural way is *superior* to religion as generally practiced in mainstream society. Though Absal hails from the island of revealed religion, Hayy is more enlightened. After bootless attempts to sway Absal's compatriots to a more enlightened faith, the two reject the island of organized religion for individualistic, contemplation-based piety.

The devout Ibn Tufayl is not rejecting Islam but critiquing a society that elevates outward observance over interior experience, adheres to ritual while blithely ignoring the prophetic call to bestow justice and mercy on others, and frustrates believers' rights and responsibilities to think for themselves. Though he speaks of his own Islam, his critique (whether or not one agrees with its substance) would pertain equally to any organized religion. Ibn Tufayl offers the faint, though genuinely intended, praise that organized religion enables the ignorant masses who are "no better than unreasoning animals" to absorb some measure of truth. He is implicitly challenging the authority of religious leaders who proclaim themselves truth's unchallengeable guardians. Ibn Tufayl's argument is extraordinary, and all the more so as he was no renegade outsider but a government functionary at a Muslim court.

Ibn Tufayl's allegory, a mere sixty or so printed pages, broaches another visionary warning that ranges far beyond religion to map out duties incumbent on all humanity. Like others schooled in the Greek philosophical tradition, Ibn Tufayl believed the planets were not passively pulled along circular orbits by gravity but were intelligently guided by heavenly spheres. The heavenly bodies were perceived as evolved and superior "intelligences," and Ibn Tufayl accordingly seeks to pattern his behavior after them. The heavens sustain life through the sunlight and rain that nourish vegetation, so enlightened humans should preserve life as well: "[He] imitated the [heavenly bodies'] action by never allowing himself to see any plant or animal hurt, sick, encumbered, or in need without helping it if he could." Hayy's ecological code surpasses what even committed environmentalists dare advocate: "Thus he could eat such things as the meat of fully ripened fruits, with seeds ready to reproduce, provided he was certain not to eat or harm the seeds or throw them in places unfit for vegetation . . . being careful to take only from the most abundant and not root out a whole species."

Ibn Tufayl's medieval astronomy leaves much to be desired: no one today regards the sun and planets as intelligent. But his overarching vision is nonetheless acute. Humans inhabiting his underpopulated, technologically primitive twelfth-century planet were unlikely to "root out a whole species." Today's human population has swelled, and humans have developed technology sufficient not merely to root out a species but indeed to obliterate the planet. Ibn Tufayl sees humanity for what we have become: cocreators and preservers of God's universe. With that exalted power comes a vocation to preserve the planet, a vocation more strikingly relevant today than when Ibn Tufayl first conceived it.

––––––––––––––––

The fictional Hayy, in withdrawing from the inhabited island of mainstream Islam to end his life in contemplation, parallels author Ibn Tufayl's own life experience. Late in life, Ibn Tufayl began resigning his prestigious court positions, including as the sultan's physician. He nominated as successor a brilliant protégé named Ibn Rushd, or Averroes (A-vér-oh-ease) as transcribed in the Latin West. Amateur astronomer, judge, physician, philosopher, political scientist, and theologian, Averroes was a Renaissance man before civilization knew the term. Underlying his manifold vocations, however, was the same unshakable conviction in human reason that so animated the Jewish Maimonides.

The relation of reason to faith was straightforward, Averroes believed. Truths discovered about the world illumine the God of truth who created it: "If the function of philosophy is none other than to study and reflect upon the facts of existence, as they provide evidence of the Maker . . . then the more complete such knowledge is, the more consummate will be our knowledge of the Maker." Divine Law and human reason enunciated truth in their own respective ways. Both are necessary.

But what Averroes called in the title of one seminal work *The Harmony of Religion and Philosophy* seems to tilt in philosophy's favor: "Since scripture is a truth and invites the inquiry that leads to knowledge of the truth then we, as Muslims, can be absolutely certain that no proposition based upon logically demonstrated proof will entail any contradiction of scripture." If any Quran passage seems to contradict what natural reason or science can demonstrate, "then scriptural interpretation is required." Writing at a time when philosophy was attacked throughout the Islamic world as a secularizing, godless discipline, Averroes boldly argued that forbidding its study "is to bar the door through which scripture invites men to knowledge of God—namely, the door of rational speculation."

Averroes was prying open a can of worms jurists had sealed tightly shut nearly two centuries earlier. Nothing was (or is) more vital to Islam than *sharia* (i.e., its "path" or "law"). Whereas Chrstianity's creed focuses on *beliefs,* four of Islam's five defining pillars dictate *actions:* almsgiving, daily prayer, the Meccan pilgrimage, and the Ramadan fast. Islam is a total way of life, and the all-encompassing code of sharia law guides right practice.

But the Quran is uncomfortably silent or ambiguous on many practical questions. Muhammad's revelation was not structured as a legal code, much less a blueprint for a multicultural, multinational empire. As early jurists relied on their wits to settle disputes, accepted Muslim practice began varying from one region to another, presenting an unsettling, even scandalous, dilemma: How could the one God's law differ from one country to another?

Judge-theologians attempted to reconcile differing approaches, eventually establishing four widely accepted bulwarks of Islamic law: the Quran, the *hadith* (sayings and events from the Prophet's life verified through a reliable chain of sources), analogous reasoning based on well-established principles, and the consensus of the Muslim community at large. There was, however, disagreement over the continued validity of reasoned case-by-case rulings by judge-theologians. Though this practice of reasoned interpretation, *itjihad* ("intellectual struggle"), retained legitimacy for a time, by the early tenth century Islamic law was considered so well-codified that judges were therafter expected to apply rather than proactively interpret it. The door of itjihad, it was said, swung closed forever.

Except that Averroes seemed to shove it back open by arguing that sacred texts—and by extension, religious law—were subject to interpretation when reason established the need. More controversial, he claimed that philosophers and others skilled in using natural reason were better qualified than theologians to make such determinations.

Averroes was essentially advocating a degree of academic freedom scandalous in his own time and unusual even today across much of the Islamic world. He plucked Quranic verses to bolster his case that God wills humans to use their powers of reason to the fullest: "You who have eyes to see, reflect!" The religious establishment should not frustrate the efforts of qualified philosophers, lawyers, and scientists (if devout) who were using their God-given intellectual eyes to search out truth.

Averroes' own penetrating intellectual gaze focused not only on religion but also on Muslim society. Even today it is controversial and sometimes taboo to question the customary status and limited roles open to women in traditional Islamic societies, but medieval Averroes confronted that question forthrightly, arguing that women's talents were badly underutilized: "The ability of women is not known, because they are . . . placed at the service of their husbands and [relegated] to the business of procreation, rearing and breast-feeding . . . they resemble plants." Indeed, Averroes conjectured, "it is not impossible that there may be among them philosophers and rulers."

Nor did Averroes' *Commentary on Plato's Republic* spare Muslim society's ruling elite his trenchant scrutiny. Plato had imagined a republic benevolently led by a philosopher-king, and Averroes believed Islam's theocratic states, if guided by well-educated and devout sultans, could fulfill Plato's ideal. But he charged the leaders of his own day with squandering such promise, drifting from fervent embrace of Islam to indulge their whims and amass personal wealth rather than improve their subjects' living conditions. He complained that political dynasties inevitably tended to deteriorate into tyranny, including the very one he served as a political appointee: "So seems to be the case with the constitution that exists now in these islands."

Taken together, Averroes' writings could be interpreted as undermining the authority of the sultan, theologians, sharia, and perhaps even the Quran itself. The one-time chief judge, perhaps predictably, eventually found himself on trial for heresy. He was banished from Córdoba. Though rehabilitated within a year, the unfettered style of philosophizing he had championed had been snuffed out. Averroes' spirit was likely snuffed out with it; he died two years later. Adventurous philosophizing in the medieval Islamic world died with him: the study of philosophy, already proscribed in much of the Islamic East, was soon after prohibited in North Africa and Spain. Averroes' commentaries on Aristotle were reduced to ash not long after his death in a great bonfire of philosophical texts designed to rid al-Andalus of such pernicious ideas.

Uprooted from Islam, philosophy caught on among what would have struck Averroes and Maimonides as a most unlikely community: scholars at Christendom's foremost academic center, the University of Paris. Aristotle's works, rendered into Arabic in the Near East and from Arabic to Latin by translator-scholars in Spain and elsewhere, reignited in the West the very same spirit of open intellectual inquiry that was dying in the Islamic world. One noted historian of philosophy credits Averroes and other Muslim thinkers for sparking the West's "rediscovery of the philosophical world, which the Christians had lost sight of ever since the second century . . . a turning point in the history of Western thought."

Paris scholars typically studied their Aristotle with their Averroes close at hand. Aristotle was known simply as "the Philosopher" (as if no other existed); Averroes was almost equally awed as "the Commentator." Medieval Christendom's greatest theologian, Thomas Aquinas, cited Averroes copiously (albeit often skeptically). Other leading thinkers—Siger of Brabant, Boethius of Sweden, Goswin of La Chapelle, and Bernier of Novelle at the forefront—made Averroes their muse, following his interpretations of Aristotle almost unquestioningly as they explored Christian theology.

Those explorations led to unusual places as far as the Church establishment was concerned. Siger of Brabant endorsed Averroes' notion that the *individual* soul was not immortal but merged after death into a common greater intellect. And if the soul (hence individual self-consciousness) didn't survive death, it followed that the key goal of human existence should be happiness in *this earthly life* through the pursuit of contemplation.

That may not sound like what mainstream Christians, ever focused on the afterlife, are supposed to believe. It isn't. Siger's twisted version of Averroes didn't thrill the canons overseeing the University of Paris. At Pope John XXI's behest to investigate, the Bishop of Paris, Stephen Tempier, fired off in 1277 a blistering condemnation of 219 heretical propositions purportedly advocated by the Paris renegades.* He excommunicated not only those guilty of teaching the condemned ideas, but even students unfortunate enough merely to have listened if they didn't scurry to confessionals for absolution.

Long after Siger of Brabant, Paris's Bishop Tempier, and the good Pope John XXI became historical footnotes, Averroes defied determined efforts to stamp out his influence. One fourteenth-century Christian scholar gushed that Averroes was the "most perfect and glorious friend and defender of philosophical truth." Take that, Bishop Tempier.

---

*Even before the dust had settled on the Paris controversy, a good deal of dust settled around poor Pope John XXI: the roof of his summer palace caved in and crushed him. His ill-starred papacy, lasting less than a year, had begun inauspiciously. When the pope-elect chose the name John, some long-ago scribe's error misled church bureaucrats into thinking it was time for a twenty-first John; historians have never uncovered the twentieth. Thirteenth-century databases, it would seem, did not quite meet modern standards. Still, providence sometimes compensates: there were *two* John XXIIIs. The first was a notorious fifteenth-century antipope who so discredited the venerable name that no successor dared touch it until the beloved twentieth-century version of Pope John XXIII.

For most moderns, the term "medieval philosophy" conjures up sleepy images of musty tomes and academics pondering such irrelevancies as angels dancing on the heads of pins. In fact, rarely does a year pass without some small aftershock reverberating from this extraordinary moment in the history of human thought—in mosques and churches, on newspaper editorial pages, and among diplomats pursuing Mideast peace. Maimonides, Ibn Tufayl, and Averroes explored the relation of faith to reason, the proper interpretation of revealed texts, and the basis of religious law. The same concerns convulse modern societies far more violently than they shook Averroes' medieval one. Should the Muslim, Christian, or Jewish believer understand the words of his or her sacred books as the literal word of God? And if so, *whose* revelation is God's literal word?

Traditional Jewish believers, for example, perceive the Holy Land as inviolably promised to them in Scripture; Muslims just as ardently lay claim to Jerusalem's very heart, the Dome of the Rock, where the Prophet Muhammad's night flight into heaven occurred. Fundamentalist Christians are no idle bystanders to this quarrel, convinced that the Messianic Age will be ushered in only once the Jews are all gathered into their Promised Land and converted to Christianity. Whose revelation is literal truth? As Averroes and Maimonides reverently groped for nonliteral paths through the words of their respective traditions, they pointed us toward a reasoned path through the seemingly intractable problems caused when competing religious texts collide.

No less consequential are questions over religious law that agitate each of the three faiths. Is God's law an expression of some objective, natural set of values that invite human discovery and interpretation through reason? Or, simply put, should humankind be content to obey what is pronounced right in revealed Scripture, whether or not the rationale behind prescribed or proscribed behaviors seems intelligible to the finite mind? To what extent, if ever, is the expression of truth in revealed texts conditioned by the era and context in which an inspired author wrote, the conceptual framework and limitations of a particular language, or the literary forms employed?

These seemingly abstract questions are anything but; in fact, they are consequential enough to have torn seemingly irreparable rifts through the three monotheistic communities across time. Orthodox and Reform Jews, for example, disagree whether the God who revealed Jewish law to Moses intends literal adherence today to its many dietary, social, and domestic strictures. In Christianity, Jesus's expressed wish that "all may be one" seems an ever more distant dream as denominations fragment and multiply with each passing generation, often over differences of scriptural interpretation. More than one contemporary Christian denomination, for example, teeters on the edge of schism over proper interpretation of scriptural condemnations of homosexuality. Islam also grapples with dilemmas concerning interpretation of religious law, beginning with the proper use of sharia. In some Islamic states, controversy swirls over proper dress for women; in others, jurists have had to consider whether to stone to death a woman accused of adultery, torn between what reason may convince them is just and the pronouncements of sharia law.

The thirteenth-century version of these struggles between religion and reason was cataclysmic in its outcome. Unbridled rational inquiry flowered in all three faiths as never before, then abruptly withered. The death of Averroes was all but synonymous with the death of adventurous philosophizing in Islam. The parallel crisis in Christianity precipitated the condemnations of 1277, which the Christian medievalist Etienne Gilson called "a landmark in the history of mediaeval philosophy and theology. There is no way to measure its influence . . . At that very moment, [scholasticism's] golden age came to an end." Maimonides, too, lionized by some Jewish contemporaries, was pilloried by others who condemned his ideas and agitated to have his works burned by Inquisitors.

Medieval Spaniards weren't the first to grapple with the relation of faith to reason, a struggle that has apparently preoccupied humanity since the God of Genesis explained His banishment of Adam and Eve from Eden: "Behold, the man has become like one of us, knowing good and evil." Humans have striven ever since to understand Adam's story, the story of our proper relation to God, God's word, and the faculty of reason.

As the unflinching rationalism championed by Maimonides and

Averroes seeped into Spain's intellectual groundwater, some religious believers rushed for an antidote. Hebrew Scripture, for example, revealed a loving, jealous, occasionally angered, and often compassionate God, a God hard to square with the philosophers' remote and supremely rational pure spirit. Many Jews wanted not Moses Maimonides' prescription to "lie and be still" in awed silence before their ultimately unknowable Creator, but the biblical Moses's passionate give and take with an emotionally involved Creator. The first Moses had rebuked his God, "Turn from thy fierce wrath, and repent of this evil against Thy people." And God did.

Those who rejected the approach of Maimonides and Averroes found ample guidance, profound inspiration, and alternative approaches to prayer in medieval Spain's spiritual ferment, above all in the work of two men widely regarded the most influential mystics of their respective faith traditions: Ibn Arabi, the Greatest Master of Sufi mysticism, and the Jewish Moses de León, master of the kabbalah.

14. Sufism

"My Heart Has Become Capable of Every Form"

Averroes' death in 1198 was a lonely affair. His remains were transported to Córdoba for burial. Thirty-three-year-old Muhyi al-Din Ibn Arabi (b. 1165) attended the memorial. He recounts a doleful procession, a coffin bearing Averroes' remains secured against one flank of a donkey with a bundle of his manuscripts lashed to the other side as a counterweight. As the ass tottered away from the small knot of mourners, Ibn Arabi wondered wistfully, almost pityingly, what use those learned writings had become to their author: "This is the Imam and these his works; would that I knew whether his hopes were realized."

History records a previous meeting between these two. Ibn Arabi's well-to-do family once lived in Seville, where his father befriended Averroes, then the city's *qadi* or judge. The young Ibn Arabi was regarded as a spiritual prodigy, and Averroes graciously consented to meet him. He entertained the twenty-year-old with greater politeness than the difference in their ages and status would warrant, inquiring whether the insights yielded by young Ibn Arabi's practice of mysticism were compatible with rationalism. Ibn Arabi replied enigmatically: "Yes and No. Between the Yea and the Nay the spirits take their flight beyond matter, and the necks detach themselves from their bodies."

Averroes evinces the overriding preoccupation with reason: Does the mystical insight conform to reason? If it's not reasonable, it can't be true. His straightforward question to Ibn Arabi demanded either yes or no. God is One or God is many; God is infinite or God is not; what's proven true cannot be false. All rational inquiry presupposes this simple principle as its foundation: contradictory statements cannot both be true; a thing cannot both be and not be at the same time.

Yet, from Ibn Arabi and his fellow Sufis—and the wider mystical tradition they share with so many world faiths—comes the answer, "Yea and Nay." Both Yes *and* No. God is hidden *and* God is revealed. God is completely other (transcendent) and remote from human experience, yet God is in the here and now (immanent). I am distant from God yet become one with God through prayer. Ibn Arabi's Yes *and* No defies the tidy categories beloved of Maimonides, Averroes, and their fellow rationalists. When the rationalist complains that yes *and* no simultaneously is illogical, the mystic answers that some spiritual knowledge *transcends* logic, communicable only in symbolic language freighted with layers of meaning: "The spirits take their flight beyond matter," as Ibn Arabi told Averroes.

The drab origins of the word "Sufi" belie Sufism's often exotic imagery. Devoted to lives of prayerful austerity, early Muslim mystics often clad themselves in coarse woolen garb; *suf* means wool, hence Sufi. Ironically, mystics who renounced such worldly preoccupations as elegant attire became forever known by their own austere fashion statement.

Sufism is rooted in Islam's earliest history. Islam's small community of believers rapidly became a prosperous society saddled with the headache of managing a multinational empire. But the Prophet had not envisioned a worldly empire, or so some pious Muslims argued. They retreated to lives of meditation and self-sacrifice. These mystics were pushed by alienation from worldly society and pulled by the tantalizing prospect of personal spiritual encounter with God. Like Hayy ibn Yaqzan on his deserted island, the would-be mystic purges all obstacles that hinder prayerful communion with God: base drives like greed and lust, then distractions like idle chatter and preoccupation with work and chores. The Sufi ultimately aims to "die to self," rooting out the consciousness of self as separate from God. Spiritual disciplines help induce the meditative state that can spark a transcendent experience: rhythmic breathing, slow repetition of the divine name, or even the more esoteric discipline of the whirling dervish. The fictional Hayy ibn Yaqzan, for example, "would spin around in circles until he got dizzy . . . fix his mind on the Necessarily Existent Being [God], cut away the bonds of all objects of the senses . . . and try with all his might to think only of Him."

"At last it came," Hayy continues. "Drowned in ecstasy," he witnessed "what no eye has seen or ear heard, nor has it entered into the heart of man to conceive." Ibn Tufayl describes Hayy's peak mystical experience with words that resonate deeply for Jews, Christians, and Muslims alike. Hayy echoes the Jewish prophet Isaiah: "From of old no one has heard or perceived by the ear, no eye has seen a God besides thee." Christians recall the apostle Paul's New Testament gloss on the very same Scripture passage: "What no eye has seen, nor ear heard, nor the heart of man conceived, that God has prepared for those who love him." Muslims recognize in Hayy's words the *hadith* (or "sacred tradition") wherein the Prophet Muhammad describes a beatific vision. Is Ibn Tufayl suggesting that those privileged to enjoy the mystic's clear gaze find a bridge beyond the stark differences that seem to divide the three faiths?

Though Sufism was rooted in the Islamic East, it flourished in Spain's fertile spiritual terrain. Worldly al-Andalus inevitably spurred some to seek a more authentic Islam, and the pilgrimage to Mecca first exposed pious Spaniards to Sufism. Though little is known about its subsequent spread throughout Iberia, Ibn Arabi provided precious glimpses through dozens of short biographical portraits of Spanish mystics. With no profile longer than a few pages and many only a paragraph, each Sufi's visage seems to dissolve into the next before any clear image becomes fixed in the reader's mind.

One nonetheless senses a rich spiritual undercurrent coursing through Muslim Spain, touching young and old, rich and poor, well-educated careerists and barely literate menial laborers. Extraordinary though their spirituality may have been, these Spaniards pursued ordinary day-to-day occupations as, among others, jurists, ship caulkers, scholars, teachers, tanners, tailors, and potters. Yusuf B. Taizza of Carmona was "so devoted to the reading of the Quran that he spoke to no man." Abd al-Salam al-Aswad was a black man who "never settled in any place" because he "found a good spiritual state in moving about." Abu Muhammad Abdallah, whose "nights were spent in prayer and his days in fasting," used to beat his legs with sticks when he grew tired from standing during prayer. Ibn Arabi reserves his fondest recollection for "one of the lovers of God, a gnostic, a lady of Seville called Fatima bint al-Muthanna . . . I served her for several years, she being over ninety-five years of age . . . She used to say to me, 'I am your spiritual mother and the light of your earthly mother.'"

Ibn Arabi's spiritual quest spurred a years-long pilgrimage through Cairo, Jerusalem, Baghdad, Damascus, and Mecca. He absorbed Sufi wisdom, eventually sharing his own vision in prolific writings, by his own count authoring some 250 tracts and treatises. Some are brief; others are monumental: a handwritten edition of his *Meccan Revelations* sprawls across thirty-seven volumes and nearly three thousand manuscript pages.

Not for Ibn Arabi the disciplined prose of a Maimonides. He effortlessly leaps from extended metaphorical images to interpretations of the Quran to ideas borrowed from ancient philosophers. His opaque prose has much to do with his elusive subject: How does one reduce the inexpressible, the infinite, to mere words? His *Bezels of Wisdom* attempted exactly this task, using the image of a bezel (the setting securing a gemstone to a jewelry piece) to convey analogously the relationship between prophets and God. Each of twenty-seven prophets portrayed—starting with Adam and including Noah, Job, John the Baptist, Jesus, and Muhammad—is a "setting" for one manifestation of the "gemstone" that is God.

For Maimonides, the finite mind's limitations opened an unbridgeable chasm between Creator and created, ultimately reducing the devout to humble silence. No such chasm separates Ibn Arabi's Abraham from God in the *Bezels*. Instead, the ancestral father of Judaism, Christianity, and Islam utters these words: "I have penetrated the course of the spirit within me,/And thus was the Intimate [of God] so called."

Islamic theologians were scrupulous to avoid "associating" the merely human with the divine. For this reason, Muslim artists decorated mosques with abstract geometric decoration rather than depicting saints or prophets, as Christians did. Ibn Arabi courts this blasphemy of associationism by proclaiming all of creation God's self-expression and the path to God's *self*-knowledge. God and creation *need each other:* "You [created beings] are His nourishment as bestowing the contents of His Self-Knowledge, while He is yours as bestowing existence." Ibn Arabi's poetic imagery ennobled the human being, yet shocked traditionalists:

> He praises me and I praise Him,
>   He worships me and I worship Him . . .
> He knows me, while I know naught of Him,
> I also know Him and perceive Him.
> Where then is His Self-sufficiency,
> Since I help Him and grant Him Bliss?
> It is for this that the Reality created me,
> For I give content to His Knowledge and manifest Him.

Because of such bold, some would say blasphemous imagery, Ibn Arabi's works were banned in parts of the Islamic world as late as the twentieth century, even as he is hailed elsewhere as al-Shaikh al-Akbar, Sufism's "Greatest Master," and regarded the "greatest mystical genius of Islam" by many academics.

The *Bezels* culminate by comparing the relationship binding God and creation to the union of man with woman. The Quran teaches that God created woman from man, much as the Hebrew Bible does. Man therefore longs for woman as something "yearns for itself," while woman longs for man as "that place to which one belongs."

> The Beloved longs to see me
> And I long even more to see Him,
> The hearts beat fast, but destiny bars the way,
> I groan in complaint and so does He.

So too the relationship between God and human: "Thus . . . the man yearn[s] for his Lord who is his origin, as woman yearns for man."

Ibn Arabi has taken the most intense relational experience humans know as his model of prayerful union with God.

At prayer's sublime peak, all distinction between God and worshipper, between lover and beloved, falls away. So too, it seems, do distinctions among religions, as Ibn Arabi describes in a later poem:

> My heart has become capable of every form,
> it is a pasture for gazelles and a convent for Christian monks,
> And a temple for idols and the pilgrim's Ka'ba and the
> Tables of the Tora and the book of the Quran.
> I follow the religion of Love . . .

15. The Kabbalah

"An Instrument for Peace in the World"

Ibn Arabi died in 1240; Moses de León was born that same year.

It seems a delicious coincidence, Sufism's greatest master symbolically passing the torch to Judaism's great mystic. In the mystic's universe, contradictions hang together in symbolic tension: God is present yet transcendent, hidden and revealed. So, too, 1240 brings death and birth: the Spanish Muslim Ibn Arabi yielding to the Spanish Jew Moses de León.

Moses de León was a wanderer, surfacing in Guadalajara, Ávila, Valladolid, and Arévalo as he pursued Jewish wisdom. By 1280 he was selling what he claimed were copies of an ancient composition by the revered second-century Rabbi Shimon bar Yohai of Jerusalem. One skeptical Jew, investigating the unlikely story, made his way to Moses de León's home in Ávila. (Devotees of mysticism and lovers of coincidence will immediately associate Ávila with two of Catholicism's most famous mystics: St. Teresa of Ávila and St. John of the Cross, both said to have been descended in part from Jewish forebears; alas, though their writings sometimes echo Moses de León's imagery, no tangible signs reveal his direct influence.) Moses's wife, recently widowed, explained that she had once confronted her husband, demanding to know why he presented his own work as that of a second-century rabbi. "If I told them my secret," Moses de León answered, "that I am writing from my own mind, they would pay no attention to my words, and they would pay nothing for them."

"Paying no attention to my words" was the last thing Moses needed to worry about, for the *Zohar* (i.e., splendor or brightness) attained extraordinary prominence within and beyond Judaism. For much of the sixteenth through eighteenth centuries it stood alongside the Hebrew Bible and Talmud in a holy triumvirate of Jewish sacred texts. The *Zohar* remains central to the Jewish spiritual tradition of kabbalah. (Its Hebrew root meaning "take" or "receive," the word kabbalah connotes spiritual wisdom received or passed down from one Jewish generation to another.)

Beaten down periodically, the *Zohar* and kabbalah invariably rise again. Renaissance Christian kabbalists teased from the *Zohar*'s complex imagery purported allusions to the Trinity and other dogmas. More recently, the *Zohar* and kabbalah have become intensely popular among twenty-first-century believers of various faiths who pursue personal enlightenment and reject institutional religion; an Internet query on the word kabbalah, for example, generates some 200,000 references.

Kabbalah flowered spectacularly in twelfth- and thirteenth-century France and Spain. While Maimonides was erecting a philosophical framework with which all rationalist Jewish theologians would have to contend, other devout Jews were laying kabbalah's enduring but radically different foundations. Central to the kabbalists' vision was the tension between the notions of God hidden and God revealed, or, as the *Zohar* expressed one pole of this dichotomy:

> He is hidden, concealed, far beyond.
> There is no one in the world, nor has there ever been,
> Who can understand His wisdom or withstand Him.

Yet these mystics were equally convinced that God was knowable. Imagine the Godhead as a fountain fed by an infinitely deep wellspring. Unfathomable at its source, but overflowing at the font, God becomes known through the outpouring of creation and in Scripture's inexhaustible store of meanings. For Scripture, too, is at once revealed yet hidden. Kabbalists searched out symbols, patterns, and images in the Hebrew Bible's verses, comforting themselves that Scripture would always harbor yet-undiscovered wisdom, sufficient to tide each successive Jewish generation through life's afflictions.

Moses de León and the kabbalists, looking to rescue Jewish spirituality from the remote God of the Maimonidean rationalists, championed a daring spirituality in which the human community deeply affected God. Indeed, the fullness of divine life came to full fruition only with the prayer and good works of the faithful. Nowhere is this clearer than in the *Zohar*'s extended meditation on male and female conjoined as exemplar of the relationship between God and creation, the same image that Ibn Arabi explored so powerfully. Just as male and female complete each other, the human community completes God. "Male and female He created them," says Genesis; the *Zohar* proclaims, "Any image that does not embrace male and female is not a high and true image . . . The Blessed Holy One does not place His abode/ in any place where male and female are not found together."

The *Zohar* tells of a rabbi undertaking a journey. Temporarily separated from his wife's companionship in this lower, earthly world, he nonetheless remains united with the (feminine) Divine Presence in the upper world through prayer and good intentions during his travels: "He is now male and female in the country, just as he was male and female in the town." Moreover, concludes the story, "It is his duty, once back home, to give his wife pleasure, inasmuch as she it was who obtained for him the heavenly union . . . this pleasure is a religious one, giving joy also to the Divine Presence, and it is an instrument for peace in the world, as it stands written, 'and thou shalt know that thy tent is in peace; and thou shalt visit thy habitation and not sin' [Job 5:24]."

The divine life reaches full fruition when complete harmony reigns between God and creation. The human community therefore bears the extraordinary responsibility and privilege of bringing the Divine to fullness through prayer, good works, and meditation. Humans complete the Godhead, as female completes male, by living holy lives and ensuring that peace and love reign in their homes.

God is unknowable yet knowable. All creation is an outpouring from an Infinite God. Love between man and woman is a metaphor for mystical union with the Divine. If it seems that Jewish Moses de León is echoing beloved themes of Muslim Ibn Arabi, that's not coincidence. Not that Moses de León copied Ibn Arabi (or even read him, as best we know). Rather, both drew from a deep reservoir of images and ideas that found equal voice in Christianity. The sixteenth-century Spanish Christian mystic St. John of the Cross, for example, charted a mystical journey reminiscent of the Sufi path, culminating only when consciousness of self as separate from God melts away.

The imagery that so profoundly influenced Muslim, Jewish, and Christian spirituality reached Spain after wholly improbable detours through ancient and medieval civilizations: quashed by Christian emperors, preserved by heretics, nurtured by Muslim caliphs, and finally revived in Europe. Ideas wound some five thousand miles and eight centuries through Greece, Egypt, Turkey, Syria, Iraq, and North Africa before blossoming in Spain after an unimaginable combination of luck, spiritual devotion, competing religious faiths, and changing political dynasties. Ideas leached into humanity's intellectual groundwater and bubbled up centuries later in a Spanish civilization far removed from their origin.

Like the mystic Moses de León who roamed Spain and Ibn Arabi who wandered the Islamic East, a third-century Egyptian named Plotinus ranged the ancient world seeking wisdom. He studied pagan Plato alongside a mentor who despised Christianity and a classmate devoted to it. He finally settled in Rome, absorbing and filtering the stream of ideas coursing through the ancient world's cosmopolitan capital. Plotinus hatched his own grand synthesis, postulating a cosmos where all creation emanated from a supreme infinite being he called the One or the Good. He described creation through the image of a fountain: Infinite Being necessarily overflows and pours all reality into existence. All creation, proceeding from the One, is innately gripped by the impulse to turn back toward its source. The human soul does so by shedding worldly attachments and undertaking a loving contemplative ascent to the One, eventually attaining mystical union so complete that any consciousness of distinction between the soul and the One is completely obliterated.

It is easy to see how such ideas influenced the Spanish mystics but difficult to trace the transit of these ideas to Spain. Plotinus's theories were debated in the famous Academy of Athens that had been founded by Plato in 387 B.C.E. and shut down in 529 C.E. by the Roman emperor Justinian, anxious to stamp out Greek philosophy and all pagan ideas. Some philosophers fled to Persia, finding an intellectual haven among descendants of earlier exiles, followers of a heretical fifth-century Christian bishop named Nestorius. Nestorians in Persia worshipped Jesus as they understood him, and, crucially for humanity, preserved Greek wisdom in their native Syriac translations. (Even today, thousands of intrepid Nestorians still worship in Iraq, Syria, and elsewhere. A raft of Christians on the Mideast's ocean of Muslims and a slender orphan branch of Christianity's family tree, they are doubly a religious minority.)

Nestorians attained unlikely yet vital prominence on civilization's stage when a ninth-century caliph founded the House of Wisdom in Baghdad. Scholars flocked from across the Islamic world to hear Nestorians teach Greek wisdom. The texts they once translated into their native Syriac were retranslated into Arabic. The transition across languages, cultures, and centuries was anything but smooth; much was lost, and much was corrupted as one hand-copied edition followed another. Some of Plotinus's work was mistakenly relabeled the "Theology of Aristotle." Though Plotinus was robbed of his byline, his ideas enjoyed a credibility boost by association with the finest "brand name" in ancient philosophy.

Baghdad-based scholars nurtured a revival of classical learning just when Dark Ages Europe had lost almost all touch with it. Later generations of Muslim scientists, theologians, philosophers, and medical researchers further developed ideas inherited from Aristotle, Galen, and other classical authors. The new and newly rediscovered ideas snaked across trade routes that linked the Islamic world, eventually reaching Muslim Spain, where translation into Latin spurred dissemination across Christian Europe.

Such was the unlikely preservation and transmission of some of humanity's most precious intellectual heritage: pagan Greek thought, suppressed by a Christian emperor, preserved by heretic Nestorians, promoted by Baghdad's caliphs, was welcomed by the Muslim successors of those who wrested Spanish rule from Visigoth Christians. As

Reconquest monarchs slowly reclaimed Iberia, Christian scholars followed in their wake, appropriating the intellectual gifts mediated by Islamic civilization.

Medieval Spain was blessed with an extraordinary quartet of towering religious figures whose ideas play off one another in a holy, eloquent, learned fugue: Maimonides, Averroes, Ibn Arabi, and Moses de León—the second Moses, the Commentator, Sufism's Greatest Master, and Judaism's greatest kabbalist. They show us that just as sacred Scripture is a divine gift, so too is the human mind's wondrous capacity to interpret its intended meanings, celebrate its spiritual beauty, plumb its profundities, and reason through the painful dilemmas that arise when faith traditions collide.

Each was unshakably devoted to his respective faith. Yet each stretched the traditional boundaries of how that faith could be expressed and interpreted. Each one's work bears its author's distinctive, inimitable stamp, yet each echoes themes dear to one of the others. Muslim Averroes harmonizes well with Jewish Maimonides under the baton of their common inspiration Aristotle, while Muslim Ibn Arabi and Jewish Moses de León take common mystic flight beyond the soberly rational philosophers. Divided by their religious beliefs, Spain's philosophers and mystics nonetheless explored values and ideas within each faith tradition that could have—and still can—surmount divisiveness.

Though all were Spaniards, all but Moses de León generated their most inspired work while living outside Spain. Spain claims their greatness as the society where ideas, beliefs, and cultures rubbed against one another to generate the vital friction that sparks brilliance. Each was forced—or privileged—to hear both the Muslim call to prayer and the tolling of church bells. Each recognized that no single tradition has monopolized every human expression of truth. As Averroes once put it, "We avail ourselves of what our predecessors may have said. That they were or were not our coreligionists is of no account . . . Whatever accords with the truth, we shall happily and gratefully accept and whatever conflicts, we shall scrupulously but generously point out."

Averroes teaches us to love the truth, to seek it fearlessly, and to welcome all who might enlighten us: "That they [are or are not] our coreligionists is of no account." Muslim, Christian, and Jew have truth to share. The enemies of truth are those demagogues, pundits, and religious fanatics who, certain that they alone posssess all truth, bark out their own opinions while shutting their ears to Muslim, Christian, or Jewish neighbors. The enemies of truth are those who would impose standards of behavior or a political future by resorting to terror, brute force, or overwhelming power and wealth, eschewing the reasoned discourse that respects another's human dignity and freedom. Averroes the truth-seeker would have us stand against all those who insist that their religious conviction or political standing renders them exempt from reasoned discourse with others.

Maimonides, brilliant yet chary of the finite human mind's limitations, ultimately fell silent before God, warning us against the self-idolatry of presuming to speak on God's behalf, of manipulating God's revealed word to serve a political agenda, or, most offensively, of doing violence to the innocent while invoking God's name. The mystic Moses de León instead outlines our proper role in God's plan: to complete the Godhead and bring God's reign to fullness by bringing peace to our shared global home. Everyone participates in this vital task, at a minimum by praying earnestly and daily for that peace and by extending to every Muslim, Christian, and Jewish neighbor the profound respect all are due as beings fashioned in God's image and likeness.

None of medieval Spain's mystics or philosophers aspired to what today is called interfaith dialogue, yet each drew ideas and influences from beyond his own religious tradition. They were born into a culturally mixed Spain that functioned only through the combined contribution of Muslim, Christian, and Jew. Uncomfortable necessity, rather than some higher-minded ideal of tolerance, first spurred the accommodation that scholars hail as Spain's era of *convivencia* ("common life").

Yet the roots of convivencia's demise grew never far beneath the surface. Almohad intolerance, after all, rousted Maimonides from Córdoba, spurring the odyssey that ended at an Egyptian sultan's court. By the time of Moses de León's death, Christian Spain had broken the centuries-long seesawing stalemate between Christian and Muslim Spain. A resurgent Christian Spain was rapidly asserting dominance over Iberia. Spain was on the verge of becoming a place where it was no longer necessary for adherents of one faith to accommodate the others.

Two great kings presided over a crucial turn in that long Christian Reconquest. Fernando III and his son Alfonso X between them reigned for over seventy years, presiding over the surrender of some of Muslim Spain's greatest cities into Christian hands. Yet, longevity—and Christianity—were almost the only things these extraordinary monarchs shared in common.

16. Fernando III

"Who Broke and Destroyed All His Enemies"

While Averroes, Maimonides, Ibn Arabi, and Moses de León were pondering God, God's creation was being marred by the religious wars waged in His name. The centuries-long struggle to dominate Iberia culminated in the mid-thirteenth century. And its decisive turn owed less to Spain's philosophers and mystics than to a rock.

The rock struck the child king Enrique I of Castile while he played with friends, and he died at age thirteen after a three-year reign. If the boy king's life was cut tragically short, at least his guardians had not so thoroughly saddled him with the adult world's concerns as to deprive him of all childhood pleasures. And if a thirteen-year-old must die, better in the midst of horseplay than heading an army waging religious war.

With Enrique's death his older sister, Berenguela, might legitimately have claimed Castile's throne. Spain's diverse pageant of cultural and political leaders had included Christians and Jews, light-skinned Arabs and dark-skinned North Africans, converts to Islam and converts to Christianity, royals boasting centuries-old dynastic pedigrees, usurpers like Almanzor, and renegades like the Cid. But medieval Spain would cast few women in public leadership until Queen Isabella seized her chance with gusto in the late 1400s. Berenguela yielded her claim to her son, Fernando.

191

Not everyone applauded eighteen-year-old Fernando's elevation as king of Castile in 1217. Foremost among the disgruntled was Fernando's own father (and Berenguela's ex-husband), King Alfonso IX of León. Alfonso campaigned to usurp his son's throne and crown himself king of a united León and Castile. His machinations honored a long-standing ancestral tradition; war against infidel Islam, and good governance for ordinary Spaniards, had often taken a back seat to messy dynastic squabbles. But for once, Spain's nobles refused to indulge in the internecine strife that had so often drained their finances and hamstrung efforts to reassert Christian dominance throughout the Peninsula. Alfonso's plot sputtered; the chastened father patched up relations with his son.

Alfonso died a dozen years later, prompting Fernando to seize León's crown and thereby fulfill his father's dream of uniting León and Castile (albeit not exactly as the dead Alfonso had hoped it would happen). The two kingdoms were never again separated. León-Castile sheltered the majority of Iberia's population and blanketed its largest landmass. As León-Castile increasingly dominated Iberia's politics, a constellation of lesser kingdoms—Portugal, Navarre, and Aragon—were pushed to an ever wary and often cranky peripheral orbit.

Fernando III might never have reigned but for the freak accident that killed his boy uncle Enrique, and Fernando would not have ruled for long had his father engineered a savvier plot to supplant him. Yet, notwithstanding his reign's shaky launch, Fernando went on to rule for thirty-five years. This greatest of Spain's Crusader kings conquered al-Andalus's crown jewel cities of Córdoba and Seville while whittling Muslim Spain's territory to one embattled province surrounding Granada. Indeed, by one measure, Fernando outshone all Europe's Crusader kings and warriors combined. What Fernando conquered in little over a decade, Christian Spain never again lost; in contrast, all medieval Europe's multinational Crusader armies were left with virtually nothing to show for centuries of slaughter and pillage once Muslim armies reclaimed the Mideast by the late thirteenth century.

Fernando could thank both his predecessors and his enemies for paving his path to military glory. The centuries-long Reconquest had sapped Muslim Spain's defenses and shaken her political will. Once al-

Andalus did Christian Spain the favor of splintering into petty principalities, Christian princes secured their diminutive kingdoms in the north, then clawed back chunks of largely empty and worthless frontier, and finally reclaimed Muslim Spain's heartland.

The battle of Las Navas de Tolosa (1212) is generally considered the engagement that once and for all shattered Muslim Spain's capacity to resist. Fernando's grandfather King Alfonso VIII led a multinational expedition from Toledo into al-Andalus. Well, briefly a multinational expedition. Once Alfonso prohibited wanton sacks of Muslim towns captured along the way, most of the foreign knight-adventurers abandoned the crusade, disgruntled that those who liberated Muslim territory for Christendom were not permitted to liberate Muslim possessions as reward.

The knight-tourists were hardly missed. Alfonso's diminished forces engaged an Almohad army some sixty miles south of Toledo. One account depicts the Christian forces hacking their way through a human fence of slaves chained one to another in desperate defense of the caliph's tent. The Christians scored an overwhelming victory, and a jubilant King Alfonso VIII apprised Pope Innocent III of a miraculous triumph: "On their side 100,000 armed men or more fell in the battle . . . [But] unless it be a miracle, hardly 25 or 30 Christians of our whole army fell. O what happiness! . . . though one might lament that so few martyrs from such a great army went to Christ in martyrdom."

Two decades drifted by before Christian Spain raised in Fernando a military leader resolved and aggressive enough to press home its advantage. Fernando captured Córdoba in 1236, liberating Santiago de Compostela's cathedral bells from 230 years of forced service as lamp fixtures in Córdoba's grand mosque. Whereas Almanzor had abandoned a cold, damp Santiago de Compostela after looting what little of value he found there, Fernando had no intention of abandoning a Córdoba that was, after all, as fine a city as any in his kingdom. He expelled its Muslim populace, rechristened its mosque as a cathedral, and began recruiting Christian immigrants to resettle the city.

A decade or so later, Fernando turned his attention to Seville, among Spain's and Europe's most populous, affluent cities. Its 100,000 inhabitants were sheltered by an extensive network of walls and moats. The

Guadalquivir River, the ocean outlet that won Seville's prosperity as a trading depot, became in war the watery lifeline to the outside world that greatly complicated Fernando's siege plans. Late medieval warfare could be a long-drawn-out enterprise, steeped in what modern warriors antiseptically call collateral damage. Simply put, the technology for erecting strong walls had outpaced the technology for knocking them down. Hunkered down in their protective cocoon, besieged inhabitants could survive indefinitely.

Provided, of course, they had food and water.

Unable to scale, batter down, or tunnel under well-constructed municipal fortifications, medieval armies camped outside at a safe distance, intercepted all trade, and waited for the enemy within to starve. By the summer of 1247, Fernando had sealed the land routes into Seville and blockaded its river link to the outside world, giving its inhabitants, as one Muslim chronicler put it, their first "taste of disaster."

Sevillians struggled to break the siege, floating burning barges down the Guadalquivir in the hopes of immolating the blockading ships. Nighttime patrols sneaked outside the city walls to scavenge food in fields that Fernando's crusaders had scorched barren. Sevillians were slowly starving, while Fernando's six or seven thousand besiegers, according to one Christian chronicler, patiently maintained their vigil from a camp that "had the appearance of a great city, noble and very rich," served by "rag-and-bone dealers and money changers . . . grocers and apothecaries . . . armorers and bridle-sellers . . . butchers and fishermen; and so on for every need that can exist in the world."

Fernando's armies futilely pounded stone walls that proved far sturdier than the flesh-and-blood humans cowering within. After failing to penetrate Seville's defenses, they catapulted stones and flaming debris into the city proper, "destroy[ing] all amenities, both small and great, except what was in the houses of a few rich people." With the advent of sophisticated modern weaponry, the catapult may seem a Tinker Toy that amuses little boys yet terrifies no one. But medieval catapults could lob some two hundred pounds of matériel the length of a football field, showering towns with bombardment both terrifying and damaging. Well aware that warfare is psychological no less than physical, Christian armies occasionally launched the severed head of a Muslim captive into the midst of a besieged town.

Seville's inhabitants were too hunger-crazed to appreciate the irony that the same defensive walls that sealed out Fernando's armies were effectively guaranteeing their own starvation within; they "stagger[ed] around like drunkards even though they weren't drunk," the chronicler continued, "resigning any hope of corn or barley, the people began to chew [animal] skins." "Squeezed in the grip of the enemies of God," anguished Sevillians appealed to Muslim North Africa, bewailing "the terrible struggle and the severe and excruciating distress that had overtaken them." North African Almoravids and Almohads had rallied more than one jihad to deliver Muslim Spain from previous crises. But this time an Almohad dynasty on the verge of collapse was too preoccupied with its own worries; nor was help forthcoming from elsewhere in al-Andalus. Indeed, the besieging armies camped outside Seville's walls included a five-hundred-strong contingent from Muslim Granada, dispatched by its emir.

Nearly eighteen months passed before Seville's magistrates bowed to the inevitable and negotiated surrender terms. Suffice it to say that their bargaining position was by that point weak. Fernando allowed Sevillians one month to depart with whatever they could carry. An emaciated populace barely able to stand wasn't about to carry much; most sold what they could at distressed prices—who was there to buy?—before staggering forth. Many joined a waiting convoy that sailed to North Africa. Others trekked the one-hundred-odd miles to Granada, now the last remaining principality of size in Muslim hands. Ironically, they were taking refuge in a kingdom lorded over by the same Granadan emir who had helped starve them out of Seville.

King Fernando and his retinue entered a deserted Seville a few days later, taking possession of well-constructed but empty residences and shops, a stage set on which Christian immigrants would try to recreate what had been one of Europe's most populous and prosperous cities. They began by rechristening its central mosque as a cathedral.

Muslim Spain's fearsome shadow once loomed over even the Compostela pilgrimage route in Iberia's far north. With Seville's demise,

Muslim Spain shrank to a far less fearsome pocket of land surrounding Granada. Yet the diminished kingdom would linger on for more than two centuries in near permanent subservience to surrounding Christian kingdoms. Though Granada's Nasrids (1232–1492) reigned longer than any other Muslim dynasty in Spain, the distinction was hollow. They launched a dynasty by joining the siege of Seville and secured Fernando's forbearance by selling out Muslim coreligionists. The Nasrids essentially reenacted a morality tale often played in medieval Spain's long drama, and countless times elsewhere in centuries since, where raw pursuit of power determines one's allies and actions, with religion's dictates ignored when convenient or cynically overlaid when helpful in currying popular support.

A determined Christian push might have surmounted Granada and entirely swept Muslim rule from Spain at almost any point over the ensuing 260 years. That the coup de grâce was delivered only in 1492 had less to do with Granada's might than Christian Spain's priorities. True, Granada was a challenging military target, nestled picturesquely, and inaccessibly, within the Sierra Nevada mountains. And Granada's Mediterranean coastline held the ever present yet fading threat that a Christian assault could draw North African armies into the fray.

But Christian Spain's monarchs had other reasons for tolerating a largely emasculated Granada. Fernando III's thrusts had engulfed Muslim cities far larger than the towns of the Christian north. His governors found themselves minority rulers of large Muslim populations, much as Spain's Muslim conquerors once governed large Christian majorities. Muslim Granada unwittingly abetted re-Christianization of the newly conquered territory by siphoning off refugees and disgruntled Muslim émigrés unwilling to bear the ignominy of Christian rule. There was also financial incentive to tolerate Muslim Granada: the vassal state bought off the threat of invasion by paying a handsome annual tribute to Castile's perennially cash-strapped monarchs.

The warrior-king Fernando died a natural death. So often girded in battle armor during life, in death he was garbed in a friar's habit and entombed in Seville's great mosque. Or, more accurately, he was entombed (and lies still) in the great mosque he had rechristened as a cathedral after Seville's surrender. His tombstone epitaph communicates a curiously mixed message. It is chiseled in Latin, Hebrew, Arabic, and Castilian, as if celebrating the very diversity of his kingdom; yet its words tell a different story, praising the king "who conquered all Spain . . . who broke and destroyed all his enemies."

Fernando's Castile had overrun great chunks of Muslim Spain, as had the neighboring Christian realms of Aragon. Christian governors now often found themselves minority rulers of large Muslim populations, exactly paralleling the predicament faced by al-Andalus's first Muslim princes many centuries earlier. The harsh rhetoric hammered into Fernando's gravestone and his banishment of Seville's conquered Muslims might suggest that the Christian Reconquest ushered in only conflict and discord among Muslims, Christians, and Jews in the newly conquered territories. In fact, after centuries of struggle and despite every possible rhetorical inducement to hate each other, many medieval Spaniards were to find in themselves and neighbors sufficient reservoirs of goodwill to build a shared life—and leave humanity's later generations a lesson about the capacity of ordinary humans to give priority to what unites them rather than what divides them.

17. A Common Life Shared Among Three Faiths

"Damnable Mixing"

In the nearly two thousand years since Jesus died, popes have convened only twenty-one Ecumenical Councils of the Catholic Church. Delegates to the first, at Nicea in 325, hammered out a creed enunciating the still-intact formulation that Jesus is "true God of true God . . . of the same substance as the Father." In 1962, some two thousand bishops gathered for Vatican Council II, the most recent council, which Pope John XXIII envisioned as an *aggiornamento*, or "updating" of the Church for the modern world. The Council fathers frankly acknowledged unhappy chapters of Christianity's past relations with other religions. One document greeted the Muslim people "with esteem," acknowledged the "many quarrels and hostilities" that had marred Church-Muslim relations, and "urged all . . . to strive sincerely for mutual understanding." The same document addressed the Jewish people: "Mindful of her common patrimony with the Jews . . . [the Church] deplores the hatred, persecutions, and displays of anti-Semitism directed against the Jews at any time and from any source."

The Council fathers may have been recalling the work of predecessor bishops at the Fourth Lateran Council of 1215, who had condemned what they called "damnable mixing." One decree lamented that "by mistake Christians join with Jewish or Saracen women, and Jews or Saracens with Christian women." The Council fathers prescribed a remedy: "That such persons [Jews or Muslims] of either sex, in every Christian province and at all times . . . are to be distinguished in public from other people by the character of their dress." Within a few years of the Council's close, Jews in Sicily and England were getting used to sewing distinguishing patches to outer garments, while Jews in some Germanic principalities were unmistakable in their conical hats. In many regions, the Council had merely legitimized policies already practiced in and beyond Christendom. Jews in Paris, for example, had long endured the humiliation of a distinctive dress code, as had Jews in Muslim-ruled North Africa.

While much of Christian Europe complied with the Lateran decrees, Fernando III's Spain proved recalcitrant, provoking a steady stream of reprimanding correspondence from Rome. In 1221, Pope Honorius III complained to Toledo's archbishop that the "Jews of your diocese do not observe [distinctive dress statutes], with the result that under the veil of error this damnable sin of intermingling may be committed." A decade later, Pope Gregory IX futilely pressed Castile's king to comply and also proceeded to "beg and earnestly warn" King Sancho VIII of Navarre to fall into line. In 1239, the exasperated pope wrote the Navarrese again, even detailing the precise insignia that papal authorities had in mind: "one round patch of yellow cloth or linen, to be worn on the uppermost garment, stitched over the heart and another behind it, in order that they [Jews] may thus be recognized. The full size of this sign shall be four digits in circumference." But the mounting pile of disapproving papal correspondence only confirmed what prelates from Castile and León had earlier concluded in stunningly plain language at their Council of Valladolid: the Lateran Council's discriminatory dress decrees were "in large measure neglected" throughout much of Spain.

Why? Correspondence between Pope Honorius III and King Fernando sheds light on Spain's defiance. Fernando worried, as the pope summarized it, that "serious misfortune may befall [his] kingdom" were he to subject Spain's Jews to conspicuous badges, conical hats, or other humiliating paraphernalia. The monarch guessed that Jews would "choose rather to flee to the Moors [i.e., to Spain's Muslim-ruled south] than to be burdened with such a sign." If they emigrated, León-Castile would suffer the "serious misfortune" of losing the Jews—and their tax revenues.

Fernando's motives for refusing to adorn Jews with humiliating badges were plainly self-serving. No lofty human rights rhetoric elevates his correspondence with papal authorities, nor does he protest that stigmatizing dress would fundamentally demean the Jews. The monarch's brand of religious tolerance features no paean to cultural diversity and issues no idyllic appeal for interfaith dialogue. Indeed, one senses that he might willingly enough have subjected Jews to the humiliation had he been certain of preserving their tax revenues and commercial savvy.

Fernando's was the imperfect, even grudging acceptance of one's neighbor simply because one must. England and France could better afford to pin badges on Jews, tiny minorities bearing scant impact on their overall economies. Many English and French villagers had never met a Jew or a Muslim; it was far easier to discriminate against those known abstractly as blasphemers and heretics rather than flesh-and-blood neighbors, merchants, or customers. Fernando's kingdom, on the other hand, was everywhere dotted with Christian towns and villages deeply accustomed to the religious other in their midst. The Lateran Council's bishops may actually have believed that "damnable mixing" among Muslims, Jews, and Christians was happening, as they put it, "by mistake." But the mixing that took place across Iberia was no mistake at all. No yellow cloth patch, dunce cap, or other warning beacon could have preempted commercial, social, and even intimate relations among Spaniards of diverse faiths.

Nowadays, Muslims, Christians, and Jews most typically interact in great urban centers like London and New York, vortexes that in every generation draw the ambitious and the desperate, those desiring fame and those desiring only a day without hunger. But Spanish portraits of common life can be sketched not only in Toledo's libraries, where multifaith translation teams toiled, but just as vividly in tiny Cuenca, even today a fairly isolated town perched in the foothills of mountainous terrain some hundred miles east of Madrid. Medieval Cuenca was neither populous, nor wealthy, nor particularly fertile. Yet, straddling as it did the frontier fault line between Muslim and Christian Spain, this otherwise charmless town exerted endless fascination for would-be Crusaders and conquerors. First established by Muslims, Cuenca was later captured by Christians, reconquered by Almoravid fighters in the early 1100s, and reclaimed once and for all by Christian Castile's King Alfonso VIII in 1177. With each change of control some Cuencans fled rather than submit to new rulers espousing a contrary faith. Yet many others remained and persevered, resilient fatalists grown genetically accustomed to watching and coping as cross yielded to crescent (or vice versa) each generation or so.

When royal counselors codified this twice Muslim–twice Christian town's laws and privileges, one might have expected wary treatment for non-Christians who had so recently been the enemy. Yet, the Code of Cuenca pointedly instructs that "whoever may come to live in Cuenca, whatever condition he may be, whether Christian, Moor, or Jew, free or servile, should come in safety." Odd though it may seem to welcome Christianity's perceived antagonists, the practice evinces what might be called frontier logic. Christian monarchs were anxious to establish viable frontier settlements as bulwarks against future attack. Alfonso, like his contemporaries, had virtually no standing army and limited financial resources with which to defend each newly won chunk of frontier. A thriving local community prosperous enough to equip a militia and maintain town walls was any Christian monarch's best hope of securing freshly conquered territory.

The same approach was followed all along the frontier. The town of Chivert had a legal code that instructed Muslims and Christians to man the town ramparts and fight side by side against Muslim raiders or foreign invaders. "The Moors of Chivert should defend themselves and their property together with the [Christian] Brothers [Hospitaller] as best they can," it declaimed. When French armies attacked Gerona in the late 1280s, hundreds of Muslim archers and lancers converged from nearby towns to assist its besieged Christian and Muslim defenders.

Cuenca's law code was, of course, an abstract document. That the code prescribed certain behaviors hardly guarantees that daily life unfolded accordingly. Modern statutes urging pedestrians not to litter, for example, have hardly brought spotless sidewalks to urban America. But even individuals who shunned the idealized behaviors enshrined in Cuenca's code bowed to the economic necessities of life in small, mixed-faith villages. Iberian towns and villages were often hamlets of fewer than one thousand persons; cooperation with neighbors—whatever their faith—was virtually unavoidable.

There was, for example, not the least bit of idealism in King Jaime I of Aragon's 1258 decree that one municipal bakeoven would serve the small Valencian town of Navarrés, "to which both Christians and Saracens, present and future, are bound to come for baking their bread." Few if any medieval peasant homes had a bakeoven. The balky contraption was too large for a peasant dwelling, and stoking it to a temperature suitable for baking bread would have entailed an uneconomic, laborious investment merely for one or two daily loaves. The King Jaime who licensed Navarrés's one oven was recognizing the same economic reality that governed countless other Iberian towns, where day after day some three dozen loaves shaped at home by Muslim, Christian, and Jewish hands would rise peaceably alongside one another in the municipal oven.

The floury substance of these loaves reflected another elaborate experiment in interfaith relations. With water so scarce in much of al-Andalus, its Muslim overlords had imported irrigation technology from the similarly water-poor Mideast to construct elaborate canal networks. Disputes inevitably erupted between upstream farmers suspected by their downstream neighbors of hogging water; Muslim rulers accordingly established local water councils to mediate such quarrels. As the Christian Reconquest subsumed one Andalusian town after another, Christian and Muslim villagers learned to share life-giving water not only across farms but across faiths. Arab-engineered canals snaked through Muslim and Christian fields alike, and water councils brought Muslim and Christian farmers together to sort through disputes.

As the harvest approached and burgeoning fields beckoned would-be crop raiders, other opportunities for interfaith cooperation emerged. Farmers in Daroca for a time pooled their funds and paid a night watchman to guard both Muslim and Christian wheat fields. Harvested grain became grist for mills that in smaller towns were shared by Muslim, Christian, and Jewish farmers alike. Elsewhere along the winding course of the streams powering these mills, wives and slaves of these Christian, Muslim, and Jewish farmers could also be found working in close proximity, laundering clothing at some location outside the town walls designated for this purpose. The most intimate, vulnerable, watery engagement of all was the custom of stripping down and sinking into a shared communal bath. Bathhouses, inevitable fixtures of Andalusian towns, were unheard of luxuries to Christian immigrants following the Reconquest's wake. Ripe northerners who once contented themselves with one or two cold water baths each year suddenly looked forward to luxuriating, weekly hot water soaks.

But first, religiously mixed communities had to sort out the nitty-gritty logistics of sharing this treasured resource. Larger cities like Seville could afford segregated facilities, designating some for Christians and others for Muslims. Smaller towns had no such alternative, especially after restricting certain days each week for women bathers. Christian men used Teruel's bathhouse on some days and Jews and Muslims on others; in Valencia and Tortosa, Jews, Muslims, and Christians all soaked at will, with no segregation by religion (which seems to have been the convention practiced all along in Muslim-ruled al-Andalus). Interreligious bathing days seem to have been most customary for women, perhaps because no obvious sign like circumcision constantly reminded the bathers of the religious differences that separated them.

These Jews, Muslims, and Christians did not purposely seek each other's company to build a richer common life. Indeed, each community typically preferred to segregate itself where circumstances allowed. The five hundred Jews who made up some 10 percent of thirteenth-century Burgos's population could do just that. They lived, shopped, worked, and worshipped in the comforting confines of their own religious culture, a substantial enough community to provide a livelihood to Jewish merchants. But smaller Ávila, like most Iberian towns, afforded no such critical mass. A medieval census reveals Jews sprinkled throughout the town, occupied as locksmiths, weavers, blacksmiths, shopkeepers, a butcher, quilt maker, carpenter, and a chair maker. Few to none of these craftsmen could have made a decent living without cultivating non-Jewish customers.

A medieval craftsman learned his trade and its secrets from a father or mentor. Under the circumstances, certain regions or religious communities occasionally came to dominate a given trade. Valencia's Muslim dye masters, silk processors, potters, and glass makers were so highly esteemed by Christians, Muslims, and Jews alike that King Jaime I of Aragon dissuaded these uniquely skilled craftsmen from migrating to Muslim Granada by granting exemptions from certain taxes. Similarly, Jewish physicians were so deeply respected that their presence at the royal court was more commonplace than remarkable. Indeed, they supplied their healing arts in even the most intimate and privileged of settings, exemplified in a thirteenth-century court document referring to the Jewish physician who served the cloistered nuns of Las Huelgas monastery.

If monastery walls and the status of consecrated religious virgins proved no barrier to the "damnable mixing" of commerce among the faiths, neither did the strict dietary regulations stipulated by Muslim and Jewish law. Then, as now, it seems, a good butcher could draw clientele regardless of faith. One Granadan poet ranted that Jewish butchers "slaughter beasts in our markets" and sell to Muslims. Christian butchers in Valencia similarly complained that Muslim and Jewish competitors were successfully poaching Christian customers.

Indeed, some savvy Muslims, Christians, and Jews even partnered in interfaith businesses, pursuing customers from multiple faith communities while remaining open on each partner's respective Sabbath. Such ventures presented theological conundrums, and even the great Maimonides, when not ruminating on God's nature, grappled with the more mundane dilemma of dividing profits from a Jewish-Muslim business partnership. The "second Moses" suggested the eminently logical arrangement that the shop's Friday revenues go to the Jew (who could work on the Muslim holy day), and Saturday sales accrue to the Muslim partner. The fourteenth-century Muslim Mahoma Abenfo and the Jew Abraham Avenrrabi trusted each other enough to sign for a business loan in Saragossa as cocreditors. In nearby Borja, Christian and Muslim partners jointly ran an inn situated in the town's Jewish quarter.

Some of these interfaith relationships inevitably soured, and the ensuing legal repercussions demonstrate that Jews, Muslims, and Christians not only did business together but made mischief together. We know that Muslims and Christians jointly patronized certain taverns from legal records of tippling bouts that ended badly. In Elche, inebriated Muslims and Christians were more than once tossed into jail to sleep off drunken rows that erupted in a tavern. The incidents spurred a Muslim petition that the king forbid Muslims from drinking in Christian-owned inns—not out of some pious desire to enforce Muslim bans on drinking alcohol, but as a clever maneuver to secure a monopoly on Muslim business for Muslim barkeeps!

Legal records expose more sinister sorts of interfaith cooperation. A late thirteenth-century Tarazona gang of Christians and Muslims was accused of abducting a Muslim woman to sell into slavery, a reprehensible crime ideally suited to interfaith partnership: because frontier Christians would typically buy Muslim slaves, and vice versa, one partner would be well positioned to procure the human goods and the other the "customers."

The constant friction of shared village life occasionally generated sparks of misunderstanding and resentment, but also inevitably kindled mutual understanding and accommodation born of countless daily interactions at bakeoven, mill, butcher stall, tavern, and water council. To be sure, believers of each religious tradition never forgot the confessional differences that separated them from neighbors. It would have been unthinkable, even blasphemous, for medieval Spanish religious leaders to engage in the interfaith dialogue pursued in a modern world anxiously groping for harmonious interfaith relations. But daily conversations about the weather, prices, the quality of produce, or the latest village scandal enabled each to perceive others as multidimensional human beings, rather than objectified as caricatures of Jew, Christian, or Muslim. If close interfaith friendships were far from normal, they were not unheard of. Witness the poignant story of a thirteenth-century Christian girl who fled an abusive forced marriage to take refuge with a sympathetic Jewish friend. Who knows how many other stories of kindness or friendship remain untold; illiterate medieval peasants in small, paperless villages left no diaries of daily life's adventures, concerns, and amusements.

Of course, the "damnable mixing" that the Lateran Council's bishops most abhorred was sexual, and such mixing occurred far too regularly to be "by mistake." To be sure, most such liaisons show medieval society at its worst. Prostitutes found clients outside their own religious tradition. Slave owners of all three faiths purchased slaves outside their faith group, and owners slept with female slaves as a matter of common practice. Sexual revulsion of the religious other was surmounted in such cases only to exploit, humiliate, and degrade another human being.

But one also finds signs of more genuine intimate relations. One Moorish poet encapsulates in a single couplet both his infatuation with a Christian girl and society's disapprobation of their liaison: "I have a girl among the Christians, who bolts like a shy gazelle round the churches. I am in raptures over her; but passion among the cloisters and the churches is a sin." The eleventh-century Jewish poet Moses Ibn Ezra of Granada was just as deeply enthralled by a young Muslim woman: "By the hand of the Muslim doe [female] is my soul destroyed and my heart by her eyes is torn." Many such relationships remained clandestine. When they became public, the lovers instantly became outcasts from their respective communities. Fear of social condemnation invariably crushed most such relationships before they fully blossomed. But more than a few medieval Spaniards chose love over faith and family, like a young Muslim girl of Liria who left behind an angered and stunned father to begin a new life beside her Christian beloved.

Such reflections of common life among Christians, Muslims, and Jews, plucked from across towns and across centuries, are in one respect exceptions that prove a rule. Coexistence was fragile; members of each faith group preferred to build their own homogeneous society than to forge a mixed one. Frequently enough, however, that choice was unavailable. In consequence, an eloquent interfaith dialogue was occurring all over Spain every day in countless ways, the pedestrian but rich dialogue of daily life where one learns to accommodate the customs and beliefs of another through myriad quotidian interactions while baking, laundering, buying, selling, sowing, and reaping. Unfortunately, glimpses of these everyday victories of goodwill over hate are rare and fleeting. History inordinately concerns itself with the affairs of society's "great and good"; few medieval scribes were inclined to waste a scrap of parchment on the unremarkable lives of illiterate commoners. Still, the few anecdotes that can be pieced together suggest that ordinary Muslims, Jews, and Christians sometimes triumphed to forge accommodations with neighbors of different faiths, creating a common life unlike any other achieved or even imagined elsewhere on Europe's continent in the medieval era.

King Alfonso X inherited this Christian Spain, greatly increased in size through his father Fernando's conquests and including an Andalusia dotted with rural villages where majority Muslims adjusted to life under Christian rule. A thirteenth-century chronicler recounted Fernando's purported deathbed challenge to his son and heir. After rehearsing his many conquests, Fernando told his son, "If you know how to preserve in this state what I leave you, you will be as good a king as I, and if you win more for yourself, you will be better than I, but if you diminish it, you will not be as good as I."

But Alfonso was a man unwilling to measure his life by his father's yardstick.

18. Alfonso the Learned King

Alfonso's contemporaries called him El Sabio, Alfonso "the Learned" or "the Wise." Thanks to the military successes of his illustrious father and storied ancestors, he appended quite an impressive coda to official pronouncements: Alfonso, King of Castile, Toledo, León, Galicia, Seville, Córdoba, Murcia, Jaén, and the Algarve. Yet Alfonso often seemed less absorbed by military campaigns than by his lavish project to gather every bit of astronomical knowledge available in the medieval world. Alfonso aspired to be emperor of all Christian Europe, a dream he chased even as rebellion at home nearly cost him a slice of Spain. He battled Muslim armies, yet later allied with those same armies to attack his own kingdom. He included Jewish scholars among his innermost circles even while reviling the Jews in his poetry. Alfonso's reign was farsighted yet misguided, inspired yet clumsy, and ultimately, in many important respects, world-changing.

That Alfonso even dared dream of empire beyond Iberia shows how far Christian Spain had come since the humiliating Muslim invasion of 711. After all, the last Iberian rulers to pursue territorial expansion weren't Christian, but Muslim warriors giddily confident after overrunning Visigoth Spain. They had raced to within two hundred miles of Paris before they were halted.

That was five centuries earlier. In the interim, Christian rulers generally had their hands full warding off Muslim armies threatening their own backyards. Yet, thanks to his father's stunning takeover of Seville, Córdoba, and much of Andalusia, Alfonso could resurrect long dormant dreams of empire, mounting a two-decade, treasury-draining chase after the Holy Roman emperor's crown. Charlemagne had been first of these emperors, crowned by a Pope Leo anxious to enlist a pious monarch mighty enough to intimidate papal enemies. Both pope and Charlemagne had envisioned as glorious an empire as the first Rome, with the emperor's temporal sway over all Christendom perfectly complementing the pope's spiritual reign.

It never quite worked out. The Holy Roman emperors never commanded servile obeisance from Christendom's monarchs, unless the emperors also happened to command armies substantial enough to instill respect. Still, European monarchs inevitably chased the crown, and Alfonso was one of them. In retrospect, few greater disasters befell his reign than that unlucky day when a faction of electors backed his claim to the imperial throne. For if the value of the emperor's crown was not obvious, its cost was to the noble subjects Alfonso saddled with the bill. Holy though the Roman Empire supposedly was, candidates secured its crown only after thoroughly *un*holy diplomatic maneuvering, double dealing, and bribery. As Alfonso finagled tax levies to finance his campaign, Spain's nobles grew disenchanted with their profligate monarch.

Worse, bewitched by his imperial dream, Alfonso was oblivious to conspiratorial stirrings among restive Muslim subjects. North Africa's Marinid sultan launched a jihad into Iberia, following the tradition that proved the mettle of so many Almoravid and Almohad warriors before him. While North African invaders and Andalusian Moors ravaged Spain's south, King Alfonso was in France beseeching the pope's backing for his imperial candidacy. Alfonso's nineteen-year-old son and heir, Fernando, rallied Spain's defense, but with Christian Spain's fate in the balance, the prince chose this extremely unpropitious moment to keel over and die before ever actually engaging the enemy.

The demoralized Christians were routed in the battles that followed. The Marinids' gruesome war trophies included the severed heads of Governor Don Nuño González de Lara and the warrior-archbishop

Sancho II of Toledo (and, for good measure, the hacked-off hand bearing his episcopal ring). The high-profile souvenirs headlined a grisly haul: one Muslim chronicler exaggeratedly brayed that the invaders amassed some 18,000 severed Christian heads; as if that image alone is not loathsome enough, he further depicts a muezzin clambering atop the piled skulls to sound the Muslim call to prayer.

Alfonso's second son, Sancho, stormed into the breach and checked the Muslim advance until the king straggled back to Spain. All in all, this can't have been the happiest trip Alfonso ever took. Already disconsolate that the pope had rebuffed his imperial bid, Alfonso returned home to a full-blown invasion and the death of his heir. Fighting dragged on intermittently for another two years. Alfonso's siege of the Marinid-held Spanish port of Algeciras demonstrates just how imperiled his armies were. Alfonso had underestimated the Algecirans' resourcefulness, and as the siege dragged on his finances dwindled. He scoured Seville for financing while his unpaid troops maintained the blockade throughout the winter of 1279–80 with "no renewal of clothes or food when they needed them . . . [they] became seriously ill . . . their teeth fell out, and they suffered very great hardships." Such were the sufferings of the besiegers, mind you. Algeciras's famished inhabitants had it worse, "falling dead in the streets of the city." Alfonso's wasted navy might have outlasted the dying Algecirans, but a Marinid fleet sailed to Algeciras's relief and easily scattered Alfonso's demoralized, malnourished soldiers, "so few and injured that not a single one of them thought to defend himself."

Alfonso the Wise's ambitions proved Alfonso the Wise's folly. Nothing came of his quest for an imperial title or his siege of Algeciras. Instead, his financial resources frittered away and his focus distracted, he found himself frequently on the defensive. Christian Spain ultimately repulsed the Marinids, but the strife cost Alfonso his first-born son and scores of warrior-nobles.

The strife's aftermath tore apart his family and cost him his crown. He named Sancho heir upon Fernando's death, disappointing the deceased prince's relatives, who vociferously argued the claims of Fernando's own sons (Alfonso's grandsons). Alfonso then alienated Sancho, clumsily patching up relations with Fernando's relatives by carving them a slice of Sancho's inheritance. The disgruntled Sancho rebelled, declaring his father mentally incompetent to rule and winning the backing of nobles fed up with Alfonso's erratic reign. Compounding the indignity yet further, even Alfonso's wife, Queen Violante, supported Sancho's claim.

Now age sixty in a society where most were happy to reach forty, his face disfigured by a painful degenerative cancer, rejected by his nobles and family, his treasury all but exhausted, Alfonso cut a tragic figure yet refused to retire and rage in Lear-like impotence on some windy expanse of meseta. With nowhere else to turn for support, Alfonso concocted an alliance—unbelievably—with the very same Moroccan Marinid dynasty that had brought him such grief by invading Spain, occasioning his son Fernando's premature death, butchering hundreds if not thousands of Christian Spain's knights, and (if legend be believed) scaling their skulls at prayer time. He negotiated a massive loan from the Marinid sultan, tendering his own crown as collateral. (A fifteenth-century Muslim chronicler delightedly crowed that the crown was still being displayed in a Moroccan palace.) Theoretically now Alfonso's allies, the Marinids invaded Iberia at his invitation, rampaging through southern Spain and gorging themselves on booty while paying little attention to securing Alfonso's strategic advantage.

Alfonso, Sancho, and Spain's nobility soon enough realized what havoc they had wrought upon their homeland. Father and son reconciled before Alfonso's death in 1284, although the king overlooked the minor detail of redrafting his will. Sancho remained disinherited, an inconvenient fact that Spain's nobility, churchmen, and lawyers ignored in recognizing King Sancho IV as Alfonso X's successor. Alfonso's will instructed that he be entombed at the feet of his parents in Seville's cathedral, though, envisioning greater conquests ahead for Christian Spain, directed that his heart be removed from his body for eventual burial in the Holy Land.

If Alfonso the politician seemed at times less than Wise, he reigned alongside Alfonso the truly Wise, whose cultural agenda was every bit as grandiose as his imperial dreams yet, in contrast, was splendidly implemented. This wiser Alfonso revolutionized the arts, sciences, law, and even the very language his subjects spoke. Scholars who routinely disparage Alfonso the politician heap praise on this other Alfonso.

He was the master architect of a law code that was consulted across a wider swath of the globe than any other law book in history when chunks of the Americas, Asia, and Africa began falling under Spain's imperial sway. Indeed, Alfonso's visage peers out from above the gallery doors of the U.S. House of Representatives, appropriately commemorating him as one of world history's most influential lawgivers.

That law code was composed not in Latin, but in the vernacular Romance dialect prefiguring today's Castilian (Spanish). By recognizing Spanish as a formal language of government, Alfonso engineered a momentous break from Latin's centuries-long monopoly and accelerated the development of one of humanity's most widely spoken languages.

The spread of Spanish owes much to the explorers who colonized the Americas for Spain, but those sixteenth-century explorers owed something to Alfonso. Well over two centuries after he died, navigators still used his "Alfonsine tables" as their authoritative map of the night sky, and some of them calibrated the position of stars overhead with astrolabes fashioned from instructions laid out in Alfonso's astronomical treatises. Both astrolabe and tables were products of Alfonso's focused effort to consolidate the world's astronomical knowledge in Spain.

This far-flung cultural agenda may seem a scattershot product of undisciplined genius, all the more so considering that Alfonso's interests also encompassed literature, poetry, arts, history, comparative religion, and even chess and backgammon. But such varied interests were bound together by a far-sighted vision of a better-unified, more learned, and fairer Iberia.

King Alfonso had inherited Babel. His chroniclers chronicled and commoners chattered in an unwieldy hodgepodge of languages: Latin, classic and colloquial Arabic, Berber dialects, Hebrew, Arabic written in Hebrew script, Castilian, Galician, and Basque (to name but a few). Portuguese, Catalonian, French (to name a few others) predominated along Castile's borders. Who knows what dialect amalgams of these still-evolving languages were spoken in myriad isolated towns and villages. Spain's kings and chroniclers proudly crowed about the Reconquest that was inexorably unifying Christian Spain, ignoring the uncomfortable reality that their Latin pronouncements were intelligible only to the smallest handful of Spaniards.

Alfonso's adoption of Castilian for his law codes, histories, and government records helped establish a common tongue for a kingdom coping with more working languages than any other land in Europe. He was one of the very first European monarchs to substitute a vernacular language for Latin, thereby heading a trend that, to say the least, caught on well. By doing so, Alfonso dignified not only Spanish itself but also the commoners who spoke it. An ever-dwindling Latin-fluent elite of clerics and bureaucrats dominated not only the affairs of state but even the ability to read about them. All others prattled on in vulgar tongues, neither they nor their language worthy of participation in Spain's governmental discourse.

To be sure, Alfonso would never have described himself as striking a blow for Castile's common man. Spain, and Europe, remained rigidly stratified, from hereditarily privileged royals on top to chattel slaves at the bottom. Alfonso's embrace of Castilian did not suddenly empower commoners to claim a voice in Castile's affairs. They still had no say in choosing their leaders, nor even, to a large extent, in choosing their own futures in a feudal society where peasants rarely rose above their birth status.

And there remained the minor consideration that the overwhelming majority of Alfonso's subjects were illiterate in *any* language. Centuries more would slip away before European rulers would even consider public education a worthy goal, much less grapple with making it a reality. Still, Alfonso had sounded a democratizing note that signaled a more open if still distant future. He laid the groundwork for a society where citizens could understand and speak the language by which they were governed, a human right now taken so much for granted that no rights charter need even mention it.

Another momentous Alfonsine initiative fostered a human right that unfortunately still can't be taken for granted in much of the world today: the right to be governed by a transparent, consistent law code. Such was the goal of Alfonso's effort to prune León-Castile's overgrown thicket of royal, municipal, and religious laws and replace it with one definitive code. Alfonso inherited a kingdom cobbled together over centuries, gradually engulfing once independent kingdoms that stubbornly clung to their old law codes and towns that guarded local rights granted by municipal *fueros* (codes of laws and privileges). León-Castile was a mangled jumble of overlapping, confusing, and sometimes contradictory laws, where behavior could be criminal in one village and legal in the next. Most towns, for example, had neither the imagination nor the need to outlaw one unusual crime that vexed Cuenca's civic leaders: "Whoever puts his backside in the face of another or farts in his face should pay three hundred *solidi*."

Alfonso's scholars not only pruned Castile's unwieldy legal thicket but erected a framework to support it. They drew on Roman and Church canon law to weave through Alfonso's code the principles of consistency, due process, and individual rights that are cornerstones of every advanced legal system. After his death, Alfonso's vision of one uniform code for Spain became reality when his *Siete Partidas* (named for the "seven parts" into which it was divided) were promulgated as Spain's law code in the 1340s.

Though Alfonso's most valuable legal contribution was the big picture of a master code underpinned by a clear philosophy, his *Partidas* didn't neglect nitty-gritty details. Its laws comprehensively ranged across contracts, partnerships, relations between lords and vassals, marriage laws, rules of evidence, plaintiff's rights, and more. The *Partidas* revel in minutiae, and in so doing illuminate the oddities, foibles, and perils of medieval life. One learns when a man can take ownership of a swarm of bees on his property (when he builds a hive around it). The laws pronounce the penalty for abducting a nun (excommunication) and killing a priest (six hundred sueldos, but nine hundred for a bishop). A slave may marry a free woman so long as she understands her intended's status.

The political philosopher Thomas Hobbes famously proclaimed seventeenth-century life "nasty, brutish, and short." Alfonso's code reveals an era yet nastier, shorter, and more brutish. A man who catches his married daughter in an adulterous act should "kill both parties or neither of them." Anyone who "complains of great hunger and is so poor that he cannot have recourse to anything else he can sell" may sell his own child. This shocking law draws on a precedent that entitled a famished defender of a besieged castle to "eat his son without incurring reproach, rather than surrender the castle without the order of his lord."

If the harshness of medieval life is apparent throughout the code, so is the thorough entanglement of religious and secular concerns in a society predating the separation of church from state in many modern nations. Anything else would have startled medieval Europeans, just as secular moderns may bridle at finding in Alfonso's legal code a digest of the prayers that every Christian ought to learn.

Indeed, though Alfonso's Muslim and Jewish subjects may have thought his Christian faith utterly wrongheaded, they would have shared his understanding of law. When God enlightened Moses atop Mt. Sinai or Muhammad on Mt. Hira, the Almighty hadn't made arbitrary distinctions between the affairs of state and those of religion. Both Judaism and Islam were total ways of living, and their prescriptions accordingly regulated the marketplace, kitchen, and bedroom, not merely what transpired in synagogue or mosque. Alfonso and his contemporaries referred to each of the three respective faiths as a "law," and Jewish, Muslim, or Christian culture and identity were inextricably linked to observance of one's religious law. Outside one's law lay not the secular mainstream familiar to modern societies but the uncomfortable status of the outcast.

Even though Jesus had famously instructed disciples to render to Caesar what is Caesar's and to God what is God's, neither medieval churchmen nor lawgivers understood Jesus as intending any precise cleavage between church and state. And so Alfonso the lawgiver was saddled with a far greater challenge than either his contemporaries or modern lawmakers. Unlike medieval European monarchs ruling more homogeneous populations, he alone legislated both for Christian subjects and for large populations of Jews and Muslims. While Alfonso's modern counterparts may govern populations as diverse as medieval Spain, they believe themselves ordained to govern not by God but by constituents, and mandated to enact and protect not God's law but human laws.

Even so routine a practice as swearing in witnesses presented challenges in a medieval multireligious society. Witnesses in U.S. courtrooms pledge to tell nothing but the truth, "so help me God," allowing each to construe God as he or she chooses. Alfonso instead plunged into the complexity of multireligious Spain, drafting distinct oaths for Muslim, Christian, and Jewish witnesses. Each was obliged—privileged—to acknowledge his or her own faith. The *Partidas* instruct a presiding judge and Muslim witness to "go to the door of the mosque," where the Muslim would swear "by that God than whom there is no other, he who possesses, knows, and destroys . . . and by the Truth . . . which God placed in the mouth of Mohammed, the son of Abdallah, when he appointed him his prophet and messenger, according to thy belief." The oath not only reinforced the obligation to testify truthfully but provided any Christian bystanders a small window into the beliefs of their Muslim neighbors.

Alfonso's seventh *Partida* navigates the dilemma of delineating the rights of Jewish and Muslim subjects in a Christian state. It begins ominously, introducing its topic as "all the accusations and offenses which men commit and what punishment they deserve therefore." Thirty-four subsections examine incest, necromancy, fraud, adultery, larceny, homicide, and all manner of baleful misdeeds. Jews and Moors are lumped in among thieves, murderers, adulterers, and other miscreants. Their crime? Jews insult God's name by denying "the marvelous and holy acts which He performed when he sent His Son" into the world. Even though this is a law code, it parrots some pretty ghastly hearsay: "We have heard" that the Jews celebrate Good Friday by "stealing children and fastening them to crosses."

Yet, the laws themselves don't reflect this frightfully prejudicial introduction. Instead, Alfonso's subjects are admonished not to cause Jews any "annoyance" on their Sabbath, nor to deface or loiter around Jewish synagogues. Alfonso goes beyond the grudging tolerance of the Church law he inherited by emphasizing that synagogues are sacred places, "where the name of God is praised." Jews should live peaceably in Christian society "by observing their own law and not insulting ours," a maxim that sums up Alfonso's formula for securing coexistence among the three faiths. Jews and Muslims are entitled to live by their own laws arbitrated by their own judges, provided they don't contravene state laws. Civil disputes between Jews would be settled in the

Jewish community, though disputes between Christians and Jews would be brought before Christian magistrates.

Conversions to Christianity are encouraged, but forcible conversion is unacceptable, "for no one can love or appreciate a service which is done him by compulsion," plain wisdom that later Spanish monarchs would choose to ignore. Still, while Jews were encouraged to embrace Christianity, religious freedom was not a two-way street: "Where a Christian is so unfortunate as to become a Jew, we order that he shall be put to death." Conversion to Islam is likewise a capital offense, the only difference being that Christians choosing Judaism are deemed "unfortunate," while those converting to Islam are regarded as "insane."

If the picture seems confused, it is. Condemnation vies with tolerance. The same mixed message leaps from Alfonso's poetry, most strikingly in his groundbreaking *Cantigas de Santa Maria* (*Songs of Holy Mary*). The *Cantigas* melded poetry, music, and stylized dance into a wholly unique art form that seems a distant precursor of opera. Most of the four-hundred-odd poems recount miracles attributed to the Virgin. Mary revives the dead, saves the drowning, restores sight, cures rabies, and heals battle wounds. She undertakes offbeat interventions as well, helping a man who swallows a spider, restoring a young boy's mule to life, and enabling a poet to conjure up the missing rhyme to complete a verse.

She exerts considerable miraculous energy to reining in wayward priests and nuns. She deters one nun from eloping with a knight; after another successfully elopes, she induces both the nun and her paramour to renounce married bliss and enter monasteries. Mary deals with another cleric who seems more fetishist than sexual adventurer; he steals a beautiful fabric donated to his church in order to have "undergarments made from it with which to cover his sinful parts." Who wouldn't applaud Mary's creative vengeance on this rascal: he is jolted from sleep in dreadful pain to find his legs turned completely upside down, "both his heels pressing into his loins so tightly that he could not pull them out."

Some of the poems depict Spanish Muslims, and they are frequently more pious and honorable than this scurrilous cast of straying clerics. Alfonso's court poets knew how deeply Mary is revered in Islam, cited more frequently in the Quran, in fact, than throughout the entire New Testament. The Mary of the *Cantigas* accordingly works wonders on behalf of reverent Muslims. One Muslim general treasures a statue of the Virgin seized from a defeated Christian army. Holy Mary of Salas revives the dead son of a Moorish woman who has maintained an overnight vigil at her shrine. In another poem, Mary rescues a Muslim mother and child from a burning tower.

There is an agenda to these poems: the protagonists all convert to Christianity. Still, the very assertion that there are good, honorable Muslims recalls the heroic Cid and distinguishes the *Cantigas* from the harsher Crusading rhetoric more common elsewhere in Christian Europe. Indeed, one striking *Cantiga* is distinctly out of step with the Crusader mentality. A Muslim platoon camps for the night beside a church dedicated to Mary. By extraordinary coincidence, an armed Christian contingent bivouacs at the opposite side of the same church. "Both companies . . . led their horses to water at the fountain, but the horses did not whinny at all so that they neither heard nor saw nor took notice of each other."

With dawn's first light, the startled soldiers confronted each other and "were greatly amazed. At once they asked truce of each other when they realized what had happened." Here Mary inspires neither a Christian onslaught nor mass conversion. Instead, the combatants retire in peace, for "Holy Mary brings about harmony among those who honor Her, even though they have no love for each other, for She who is full of goodness and holiness loves peace and harmony and love and loyalty."

Unfortunately, that extraordinary sentiment predominated neither in Spain nor elsewhere in the *Cantigas,* and most especially not regarding Spain's Jews, branded in one poem as "[Mary's] enemies, whom She hates worse than the Moors." The Jews of the *Cantigas* are ghoulish, even monstrous figures. One Jew kidnaps a young boy who sang beautiful hymns to the Virgin, and "struck him such a blow with an ax that he split open his head down to his teeth," then buried him in his wine cellar. Another Jew casts his own son into a furnace after learning that the boy has taken communion at mass in innocent imitation of his Christian classmates. In an especially provocative *cantiga,* a Jew steals a painted image of the Virgin, and after throwing it into a latrine, "[he] sat down there and desecrated it shamefully."

Still, what Alfonso's laws and poetry said was one thing; what Alfonso did was another. Though the *Partidas* mandated that no Christian "shall take any medicine or cathartic made by a Jew," a sickly Alfonso most certainly heeded the advice of his own Jewish physician. Jews were integral to his court, serving as ambassadors, physicians, tax collectors, translators, scribes, and advisors. While parceling spoils of the Muslim Seville his father had won for Christendom, Alfonso allocated Jewish subjects three mosques to be reappointed as synagogues. Indeed, one scholar asserts, "Jews enjoyed their greatest freedom and well being under Alfonso X. Every historian, chronicler, and scholar . . . who has treated this subject, has testified that Alfonso's reign was ideal for the Jews."

An uncompromisingly hostile attitude often permeates Alfonso the king's laws and poetry, but Alfonso the Learned was torn by conflicting impulses that focused less on how Spaniards worshipped than whether they could help transform Castile into a better, more learned kingdom. Nowhere was this spirit more apparent than the project that won Alfonso the sobriquet "founder of Spanish science." In the early 1260s, Alfonso assembled a multicultural team to translate and update the research of the eleventh-century Córdoban astronomer al-Zarkali (Arzachel). Jewish scholars Isaac ben Sid and Jehuda ben Moses Cohen labored alongside Italians like John of Cremona and Spanish Christians like Juan Daspa and Garci Pérez. After replicating al-Zarkali's comprehensive celestial readings over years of painstakingly precise observations, the scholars produced a celestial map that was reproduced in edition after edition for centuries. These "Alfonsine tables" were definitively supplanted only in the 1600s; Johannes Kepler trumped Alfonso's thirteenth-century team only by using a relatively new, vastly more sophisticated observational tool: the telescope.

The Alfonsine Tables were but one showpiece of Alfonso's inspired effort to bring the world's knowledge and wisdom to Spain. Jewish, Muslim, and Christian translators buzzed away rendering excerpts from the Quran and the Talmud, philosophical works, mathematical treatises, and even manuals for chess and backgammon. Many of the source works were in Arabic and intended for translation to Spanish, making multicultural teamwork essential. Few Christian scholars read Arabic; Muslims and many Jewish scholars did; the Italians understood Latin but not necessarily Spanish. Thus, Arabic works were often translated first to Latin and then to Spanish by multilingual, multicultural collaborators.

In a society harshly divided by religiously motivated Reconquest, with interfaith dialogue nonexistent and interfaith relations uneasy, the very process of interfaith scholarly collaboration was almost as impressive an achievement as the output these collaborations produced. Even more impressive, however, were many acts of interfaith collaboration that were freely chosen and not spurred by royal patronage. Indeed, such collaboration touched the very touchiest of arenas: the religious belief and worship that defined the fundamental differences separating Christians, Muslims, and Jews.

Still, religious celebration sometimes *united* Christians and Muslims rather than divided them. Murcia's Christians enlivened religious festivals by inviting Muslim jugglers and musicians. Such interfaith merrymaking occurred elsewhere, and apparently thrilled the revelers more than their pastors: a church council in Valladolid eventually enacted a statute prohibiting Muslim singers from performing in Christian churches; similarly, a rabbinical ruling admonished a cantor for chanting Jewish prayers to the tune of popular Muslim melodies. Muslim clerics were likewise vexed to find their faithful celebrating alongside Christian neighbors; one Córdoba jurist reminded Muslims, "[Receiving] presents at Christmas from a Christian or from a Muslim is not allowed, neither is accepting invitations on that day."

Not that such admonitions seemed to do much good. Three full centuries later, an Almoravid jurist condemned similar practices, complaining that Muslims were incorporating Christian customs into religious festivals: "At the celebration of *al-Andara* (24 June) . . . [purchasing] fried doughnuts (*isfanj:* churros) and cheese fritters (*muabbana*), both of which are innovative foods . . . men go out mingling with the women, separately or in groups, to enjoy spectacles, and they do the same on the days of the Muslim festivals."

When a drought racked Uclés in 1470, inhabitants beseeched God's help in church, mosque, or synagogue, but some did more. Hernán Sánchez Castro "set out from the church together with other Christians in the procession, and when they reached the square where the Jews were with the Torah he joined the procession of the Jews with their Torah and left the processions of the Christians." Joyful events occasioned more formally organized interfaith processions. Princess Doña Blanca of Navarre, crossing northern Castile in the mid-fifteenth century en route to her wedding, was greeted in towns like Briviesca: "Following [the artisans] came the Jews with the Torah and the Moors with the Quran [dancing] in the manner usually reserved for [the entry of] kings who come to rule a foreign country. There were also many trumpets, tambourines, drums, and flute players."

While Christian, Muslim, and Jewish religious leaders each zealously defended their respective faiths as uniquely favored through Divine Revelation, those on the ground sometimes saw things differently. The personal beliefs of ordinary Spaniards were rarely recorded during the medieval era, but the elaborate dossiers of "evidence" compiled by Spain's inquisitors offer a precious—if sadly ironic—glimpse into the minds of fifteenth- and sixteenth-century Spaniards from all walks of life. Diego González, a priest, believed that "the Jew can find salvation in his own faith just as the Christian can in his." He was burned at the stake for such heretical leanings. Another Castilian Christian must have left inquisitors slack-jawed when he mused, "Who knows which is the better religion, ours or those of the Muslims and the Jews?"

Another Christian was convinced that "the good Jew and the good Muslim can, if they act correctly, go to heaven just like the good Christian." One peasant woman, described by a university graduate who knew her as "simple" and "ignorant," nonetheless spoke with uncommon wisdom: "The good Jew would be saved, and the good Moor, in his law, and why else had God made them?"

Some well-educated clerics agreed. The Franciscan friar Alonso de Mella was moved to write Castile's King Juan II after living amid Granada's Muslims, opining that Muslims were not only "sincere believers in the one true God," but worshipped with "faith, fear, humility, reverence, devotion" greater than sometimes found among Christians. The Franciscan's eloquently worded conclusion surely shocked Castile's monarch and de Mella's religious superiors: "We truly recognized that God is not merely the God of the Christians, but the God of all those who properly believe in Him . . . and is concerned with everybody who turns his eyes toward Him . . . nor does He take any pleasure in the damnation of the dying."

Miguel Semeno seems to have endorsed that theory; either that or his family were hedging bets on the afterlife when they erected his tombstone. "In the name of Our Lord Jesus Christ," it reads, "he died on Sunday 4 November in the Era 1194." Yet bordering the edge of the same gravestone is an Arabic inscription: "In the name of Allah, the Compassionate, the Merciful. Mikayil ibn Semeno was he who went forth to Allah, with His mercy, from the abode of this life." Similarly, the will of fifteenth-century Alfonso Fernández Samuel requested burial with a Christian cross at his feet, the Quran at his breast, and "his life and light," the Torah, beside his head.

If such free thinking seems shocking amid the religious wars ravaging Spain, consider the multicultural blood coursing through the veins of these Spanish Muslims, Christians, and Jews. Isidore of Seville had penned his *Etymologies* for a Spain that was overwhelmingly Christian. After three centuries of Muslim rule, Isidore's Seville and Visigoth Toledo and the rest of al-Andalus had become by some estimates at least three-quarters Muslim. A few centuries later, Spain was once again an overwhelmingly Christian nation, courtesy of Ferdinand and Isabella's 1492 victory over Muslim Granada and expulsion of Spain's Jews. Migration accounted for some of each successive transformation, but conversion, pressured or freely chosen, accounted for the greater part. Sixteenth-century Spain was a country of Christians who traced jagged religious lineages that often included Muslim or Jewish ancestors, or Muslim *and* Jewish ancestors.

Even those who retained one faith across tumultuous centuries participated in Spain's cross-cultural fertilization. Christians and Jews under Muslim rule learned Arabic and adopted Arabic names, dress, and customs. Periodic outbreaks of religious persecution further roiled Spain's cross-cultural ferment by unleashing tidal flows of religious exiles. No century, virtually no generation passed without Muslims, Christians, or Jews either fleeing a region turned inhospitable or resettling territory newly conquered by coreligionists. Migrants inevitably brought their architectural style, customs, dialect, cuisine, and other cultural beliefs with them. French and German pilgrims to Santiago de Compostela must have been pleasantly startled by the churches of San Lorenzo and San Tirso in Sahagún, their Moorish-style bell towers reminiscent of the minarets gracing many an Andalusian mosque, erected by masons who presumably learned their trade in the Muslim south before religious persecution or economic opportunity drove them north.

King Alfonso the Learned epitomized the best and the worst of this mixed culture, embodying in one person the contradiction-wracked reality of Reconquest Spain. Medieval Spain is the nation of Santiago the Pilgrim, embodying a vision of history that journeys forward toward a more hopeful future, "whose king is truth, whose law is love, whose measure is eternity," as St. Augustine wrote. Yet that hopeful vision competes with Santiago the Moor Killer's endless cycle of violence. The medieval era's two great epic poems embody the same contradictory impulses that afflict the schizophrenic Santiago: grim Charlemagne's insistence that "the pagans are wrong and the Christians are right" sits uncomfortably alongside El Cid's embrace of his Muslim friend Abengalbón.

These contradictory impulses are married in the one Alfonso. Though his *Cantigas* proclaim the Jews "[Mary's] enemies, whom She hates worse than the Moors," he eagerly enlisted Jewish subjects in the vast project of reverently translating excerpts from both the Quran and the Talmud. Alfonso the law giver condemns the Jews for insulting God's name, yet his same laws stipulate respect for Jewish worship.

Alfonso and his subjects had in fact discovered remedies for their schizophrenia, which could have blessed Spain with a peaceful common life. The monarch legislated respect for all houses of worship, "where the name of God is praised." His commoner subjects often shopped and worked alongside Muslim, Christian, or Jewish neighbors, engaging in the dialogue and accommodation that proceed from shared daily life. His court scholars set aside theological differences long enough to transform Spain into a more learned land, enriching their respective religious communities. The *Cantigas'* poets depicted

Muslim and Christian armies turning their backs on battle, showing that peace is possible even among those "who have no love for each other," for the one "who is full of goodness and holiness loves peace and harmony and love and loyalty." Tragically, Alfonso's kingdom never fully heeded its own wisdom. Today's Muslims, Jews, and Christians still share Abraham's common patrimony and still are divided by irreconcilable doctrinal differences. Our era, suffering the same schizophrenia that afflicted our ancestors, might heal it by embracing the wisdom that Alfonso and his medieval contemporaries uncovered yet never fully grasped.

Some historians speculate that Alfonso sank into insanity late in life. They find themselves otherwise unable to explain how a king who came to such grief at the hands of Morocco's Muslim dynasty could make common cause with them against his own son. Whatever Alfonso's mental state, he mirrored the kingdom he ruled, a land torn by contradictory beliefs and passions during the uneasy struggle to transform many Spains into one nation.

As Alfonso reigned, that one Spain had almost taken shape, and (not coincidentally) the era of coexistence among her three religious faiths was nearing its twilight. For tolerance may be regarded a value in its own right, a means of securing peace in a mixed society, or a useful expedient to trade. Medieval Spain's particular recipe for tolerance relied on the latter two ingredients rather than the first. And as an ascendant, ever more dominant Christian Spain turned into the fourteenth and fifteenth centuries, tolerance seemed less necessary and less useful. Spain no longer needed to balance the needs and interests of its religious minorities to secure its peace, prosperity, or borders. Still, though the long-deferred dream of a unified and purely Christian Spain drew closer to hand, Alfonso's X's thirteenth- and fourteenth-century heirs did little to make that dream reality.

In the late fifteenth century, Ferdinand and Isabella did.

19. The End of Spanish Judaism

"The Razor That Rips the Membrane of My Aching Heart"

Late one night in March 1369, Count Enrique of Trastámara entered the tent of his estranged half-brother, King Pedro IV of León-Castile. So much time had passed since their last meeting that Enrique first verified with a retainer that the man standing before him was indeed his brother Pedro, the king. Then Enrique stabbed Pedro in the face, wounding him "again and again" as the monarch crumpled to the ground. Enrique immediately assumed Castile's throne as King Enrique II. His brother's bloated, stinking corpse lay unburied and untended for three days before Enrique permitted a burial. Such are the bloody roots of the Trastámara dynasty founded by Enrique, great-great-grandson of King Alfonso the Wise and great-great-grandfather of Queen Isabella the Catholic.

Though Enrique had seized power through butchery, Pedro is known to history as "the Cruel." The epithet was well earned. Pedro left Castile strewn with the corpses of enemies real and imagined, his own extended family included. He had a cousin clubbed to death while he watched, then dumped the mangled corpse from a palace window onto a crowded public plaza. He had two other half-brothers slain before Enrique finally turned the tables on him.

Yet Enrique's coup was motivated by more than disgust with his brother's brutality; revenge also figured in. Enrique was one of ten bastards fathered by King Alfonso XI; Pedro was Alfonso's only legitimate son. Though marital infidelity was hardly rare among medieval monarchs, Alfonso's illegitimate bumper crop was too great an indignity for Queen María to suffer silently. She had the bastard Enrique's mother jailed and executed. Enrique's pent-up rage over his mother's unjust death undoubtedly energized the knife thrusts that felled his brother.

But the assassination was no spontaneous act of crazed vengeance. Enrique had rebelled openly for years, challenging Pedro militarily while cultivating political support. Enrique also manipulated popular prejudice and a dreadful tragedy to sow discontent among Castile's nobles. The Black Death of bubonic plague had burst upon Europe in 1348 and in less than three years decimated a third of its population in history's most horrific sustained health catastrophe. Spain suffered disastrously. Of all Europe's monarchs, only Pedro's father, King Alfonso XI, succumbed to the dread virus. As the plague ground through Spain, terrified villagers fled homes, livelihoods, and dying neighbors, transforming vibrant settlements into ghost towns. Half of the Cerrato region's 112 villages, for example, were completely abandoned.

That the mysterious plague subsided as abruptly as it had exploded left terrified Europeans not only bereft of loved ones but anxious for explanations. The Jews became a handy scapegoat, blamed by some for spreading a disease Europeans couldn't understand by means Europeans couldn't identify. A wily Enrique pounded out an anti-Semitic drumbeat to serve his rebel cause. Hadn't King Pedro bestowed unseemly benevolence on the Jews? After all, his royal treasurer, Samuel Halevi, was a Jew. And with Pedro's blessing Halevi had constructed an ornate synagogue in central Toledo and dedicated its chapel to the king.

No one could accuse Enrique's Trastámara dynasty of untoward sympathy to Jews. Two decades into the Trastámara era, Enrique's thirteen-year-old grandson, Enrique III, presided over the worst pogroms ever suffered by Spain's Jews. Spain's monarchs were traditionally the Jews' defenders of last resort in times of religious tension. As Queen Isabella succinctly put it generations later, "All the Jews in my realms are mine, and they are my Jews, and they are under my help and protection, and mine is the obligation to defend, help, and maintain them in justice."

The special status was not simply a magnanimous gesture. Spain's monarchs counted on the Jews for generous tax receipts and as talented administrators and financiers. The benefits of this symbiotic relationship were lost on the powerless teenage king who stood aside while mobs stormed Seville's Jewish ghetto and murdered thousands in 1391. Anti-Jewish riots soon after convulsed Madrid, Córdoba, Burgos, and elsewhere, motivated, as one Christian chronicler confessed, "out of a thirst for plunder rather than piety."

The violent spasm was no tragic aberration. Instead, this seminal event set in motion a slow unraveling of Spanish Jewry, culminating a century later in the Spanish Inquisition and the expulsion of Jews from Spain. Thousands were murdered during the 1391 riots; others fled Spain; still others committed suicide. In the two following decades as many as half of Spain's Jews presented themselves for baptism, bowing to intense proselytization or hoping to ward off future violence. As Spain's Jewish population plummeted, so did the morale of the faithful remnant.

Many of the *conversos* (converts), so-called New Christians, mimicked Christianity's outward ritual while living among Jewish neighbors and steeping their families in cherished religious and cultural traditions as crypto-Jews. At the same time, ambitious New Christians found long-closed doors suddenly open. Discriminatory laws promulgated throughout Castile in 1412 had barred Jews from holding many public offices and prohibited their employment as tax farmers or moneylenders. Many New Christians now assumed civil posts once denied them. Some married into well-established Christian families.

On the one hand, the merchants, churchmen, and peasants who abetted the 1391 pogroms had achieved exactly what they wished: thousands had renounced Judaism and acceded to tormentors' violent demands that they convert. But many who had clamored for conversions were appalled to see New Christians successfully integrating into civil society and even attaining better social and economic status than "pure-blooded" Christians. A new cycle of resentment began to percolate.

Queen Isabella occupied Castile's throne as such resentments lurched toward a cataclysmic resolution. Probably the most accomplished and certainly the most storied of the Trastámaras, she was an "accidental monarch" who had not been intended to rule. Her older half-brother, Enrique IV, succeeded to Spain's throne in 1454, fully intending to bequeath the crown to some child of his own after a long, fruitful reign. His younger sister Isabella was destined for the traditional role that fell to gender-challenged Spanish royals, to be served up as fodder for some diplomatically opportune marriage.

Events didn't unfold as King Enrique hoped. A complicated dynastic feud erupted. Political maneuvering among rival factions was punctuated by outbreaks of civil war. Enrique was pressured into repudiating his daughter Juana as his heir on grounds of her suspected illegitimacy; he instead named his younger brother, Alfonso of Ávila. Then Enrique flip-flopped, restoring daughter Juana's claim and rejecting brother Alfonso's. Alfonso's supporters rebelled, and an embattled Enrique shored up support from one key faction by agreeing to marry off his fifteen-year-old sister Isabella to an ally. That scheme collapsed when Isabella's intended died (not, one hastens to add, at the prospect of marrying Isabella). Alfonso of Ávila succumbed to the plague soon after, leaving the rebels not exactly without a cause, but without a candidate for Castile's throne.

Isabella had been discounted and overlooked during the dizzying rounds of politicking, rebellion, and premature deaths. Now she was courted by all sides, if for no other reason than that she was still alive. The rebels' sudden enchantment with Isabella piqued Enrique's appreciation for his sister's credentials. Don't imagine the teenage Isabella a mere pawn in this unfolding dynastic farce. She drove a hard bargain with her new-found leverage, promising to marry any husband of Enrique's choosing, but only if Enrique publicly proclaimed her heir to his throne. Enrique's own daughter Juana, once before pushed aside as heir in earlier rounds of horse-trading, was callously cast aside a second time to make way for Isabella.

Fate had served Isabella well, but the savvy teenager didn't entrust her future to destiny alone, certainly not where love was concerned. When Enrique nominated King Afonso V of Portugal as her intended spouse to cement an alliance with Portugal through marriage, an eighteen-year-old Isabella in full womanly bloom was repulsed by the prospect of marrying a widower already closing in on the advanced (medieval) age of thirty-seven. Isabella's own choice was Ferdinand of Aragon. One year her junior, the dashing Ferdinand was more appealing than the decrepit Afonso. He was heir to the Aragonese throne and still childless, so Aragon could be yoked to León-Castile through their children, creating a "superpower state" that would dominate the Iberian Peninsula. There was only one stumbling block: Ferdinand and Isabella were second cousins, related, as the Church lawyers would say, within a "prohibited degree of consanguinity."

But love and dynastic ambition found a way. Isabella and Ferdinand supplied a forged papal dispensation to enable their marriage in the fall of 1469 at a secret ceremony attended by their closest supporters. Like so many medieval betrothals, theirs skimped on courtship: Isabella and Ferdinand were married just four days after their first meeting. By defying her brother King Enrique to marry Ferdinand, Isabella once again plunged Spain into civil war. The two young royals parried military and political threats for nearly a decade until timely deaths once again served Isabella's interests. She became queen of Castile upon her brother Enrique's death in 1474; Ferdinand became king of Aragon with his father's death five years later.

The last serious challenge to their reign evaporated that same year. King Afonso V of Portugal, the suitor earlier spurned by Isabella, had since found a more willing partner in Princess Juana, she who had already been twice spurned as Enrique's heir. As Juana proved she had lost neither her ambition nor her capacity to endure humiliation, her fiancé Afonso invaded Castile to press Juana's claim for the crown. The invasion quickly sputtered, and Afonso formally surrendered all claims to Castile in a 1479 treaty. Now closing in on the hoary old age of fifty, the doleful king of Portugal announced his intention to abdicate and journey to Rome as a pilgrim before retiring to a monastery. He never consummated his engagement to Juana, who passed her own remaining days in a Lisbon convent and insisted on calling herself Queen Juana of Castile.

Even before Afonso of Portugal had relinquished his dynastic dream, Isabella was consolidating and flexing her hard-won authority. The devout queen convened Castile's clergy in the summer of 1478, deter-

mined to reform Church practices. She pushed through fines and public penalties to humiliate clerics who flouted their vow of celibacy
(things hadn't much improved since Alfonso the Wise's thirteenth-
century cantigas bemoaned Spain's wayward clergy). Castile's faithful
deserved well-educated, zealous clergy who kept their hands off the collection plate. Credit Isabella with foresight: the very abuses that scandalized her impelled an outraged German monk named Martin Luther
to break with the Catholic Church some four decades later.

Some churchmen, seconded by a cross-section of merchants and
court advisors, countered by protesting that the Church faced a more
dire threat than clerical laxity. They alleged that legions of New Christians were outwardly professing Christianity while secretly observing
Jewish practices. The so-called judaizers kept the Jewish Sabbath, circumcised male children, and gathered with Jews for clandestine prayer
services. Ferdinand and Isabella's counselors fretted that this fifth column was rotting the Church from within and mocking Christianity.
Though neither Ferdinand nor Isabella had any particular record of
anti-Semitism, the alarmed monarchs petitioned Pope Sixtus IV in late
1478 to endorse an inquisition for Castile.

Contrary to common assumption, the inquisition process itself was
not invented in Spain, nor were early inquisitions targeted at Jews or
even at ferreting out false converts from Judaism. Pope Gregory IX dispatched Dominican friars as inquisitors to France in the 1230s, anxious
to stamp out heresies promoted by Christian Albigenses (i.e., the "people of Albi"). As the Albigenses saw it, humanity was blighted by the
imprisonment of our "good" (spiritual) souls within our "bad" (material) bodies. Christian orthodoxy instead taught that the spiritual soul
complemented the material body to form the uniquely dignified, fully
integrated marvel that is the human person. The Albigenses were
hardly the first Christians to be leery of the flesh. The perils of concu-
piscence had been preached by countless Christian shepherds. But
some Albigenses pressed their revulsion of the worldly body to distressing extremes, horrifying orthodox churchmen by slowly starving
themselves to death and thereby hastening the liberation of their body-
entrapped souls to enjoy the spiritual afterlife.

The inquisitors dispatched by Pope Gregory pioneered their own methods of hastening the Albigenses' journey to the afterlife, concocting many protocols later famously associated with the Spanish Inquisition. Suspected heretics had no right to know the identities of accusers; the accused were not represented by counsel; under certain circumstances, torture could be used to extract confessions; those found guilty of heresy were liable to be burned at the stake if they refused to recant. But few Albigenses were executed. The inquisitors preferred to return repentant heretics to Christian society after seizing their wealth and possessions in punishment for espousing vile beliefs.

The two inquisitors who set to work in Seville in January of 1481 engineered few process innovations. There were, however, critical differences in Spain's particular brand of inquisition. For the first time, an inquisition operated under royal rather than papal control, relatively free of the checks and balances that papal authorities could bring to bear. Whereas previous inquisitions generally strived to extirpate all kinds of heresy, Castile's inquisitors focused almost exclusively on uncovering false converts from Judaism. Finally, and most tragically for its victims, the Spanish Inquisition was more efficiently organized than previous inquisitorial investigations. The Inquisition received virtually no papal or crown funding, but sustained itself through fines and penalties levied on those found guilty, an inherent conflict of interest that apparently never troubled those overseeing it.

But such practices did trouble the pope. Not long after inaugurating the Spanish Inquisition, Pope Sixtus IV regretted bringing the monster to life: "[It] has for some time been moved not by zeal for the faith and the salvation of souls, but by lust for wealth, and that many true and faithful Christians . . . have without any legitimate proof been thrust into secular prisons, tortured and condemned as relapsed heretics, deprived of their goods and property and handed over the secular arm to be executed, to the peril of souls, setting a pernicious example, and causing disgust to many." Sixtus's condemnation could not have been more direct (or more accurate). He demanded reforms, asserting the right of the accused to know their accusers' names and the charges levied. He attempted to wrest control of a process run amuck by demanding that anyone found guilty be granted an opportunity to appeal the judgment in Rome.

Alas, bowing to realpolitik, Sixtus was ultimately more worried about appeasing Spain's powerful monarchs than protecting its beleaguered conversos. He withdrew his critical bull after King Ferdinand's diplomatic prodding. A year later, he acceded to Ferdinand's wishes that the Dominican friar Tomás de Torquemada be named inquisitor general overseeing both Castile *and* the Kingdom of Aragon. Spain's monarchs further boosted the inquisitor general's status by inaugurating a Council of the Supreme and General Inquisition under Torquemada's leadership. What may seem an inconsequential bureaucratic maneuver was a breathtaking step: for the first time ever, an inquisitorial investigation was turned into a branch of government. The Inquisition was transformed from an *investigation* carried out by specifically delegated inquisitors to an ongoing *institution,* like, for example, the Department of Defense or any other government department.

The developments were equally breathtaking to Ferdinand's Aragonese subjects, though for different reasons. Marriage might have united Ferdinand of Aragon with Isabella of Castile, but that didn't make their two kingdoms one, certainly not in the minds of Aragonese town officials determined to defend their well-established local laws and prerogatives. Castile's population was roughly five times that of Aragon, and its landmass roughly three times as large. The prickly Aragonese resented any institution, Inquisition included, foisted on them from their larger, "foreign" neighbor Castile.

Resistance to encroaching royal power and, one hopes, sympathy for their New Christian neighbors inspired Aragonese to hunker down and resist the inquisitors' intrusion on their turf. The inquisitor dispatched to Teruel found the town gates barred against him. In an odd role reversal, the inquisitors now feared for *their* lives. The inquisitor Pedro Arbués de Epila knelt to pray in Saragossa's cathedral one night in 1485, wearing a soldier's helmet and a coat of mail beneath his religious robes. He should have brought along a small army: a posse of intruders stabbed the praying priest to death.

This was—apologies to Arbués de Epila and his loved ones—about the best thing that could have happened for the Inquisition: the cold-blooded murder of a priest perpetrated in the very town that treasured the icon of Our Lady of the Pillar so long ago entrusted to James the

Apostle by the Virgin. What Christian could still doubt the dire threat posed by the false converts? Vengeance was swift and certain. The alleged assailants were rounded up. One assassin's offending hands were hacked off and nailed to the doors of a prominent public building; as if the message wasn't clear enough, he was also beheaded and quartered, his body parts hung in the city streets.

Resistance to the Inquisition evaporated, and Torquemada's emboldened inquisitors fanned out across Spain. Their arrival in town was marked by a lengthy sermon denouncing various heresies and offering heretics a forty-day (or longer) window (the "edict of grace") to confess and be reconciled. Those able to identify others as heretics were obliged to come forward, a twist that stoked the Inquisition's perverse momentum. One never knew whether one might secretly be fingered by a friend, a neighbor, or even a family member.

Inquisitors also pressed Jews to incriminate false converts to Christianity. Many wrongly assume that *Jews* were the Inquisition's direct target, but as non-Christians they were in fact exempt from inquisitorial prosecution. Inquisitors could therefore encourage Jews to finger New Christians who were judaizing, assuring the Jews that no harm would come to them personally. For their part, many New Christians approached the inquisitors before the inquisitors came to them. Better to turn oneself in and be reconciled than risk far greater trouble if snared later by inquisitors brandishing secret testimony. Indeed, even a wholly fabricated self-incrimination sometimes seemed a better-calculated bet than taking the chance of losing one's life based on a false accusation levied by someone else. The Inquisition ground out fearful confessions; nearly 2,500 Toledans, for example, rushed forward to clear their names in one year alone. As the tally mounted, many Christians who once considered claims of a widespread judaizing conspiracy to be hysterically exaggerated began changing their minds.

Those who confessed didn't simply skip home to resume normal lives; they suffered stiff financial penalties. Reconciled heretics participated in an *auto da fe* ("act of faith"), a public procession of penitents transformed into an increasingly gaudy ritual as Inquisition choreographers fine-tuned the theatrics over the decades. The lengthy procession solemnly wound its way toward the town square as townspeople

gawked at neighbors swept up in the inquisitors' net. Inquisition officials made it easy to identify the heretics, robing each in a *sanbenito*
(*saco benedito* or "holy sack" or jacket).

The real stars of the ignominious show were those who refused to recant alleged heresies. These condemned wore sanbenitos decorated
with black crosses, flames, and images of Satan, previewing both their
hellish destiny in the afterlife and the means by which they would
shortly be delivered there. The unrepentant were handed over to civil
authorities after the auto da fe ceremony, then burned at the stake, a
practice its proponents justified by quoting no less an authority than
the Jesus of St. John's gospel: "If a man does not abide in me, he is cast
forth as a branch and withers; and the branches are gathered, thrown
into the fire, and burned."

Reconciled New Christians lived only to look forward to penury
and shame. Often impoverished by the Inquisition's monetary fines,
they suffered the further indignity of wearing their yellow sanbenitos
indefinitely as public badges of humiliation, like the scarlet letter
pinned on Hester Prynne by her self-righteous New England neighbors. One lifetime of shame didn't suffice. Aging, tattered sanbenitos
hung from the rafters of Spanish churches for generations, even in the
eighteenth and nineteenth centuries reminding townspeople which
neighbors had descended from fifteenth-century heretics.

It's impossible to judge the veracity of the scores of confessions
spilled out to inquisitors. Some were undoubtedly whole-cloth fabrica-
tions, calculated to preempt the worse fate of being accused by someone else. Other confessions were manipulated, wrenched, or tortured
from vulnerable witnesses succumbing to intense psychological pres-
sure.

But many confessions were sincere. Inquisition records depict a converso community rife with crypto-Jews struggling to keep alive some
flicker of their former faith through a stubborn devotion that often per-
dured across generations. Some New Christians lit Sabbath candles on
Friday evenings and changed linens the following morning; they ab-
stained from eating pork, honored the high holy days, and entombed
lost loved ones according to Jewish burial practices. The converso
María Díaz was accused of continuing to light Sabbath candles, prepar-

ing the Sabbath day's food in advance, and refraining from work on that holy day. Beatriz González of Toledo admitted to inquisitors in 1487 that she continued to recite Yom Kippur prayers learned from her mother, begged forgiveness from neighbors according to that day's solemn traditions, and accompanied them that night at synagogue. Constanza Núñez donated oil to help keep her local synagogue's perpetual light aflame. Blanca Rodríguez of Guadalajara fasted during the Jewish Day of Atonement, passing the whole day in reverent communion with Jewish neighbors.

These New Christian women and men likely interpreted practices carried over from Judaism in varying ways. Some were secretly Jews, desperately clinging to a cherished faith under near impossible circumstances. Others surely understood themselves as Christians, finding no contradiction in marrying Jewish practices to their new worship; both Judaism and Christianity, after all, were rooted in the same Abrahamic tradition and honored the same Hebrew Bible. Jesus himself was, of course, Jewish. The converso bishop of Burgos reportedly ended the Hail Mary prayer with a coda recalling the common heritage Jews alone shared with Jesus: "Holy Mary, Mother of God, and *my blood relative,* pray for us." Still other conversos may have attached no explicit religious significance to dietary or cultural rituals learned from parents and grandparents, but the inquisitors conducted no nuanced anthropological analyses of their victims' motivations and self-understanding. Practices traditionally associated with Judaism were prima facie and sufficient evidence of heresy.

Up to two thousand conversos may have been executed during the Inquisition's first few decades and another five hundred over the succeeding three centuries. Awful though this death toll was, however, Spain held no monopoly on religious terror during the early modern era. Just as the Inquisition's mortal toll was cresting, Europe was shredded by the Protestant Reformation. England, Scotland, France, Germany, and the Netherlands sent countless suspected heretics to the stake, garrote, gallows, guillotine, rack, and other torturous devices sadistically rigged up by authorities who perceived themselves as defenders of the true faith. Moreover, religious war claimed far more victims than retail execution of supposed heretics ever did. An estimated

8 million Europeans perished in the early seventeenth century as the Thirty Years War pitted Protestant against Catholic.

It misses the fundamental point, however, to try to calculate which of Europe's too many bouts of religious persecution and violence was most lethal: even one killing in the name of religion is one too many. The Inquisition's particularly bitter, lingering aftertaste has less to do with its death toll than with its perverse pageantry, broad reach, and insidious practices that foreshadowed techniques perfected by modern witch hunters like Stalin. Veiled by a secret process, fantastic accusations emerged and circulated unchecked. The unjustly accused stared at the specter of death while weighing the cruel calculus that false confessions might rob their dignity but at least restore them to children and loved ones. The ever mounting tally of confessions fueled further hysteria that judaizing conversos were everywhere and had penetrated all levels of Spanish society.

The ironic tragedy was that New Christian descendants of converts *had* penetrated all levels of Spanish society and become vital cogs driving Spain's economy, Church, and government. Spain's Inquisition purged some of its finest talent and paralyzed New Christian society with crippling fear, despite scant evidence that most conversos were duplicitous in their embrace of Christianity. Yet every New Christian seemed liable to suspicion no matter how devout or well connected (except, perhaps, the extended family of Grand Inquisitor Torquemada, which almost certainly included descendants of converts). Those who dared take a principled stand frequently enough suffered for it. Juan Arias Dávila, the New Christian bishop of Segovia, boldly barred inquisitors from his diocese to protest their methods. But the inquisitors eventually made their way into Segovia anyway, and as an old man of eighty Bishop Dávila found himself summoned to Rome for interrogation.

Oddly, Spain's fevered imagination was thoroughly gripped by its tiny, embattled, ultimately impotent Jewish minority, while the armed Muslim kingdom of Granada thrived to remind Christians of the still uncompleted Reconquest. But Muslim Spain was no longer strong enough militarily to command Christian Spain's unwavering, fearful attention. Granada, the rump remnant of al-Andalus, had lingered on in a prolonged twilight for over two centuries while Castile's monarchs remained engrossed with other priorities. Until political strife within Granada handed Ferdinand and Isabella the ideal opportunity to realize the reconquest dream of a united, Christian Spain. Granada's Prince Abu Abd Allah (Boabdil to the Christians) revolted against his father in 1482 and proclaimed himself king. Boabdil, his father, and an uncle wrestled for Granada's throne. Ferdinand took advantage of the turmoil to insert himself into the struggle, pursuing an on again–off again alliance with Boabdil while methodically dismantling the weakened Muslim state. His first thrust sliced Granada almost in half, lopping off its southwest territory. A year later, he hacked off the southeast, reducing the kingdom to the city of Granada and its outskirts.

Granadans hunkered down to suffer Ferdinand's siege. Though the conflict dragged on for months, its outcome was inevitable from the outset. The rest of Iberia was firmly under Christian control: Granada was an island in a Christian ocean. No relief came from overseas, as North African Muslims recognized the futility of Granada's cause, once and for all relinquishing all ambition of restoring Muslim dominance to Spain.

Ferdinand and Isabella took formal possession of Granada's Alhambra palace in early January 1492. Though flush with confidence after extinguishing Spain's last vestige of Muslim rule, they nonetheless must have been as awestruck by the Alhambra as the million or so tourists today who annually visit this most stunning landmark of Moorish Spain. The one-time administrative and residential palace showcased the artisanal, architectural, and engineering genius of al-Andalus. Sophisticated aqueducts channeled Duero River water to irrigate meticulously laid gardens enlivened by bubbling fountains. Palace interiors entranced visitors with stucco adornment worked into impossibly intricate geometric designs, offset elsewhere by color-filled bursts of polychromatic tile.

Many modern visitors wrongly assume the Alhambra was the pinnacle of Muslim craftsmanship in Spain; in fact, it was the sunset achievement of an embattled civilization. Even centuries earlier, Córdoba's Umayyads erected palaces every bit as splendid. Ferdinand and Isabella were surely taken aback while touring a more impressive masterwork than any palace in Christian Spain. For a further dose of humility, they might have noted the motto etched into the Alhambra's stone, an ironic epitaph for the Nasrid dynasty and a sobering reminder to the Christian armies that supplanted them: "Only God is Victorious."

Ferdinand and Isabella mapped out surprisingly generous surrender terms, whether mindful that this same One God watched over Muslim and Christian alike, or (more likely) to court the allegiance of their new Granadan subjects. The monarchs granted "all the common people, great or small, to live in their own religion, and not permit that their mosques be taken from them, nor their minarets nor their muezzins . . . The Moors shall be judged in their laws and law suits according to the code of the *sharia* which it is their custom to respect, under the jurisdiction of their judges and *qadis*." Nor would the Moors be subjected to the indignity of wearing "distinctive marks like those worn by the Jews." Christians were not to enter mosques without the local community's permission. Granadans who had converted from Christianity to Islam were free to follow the religion of their choosing, and children born into mixed Muslim-Christian marriages would be raised in the religion freely chosen by their parents.

Many Muslims nonetheless regarded it as a blasphemy to submit to infidel law no matter how generous the terms, or doubted the Christians' ultimate motives, or were unwilling to endure the ignominy of Christian rule after centuries of Islamic governance. The surrender treaty provided for these dissenters as well, making passage to North Africa available for the next three years to any who wished to sample Christian Granada's lifestyle before finally choosing a homeland.

Spanish shipping became busy that year.

Not only did Andalusian Muslims fleeing Granada crowd Spanish ports, but Spain's Jews were about to migrate as well, faced with far less generous terms than Ferdinand and Isabella offered Granada's Muslims. Not long after accepting Granada's surrender, the monarchs' counselors began drafting the Jewish Chapter of Expulsion of March 31, 1492. In contrast to today's subtle, spin-mastered political documents, the expulsion edict told its story frankly. Ferdinand and Isabella complained that despite their inquisitors' determined efforts to root out false converts, Spain was still plagued by "wicked Christians who

Judaized and apostatized from our holy Catholic faith." The monarchs had become convinced that the ultimate problem lay not with the New Christians themselves, but with Spain's unconverted Jews, who allegedly refused to leave the conversos to practice the faith in peace but "seek always and by whatever means and ways they can to subvert and to steal faithful Christians from our holy Catholic faith." The edict continued by explaining how the monarchs had tried to end such treachery by "order[ing] the separation of the said Jews in all the cities, towns, and villages of our kingdoms," directing that "they be given Jewish quarters and separated places where they should live." But this policy of *apartamiento* ("living apart") proved inadequate, as had the more drastic measure of expelling the Jews from Andalusia, the perceived hotbed of judaizing.

The edict announced a definitive remedy: "To order the said Jews and Jewesses of our kingdoms to depart [by the end of July] and never to return."

Spain had come late to this vision of a Christian society sanitized of Jews. The Jewish people had been expelled from England in 1290 and from France in 1306; periodic pogroms had driven waves of Jewish refugees from northern Europe. Spain had always beckoned as the obvious refuge for the French, British, and northern European exiles. It was the land of Maimonides, the military hero Samuel ha-Nagid, and spiritual geniuses like the kabbalist Moses de León. Immigrant refugees joined their talents to what was already Europe's largest, most successful Jewish population.

The painful irony unfolded that many of those straggling to deportation ports as spring turned to summer in 1492 had descended from these same English, French, and German exiles. Of course, in another sense, this was no irony at all, but the very defining mark of Spanish Jewry: some 1492 exiles were, after all, descended from forbears who had wound their way to Spain from the Holy Land in the first century C.E., scattered in the great diaspora following the destruction of the Jerusalem temple.

The expulsion order allowed Jews until July 31 to convert or depart Castile and Aragon. Though dated as of March 31, heralds only promulgated the decree throughout Spain's towns and villages a full month later. Thus, most Jews had only a scant three months to wrap up material affairs and emigrate, or to ponder the renunciation of beliefs that parents, grandparents, and great-grandparents had clung to despite mounting anti-Jewish hostility since 1391. It's estimated that as many as half of Spain's Jews converted, and between 150,000 and 200,000 chose exile (though less likely estimates range as high as 800,000 exiles).

Would-be exiles ran a gantlet of challenges even before departing towns and villages. Jews scurried to sell houses and businesses, negotiating with savvy buyers who held back from bidding, knowing that Jews would become increasingly desperate to sell as the calendar wound toward July 31. Jewish moneylenders chased borrowers who tried to run out the clock on their debts. Petty scams were rife; one Christian cowherd, for example, attempted to smuggle into Portugal some 140 cattle owned by a prominent Jew, intending to return to Spain after July 31, when his master would be long gone and unable to prosecute the theft.

The soon-to-be exiles faced a perverse dilemma. They needed to sell unmovable assets like houses and businesses, but the expulsion edict forbade Jews from removing gold, silver, jewels, or coins from Spain. Although such restrictions may seem gratuitously cruel, they reflected a crude economic logic: royal advisors feared a drain of specie wealth would cripple Spain's economy. (The logic, of course, was oddly skewed, as the loss of Jewish talent was surely the more damaging blow to Spain's economy.)

Unable to transport currency, exiles resorted to transporting their wealth in the form of merchandise or textiles. Yet the expulsion orders dealt another twist: donkeys could not be removed from Spain for fear that it would become a beast-of-burden-less economy. Whatever wealth a Jew might have accumulated was reduced to the few bundles he and his family could wear, carry, or drag across the border.

Saragossa's Jews undertook a typical journey into exile. Some set off in land caravans; others hired river boats along the Ebro for part of the month-long journey to the port of Tortosa-Ampolia. Food and lodging claimed part of their dwindling financial resources each day, as did payment to Christian mercenaries hired for protection against criminal bands haunting the route. Even in the best of times, medieval roadways imperiled merchants traveling through Spain's underpopulated, under-policed countryside; the presence of women and children rendered the exile convoys even more vulnerable.

In a sixteenth-century memoir, the priest Andrés Bernáldez depicted refugee caravans limping toward exile "in much travail and misfortune, some falling, others standing up, some dying, others being born, others falling sick, [so] that there was not a Christian but felt sorrow for them; and always where they went they [the Christians] invited them to be baptized, and some in their misery would convert and remain, but very few; and the rabbis continually gave them strength and made the women and girls sing, and play tambourines and timbrels, to raise the people's spirits." Upon reaching the port, Jews arranged onward passage in merchant ships accommodating as many as a thousand or more exiles typically destined for nearby Italian ports like Pisa and Naples. In a final, ironic twist, departing Jews sacrificed the final few coins in their purses: the crown that expelled them from their homeland levied a departure tax.

The sea voyage to Christian Italy or Muslim Turkey beckoned many from Iberia's south and east, while an overland escape route tantalized refugees from western parts of Isabella's domains. Though Ferdinand and Isabella had welded together Castile, Aragon, and Granada under their united rule, two proudly independent Iberian kingdoms flanked opposite ends of their empire: Portugal in the west and Navarre in the northeast. Neither had promulgated expulsion edicts, and Portugal's long border with Castile tempted as many as three-quarters of the 1492 exiles as a chance to refound a thriving Jewish civilization.

It proved a cruel illusion.

King João II of Portugal had promised temporary asylum to exiled Jews in exchange for an entry tax. Some refugees were subsequently pressured into converting or sold into slavery; others endured an atrocity more wrenching than expulsion from Spain. Jewish children were snatched up for a bizarre experiment in social engineering. Hundreds of young Jews were herded onto ships and transported to the remote Atlantic Ocean island of São Tomé, nearly dead on the equator and some two hundred miles off the coast of what is today Gabon. It served as a way station for Portuguese explorers picking a path along Africa's coastline in search of passage to the Indies, and João imagined his little Jewish child-colonists, indoctrinated as Christians far from the prying influence of Jewish parents, as the base of a thriving Christian outpost.

Well before King João's successor (King Manuel I) finally promulgated Portugal's expulsion edict in 1496, Spanish Jews realized how disastrously they had miscalculated by fleeing to Portugal. The remnant dragged themselves to North Africa or Turkey, their refugee ranks devastated by forced conversions and João's kidnappings.

Among those forcibly converted in Portugal was the young scion of the extraordinary Abrabanel family, whose story encapsulates the whole sorry century of Jewish history that began with the 1391 pogroms. The patriarch Samuel Abrabanel, a financier and courtier to three Castilian kings, converted to Christianity in the wake of the 1391 riots, devastating a family that proudly claimed descent from the first Jewish immigrants to Spain. While some family members converted with him, others, including Samuel who now recanted his conversion, migrated to Portugal to preserve their Jewish heritage and seek out new fortunes.

Samuel's grandson Isaac restored the clan's Jewish branch to prosperity and eventually repatriated to Spain, where this remarkable financier surfaced uncannily at every subsequent critical turn in Iberia's affairs. He financed Ferdinand and Isabella's successful campaign to capture Muslim Granada. Soon after, as the monarchs readied the Jewish expulsion edict, Abrabanel reportedly spearheaded a last-ditch effort by leading Jews to buy the monarchs from their intended course. But he could buy neither the edict nor his own exemption from it. While Jewish commoners were scurrying about selling their few sticks of furniture, Isaac Abrabanel scurried about settling one of Spain's largest loan portfolios before emigrating to Italy.

Abrabanel's one-year-old grandson and namesake, Isaac, didn't accompany the family to Italy. He had earlier been spirited away to Portugal in a panicked rush after the family caught wind of a bizarre plot to kidnap and baptize the child. Jews were forbidden from removing Christian children from Spain, and it was rumored that plotters intended to baptize the child as a way of forcing the Abrabanels to remain in Spain, thereby securing the continued benefit of the elder Isaac's financial resources and acumen. The family entrusted the infant to his wet nurse and bundled the two off to Portugal before the plot could unfold. Thus, the Abrabanels miscalculated as disastrously as every other Spanish Jew who sought refuge in Portugal. Grandfather Isaac would surely have traded all his financial success to have been spared subsequent word of grandson Isaac's forced conversion to Christianity in Portugal. The disenchanted grandfather immersed himself in Hebrew Scripture, consoling himself with portents that the Messiah would soon deliver his chosen Jewish people from their travails.

There was, however, no consolation for young Isaac's father, who composed an elegiac lament for his lost son. It speaks eloquently not only for his own pain, but for that suffered by parents of every child slain during the 1391 pogroms, or pressured into converting thereafter, or condemned by inquisitors, or converted with the ultimatum of 1492, or transported to São Tomé aboard some leaky Portuguese carrack:

> Time with his pointed shafts has hit my heart
> and split my gut, laid open my entrails,
> landed me a blow that will not heal,
>
> . . .
>
> Exiling me while yet my days were green,
> Sending me stumbling, drunk, to roam the world,
> Spinning me dizzy round about its edge
>
> . . .
>
> Yes, Time—
> my bear, my wolf!—ate up my heart, cleft
> it in two and cut it into bits,
> so that it aches with groaning, panic, plunder,
> confiscation, loss, captivity.
> But even this was not enough for him; he also seeks
> To snuff my spark, exterminate my line.
>
> . . .
>
> I sent him [his son Isaac] with his wet-nurse in the dark
> Of midnight—just like smuggled goods!—
> To Portugal, then ruled by a wicked king
> Who earlier had nearly ruined me.

. . .

My darling boy was taken, and his good name

. . .

He's twelve years old; I haven't seen him since—
So are my sins repaid!
I rage, but only at myself;
There's no one else but me to bear the blame.
I chased him from mere troubles to a trap

. . .

—But how can I control myself when he is lost?
That is the thought that sickens, strangles, slashes me;
That is the razor, sharper than any barber's blade,
That rips the membrane of my aching heart

. . .

20. Columbus, a New World, and the End of History

"A Deed Forbidden by Every Faith"

Easy to overlook among refugee-burdened ships crowding Spain's harbors in the summer of 1492 would have been a three-ship flotilla being readied for an August departure. While thousands of Jews and Muslims sailed south to North Africa or east to Turkey, ninety sailors readied the *Niña, Pinta,* and *Santa María* to head west. While King Ferdinand was slowly tightening the noose around Granada throughout the 1480s, the Italian adventurer Christopher Columbus was vainly pitching an expedition plan to Portugal's King João II. João's advisors had pooh-poohed Columbus's absurd idea of reaching the Indies by sailing directly west. João's navigators were making increasingly venturous sallies along the African coastline; they were committed to opening a route to the Indies by reaching Africa's southern tip and heading east.

Ferdinand and Isabella's initial response to Columbus's scheme had been almost as discouraging. They met him in 1486, with their crusade to drive Muslim power from Granada weighing heavily on their minds and pocketbooks. With war draining their resources, Columbus was lucky the monarchs hadn't dismissed outright his far-fetched plan. Instead, they referred it to a commission headed by Queen Isabella's confessor, friar Hernando de Talavera. Isabella trusted Talavera; he could read; he knew Scripture. That more or less sums up his qualifications to head the commission. As Columbus's son put it, "There were not so many geographers then as now, [so] the members of this committee were not so well informed as the business required."

Not so well informed indeed. Some commissioners argued that if Columbus sailed west he could never get back, for they imagined the ocean sea sloping in such in a way that Columbus "would be going downhill and so could not return . . . even with the aid of the strongest wind." Equally grave theological objections were piled on top of this "scientific analysis." Columbus's world map seemed to situate the Antipodes at the globe's far south. Yet Church tradition affirmed that Jesus's apostles had preached the gospel message "to the ends of the earth," and because no record existed of an apostolic visit to these so-called Antipodean tribes, it was obvious that neither they nor the place they supposedly inhabited could possibly exist.

There were, of course, better reasons to have doubted Columbus, starting with his badly flawed assumption that he would reach Asia after sailing a mere two thousand or so nautical miles west. Neither Columbus, Talavera, nor, for that matter, any other European understood just how large was the globe they inhabited: a two thousand-mile journey would have stranded Columbus in mid-Atlantic, a good eight thousand miles short of Asia and well short even of the Americas (which, of course, were nowhere at all on Columbus's map).

Credit Columbus with perseverance, if only the perseverance of a desperate man running out of options. While Talavera's commission dilly-dallied and Ferdinand waged war on Granada, Columbus drifted toward abject poverty and solicited support from anyone who might further his suit with the king and queen. It paid off in late 1491 with his second royal audience. The steady progress of their Granada siege had brightened the monarchs' outlook and placed them in a more expansive frame of mind. Romanticized accounts portray Columbus withdrawing from the royal court without a formal commitment, only to be chased down by royal messengers summoning him back to the monarchs' presence with the good news that Granada had just surrendered. Relieved of ongoing siege costs, it suddenly seemed no great hardship to subsidize half of Columbus's expedition expenses.

However their discussions unfolded, Columbus's fine-tuned second pitch struck economic, messianic, religious, and geopolitical chords that all rang sweetly to the monarchs. He later wrote in his diary that after promising "all of the profit from my enterprise should be spent in the conquest of Jerusalem . . . your Highnesses smiled and said that it pleased them." The Ottoman Turks had gained a menacing foothold on Christian Europe's eastern flank, and Columbus portrayed Ferdinand's takeover of Muslim Granada as prelude to a cataclysmic global showdown with Islam. His expedition would reconnect Europe with supposed long-lost Christian kingdoms cut off by Islamic territory in between. By reuniting the forces of global Christendom, Ferdinand and Columbus would unleash a unified assault that Islam surely could not withstand. Such grandiose considerations aside, there were straightforward attractions to Columbus's plan, not least the chance to leapfrog Portugal's steady imperial progress by establishing overseas colonies for Spain.

So, in August 1492, Jews and Muslims sailed toward exile and Columbus toward a New World. He brought along a fluent Arabic speaker, presuming that with Islam's broad global dominance, any peoples he encountered before finding his lost Christian tribes would likely be Arabic-speaking Muslims.

Columbus wasn't the only one concerned about effective diplomacy with Islam. Friar Hernando de Talavera, chairman of the erstwhile commission that so gravely doubted Columbus, had since been named archbishop of the newly conquered Granada. He showed considerably more imagination in the role than he had when assessing Columbus's navigational plans. Talavera met regularly with Muslim religious leaders, had Christian liturgical prayers translated into Arabic while attempting to learn the language himself, and founded a school to train Christian preachers to serve what he hoped would be a growing Arabic-speaking flock. To be sure, his initiatives were geared to lure Granada's Muslims to Christianity, not exactly embodying the spirit of the surrender treaty pledge to "ever afterwards allow . . . all the common people, great or small, to live in their own [Muslim] religion." But Talavera at least refrained from the heavy-handed approach that other royal advisors advocated in this moment of Christian triumph.

That heavier fist fell soon enough. Archbishop Francisco Jiménez de Cisneros of Toledo toured Granada in 1499. No surprise that this future inquisitor general and cardinal promoted an uncompromisingly aggressive brand of proselytization. He eschewed Talavera's patient, dialogue-based ministry, preferring the more efficient approach of pressured mass conversions. Lest any of Granada's Moors misunderstand the message, Cisneros had copies of the Quran immolated in great public bonfires. As their holy book smoldered, so did Muslim resentment. Cisneros cited the riots that inevitably ensued as proof that Talavera's tactics had been too soft for so stiff-necked a people, never mind that Cisneros's own provocations had actually incited the unrest. Goaded by Cisneros and others, Ferdinand and Isabella summarily voided Muslim rights under the decade-old surrender treaty, issuing a new edict requiring Muslims in Granada and Castile to convert or be exiled, the same dilemma over which so many Jews had earlier agonized.

As Granadans stewed over the injustice that a treaty entered in good faith had been unilaterally revoked from a community now stripped of all military power and negotiating leverage, one bitterly aggrieved Muslim appealed to the Ottoman sultan in Constantinople:

> Therefore ask their Pope, that is to say, the ruler of Rome, why they
> permitted treason after having [granted] amnesty,
> And why they harmed us with their betrayal with no wrong or crime on
> Our part?
> . . .
> As for him who grants a treaty and then betrays it, that is a deed
> forbidden by every faith.

In the event, most Granadans converted, but the same writer describes their dim view of their new faith: "It was the fear of death and of burning that caused us to convert . . . we accept neither our change of religion nor what they say on the subject of the Trinity."

Columbus's glory days lasted only about as long as the Granada surrender treaty. His October 12, 1492 landfall at the island he christened San Salvador (also known today as Watling Island in the Bahamas) vindicated his decision to sail west, even if what he had discovered was not exactly the Asian island of Cipangu (i.e., Japan), as he believed. Spain's grateful monarchs named him Admiral of the Ocean Sea and governor general of all he discovered. Yet, within a half dozen years, Spain's interest in his New World was already waning. While he gushed over the New World's incomparable promise, veterans of his voyages instead described a miserable backwater tyrannized by Columbus's overbearing rule. Columbus could staff his third voyage of 1498 only by enlisting convicts to round out his crew. Two years later, Ferdinand and Isabella dispatched a legate to the Americas to investigate persistent reports of Columbus's harsh leadership style.

The Admiral of the Ocean Sea was returned to Spain in chains in late 1500. Deeply insulted, he kept the shackles "as a memorial of how well he had been rewarded for his many services." He set out to vindicate himself, scraping together raw material for what later appeared as his *Libro de las Profecías* (*Book of the Prophecies*). Spaniards may have begun regarding him as a tyrant who had stumbled on a few worthless spits of land, but Columbus regarded himself as a man of destiny, leading a great apocalyptic journey that was hastening history toward the conversion of the whole world to Christianity. Or, as he rather grandiosely imagined, "God made me the messenger of the new heaven and the new earth of which he spoke in the Apocalypse."

His *Book of the Prophecies* teased out-of-context snippets of Scripture and Bible commentary to bolster his case. Isidore of Seville hadn't dared guess when the world might end, but Columbus seized on Alfonso the Wise's world history to argue differently. From the world's creation, Columbus asserted, "according to the account of King Alonso which is considered the most certain," only 155 years remained until the 7,000th anniversary of creation, "in which years I said above according to said authorities, the world must end." With so little time remaining, there was much to do before the Messiah's Second Coming, starting with Jerusalem's reconquest and the conversion of all humanity to Christianity. Columbus saw himself catalyzing this unfolding drama of human history careering toward its climactic close.

The *Libro de Profecías* was never circulated beyond Columbus's own intimate circle during his lifetime. But if it had been, it would probably not have been dismissed as the kooky musings of a man slowly coming unhinged. Millennial speculation was rife in Spain, and fevered predictions won currency even at the royal court. King Ferdinand's courtiers honored him with the unwarranted epithet "King of Jerusalem," a sobriquet Ferdinand apparently liked so much that he used it himself. In 1496, Pope Alexander VI christened Ferdinand and Isabella "the Catholic Monarchs." The lofty tribute was at a minimum truer of them than of Pope Alexander himself: this notorious Borgia pope, a Spaniard who remains the poster child of corrupt Renaissance pontiffs, purportedly maintained an incestuous affair with his illegitimate daughter, Lucrezia, while elevating another of his illegitimate offspring to the rank of cardinal.

Alexander's indiscretions notwithstanding, he rightly discerned the glimmer of hope that the expectations so many centuries ago invested in Spain and her monarchs might finally be fulfilled. Isidore had exclaimed that Spain was the "ornament of the world." The late ninth-century author of the *Chronicle of Alfonso III,* writing when Muslim power dominated Spain, recalled Jesus's parable of the tiny mustard seed becoming the greatest of trees and predicted that a decimated Christian Spain would rise again, and "the well-being of Spain and the army of the Gothic people will be restored."

Such prophecies may have seemed laughable when the guerrilla Pelayo was holed up in Spain's mountainous north as the last thing standing between Islam and total domination of Iberia. Or when the ninth-century King Alfonso II founded a small church in northwest Spain to commemorate the miraculous discovery of St. James's remains at Compostela, preoccupied with hanging onto his tiny kingdom, not reconquering all Spain for Christendom.

The barely flickering dreams of recreating Visigoth glory blazed to life only many generations further along Pelayo's jagged family tree, when Alfonso VI in 1085 claimed the old Visigoth capital of Toledo and the renegade Cid battled his way soon after through Muslim territory to the Mediterranean coast. Fernando III's thirteenth-century conquest of Córdoba and Seville gave that Reconquest dream concrete shape, though its promise remained unfulfilled for over two more centuries, until the Catholic Monarchs in two busy decades united Christian Spain, vanquished the last remnant of Muslim rule, expelled Spain's Jews, and opened a New World. Given all he accomplished, no wonder Ferdinand was prophesied as the monarch destined to reclaim Jerusalem for Christendom and restore Spain's place at the head of nations, as Isidore had so fondly hoped.

The Eden that was Visigoth Spain had been a homogeneous Christian kingdom, at least as reinvented in the imagination of later chroniclers. By delivering Jews and Muslims the ultimatum to convert or leave, the Catholic Monarchs had restored Spain's Edenic purity. Indeed, as a fevered Columbus saw it, Spain stood on the verge of casting the whole New World in the same pristine mold: "Your Highness ought not to consent that any foreigner do business or set foot here, except Christian Catholics, since this was the end and the beginning of the enterprise, that it should be for the enhancement and glory of the Christian religion."

Columbus saw the jigsaw of world history finally falling into place with Granada's fall, the Jews' expulsion, and his own New World discoveries. But not everyone shared Columbus's vision of the Messianic age, and not everyone saw it arriving on Columbus's timetable.

Perspective is everything, and from exile in Italy Isaac Abrabanel viewed history from a rather different vantage point. Shunted from Spain to Portugal to Italy as Europe's doors swung shut behind them, Jews lamented the pressed conversions of grandsons and grandfathers to Christianity and longed for the Messiah's promised advent to redeem the wandering Jewish nation, liberate Jerusalem, and gather the Jews into a promised land. Redemption could not come soon enough for long-suffering Jews, so it's understandable that Isaac Abrabanel divined in the scriptural tea leaves a more imminent Messianic arrival than Columbus did.

Like Isidore of Seville and Columbus, Isaac also saw world history unfolding in great epochs paralleling the biblical days of creation. Christian Isidore had believed humanity's sixth (and Messianic) age had been initiated by Jesus; the Jewish Isaac still awaited a Messiah to usher in that sixth age. He found hope in the Book of Daniel's opaque imagery, where the prophet had plaintively wondered how long Yahweh would allow His "sanctuary" to be "trampled underfoot." Isaac read in Daniel this unambiguous heavenly rejoinder: "for two thousand and three hundred evenings and mornings; then the sanctuary shall be restored to its rightful state." Abrabanel composed his *Wells of Salvation* in the year 1496, calculating that from the biblical division of the kingdom of Israel exactly 2,300 years would have passed in the year 1503, one year for each of the prophet Daniel's evenings and mornings. Isaac scratched out his calculations, consoling himself that Israel's redeemer would soon make himself known, indeed must already be alive amid the Jewish diaspora's scattered communities. Perhaps even among Isaac's own circle of Spanish exiles in Italy.

As it turned out, Israel's redeemer didn't arrive in 1503. Instead, Judah Abrabanel that year composed his doleful lament over his son's forced conversion to Christianity.

One year later, Queen Isabella died. Garbed in a Franciscan habit, she was entombed in Granada's cathedral, its one-time grand mosque. She followed the great tradition of St. Fernando III in Seville and Alfonso VI in Toledo, two other Crusader monarchs whose remains patiently await the resurrection of the dead in mosques-turned-cathedrals in the cities of their greatest Reconquest triumphs. Isabella's husband, Ferdinand, joined her a few years later. Despite the Catholic Monarchs' many accomplishments over their long reign, the epitaph chiseled onto their sepulcher pointedly memorializes just two: "Destroyers of the Mohammedan sect and the annihilators of heretical obstinacy [i.e., of the Jews]."

Columbus died in 1506. His will set aside money to fund Jerusalem's liberation from Islamic rule. It's not known whether this wish was heeded, and if so, how the fund was used.

The Messiah didn't arrive to end the world in the mid-1600s, as Columbus had confidently predicted. The world had, however, changed a good deal by then. The descendants of those Granadan and Castilian Muslims forcibly converted to Christianity in the early 1500s remained as stubbornly (though clandestinely) committed to their former faith and customs as the poet had predicted: "It was the fear of death and of burning that caused us to convert . . . we accept neither our change of religion nor what they say on the subject of the Trinity." Arabic remained a living language in Granada a century after its Muslims were forcibly converted.

By 1609, Spain's monarchs had grown exasperated with these recalcitrant *moriscos* as an embarrassing blot on efforts to mold a homogeneous Christian Spain. They were expelled from Spain starting that same year. It had become unacceptable not only to be a Muslim or Jew, but even to be descended from Muslims or Jews. The renegade Cid had regarded honor a distinction earned through deeds rather than inherited through blood: the trustworthy Muslim Abengalbón merited honor; the treacherous Christian infantes of Carrión did not. Though Spaniards still lionized the semilegendary Cid as a national hero, the code of honor he exemplified had been supplanted. *Limpieza de sangre* ("purity of blood") became more the criterion of honor than deeds, and bloodline increasingly dictated what roles one might play in Spanish society. Descendants of Jews and Muslims were barred from holding most public offices or from entering most religious orders.

With the 1492 extermination of Muslim rule in Spain, St. James the Moor Killer had seemingly outlived his militant usefulness and could have been retired to bestow once again undivided attention on the grieving, lame, repentant, or merely curious who thronged Compostela each year seeking St. James the Pilgrim's favor. But Santiago the militant was drafted to combat a new enemy. Some four decades after Columbus first dropped anchor in the New World, the Spanish adventurer Francisco Pizarro stumbled on an unimaginably wealthy Inca civilization centered in what is today Peru. As his grossly outnumbered conquistadors plunged into the battle that many surely assumed would end their lives, they howled Spain's traditional battle cry, *Santiago y cierra España* ("St. James and close [ranks] for Spain"). One soldier afterward swore to seeing St. James swoop down on a white horse to lead the miraculous Spanish victory that day, just as he had miraculously intervened to battle Islam along Spain's frontier. So the battle-weary apostle embarked on a new phase of his career, its reminders still resonant in South American atlases, from the benignly named Santiago, Chile, to the more sinister-sounding Mexican town of Matamoros ("Muslim Killer").

Thanks in part to Inca gold, Spain entered what historians typically call her Golden Age. The age was golden in one obvious respect, as precious metals lifted from New World colonies gilded Spain's altars and financed her European conflicts. Yet, in other respects, the Golden Age label is at a minimum incomplete. For this was at least the *third* Golden Age Spain had enjoyed. Spain's Islamic Golden Age had blessed Europe with new models of architecture, mathematics, ceramics, agriculture, philosophy, medicine, and astronomy, to name a few disciplines among many. Spain's Jewish Golden Age had nurtured Europe's most prosperous, accomplished, and largest Jewish population, and through Maimonides and Moses de León bequeathed masterworks that still fundamentally influence Jewish thought and worship.

The enduring contributions of medieval Spain's Muslims and Jews reveal an unfortunate gap in Spain's third Golden Age. Cleansed of non-Christians and striving for homogeneity, Spain's encounter with alien cultures now occurred almost exclusively beyond Iberia's borders, most notably in her New World colonies. And what she extracted from that Golden Age encounter with other civilizations was for the most part only, well, gold.

Tourists to Spain are everywhere reminded how profoundly Spain once benefited from her encounter with Islamic civilization, from Córdoba's cathedral rising from the roots of her dizzyingly arcaded great mosque, to the Almohad minaret that dominates Seville's skyline as its cathedral bell tower, even to Moorish churches in northern provinces never ruled by Muslim Spain. Visitors to the Inca remains at Machu Picchu can't help but note that Inca architects might have made an equally profound contribution to Spanish masonry and construction technology. But the Spain of this (third) Golden Age was no longer forced to encounter and absorb the gifts of foreign civilizations on her own home soil and perhaps had lost the knack of doing so elsewhere.

Still, if foreign cultures no longer blessed Spain, those exiled from Spain blessed their adopted homelands. By some estimates, 20 percent of the world's Jews, and half of Israel's, trace their lineage to Iberia's Jewish exiles, the so-called Sephardim, named for the biblical land of Sepharad (Obadiah 1:20) that became identified with Iberia in Jewish discourse. Many Sephardim fled to Ottoman Turkey, North Africa, or Italy after the 1492 expulsion. A few years later, many fulfilled the centuries-deferred dream of return to the promised land, albeit not accompanied by a hoped-for Messiah but with the tolerant forbearance of the Holy Land's Muslim rulers.

Some returnees settled a remote, hilly corner of the Mideast where Israelis, Lebanese, and Syrians today maintain vigil over each other's border patrols. Sixteenth-century Safed held no such interest for military strategists, or for many others except textile weavers. A few mystics climbed winding trails through infertile hills to found a community of prayer and study a half-mile above sea level and close to the traditional burial site of Rabbi Shimon bar Yohai, that revered second-century spiritual leader under whose name Moses de León had penned the *Zohar.*

Many Safed settlers traced Iberian roots; Joseph Caro's family hailed from Toledo and Moses Cordovero's from Córdoba. They nursed a revival of Jewish spirituality like the reawakening once sparked by Moses de León and the Iberian kabbalists. An Egyptian Jew, Isaac Luria, joined the Safed community after spending the better part of a decade absorbed in meditation and reflection on the *Zohar;* after two intensely productive years in Safed, an outbreak of plague cut short his life. One noted scholar has deemed the Safed movement "one of the most significant and remarkable chapters in the history of Judaism."

Like the ancient Greeks and Christian Isidore, the Safed kabbalists wondered where human history was going. Their Hebrew Bible taught them, like Isidore, to regard human history not as a meaningless cycle but as the journey forward of fallen humankind toward redemption. Yet it was not easy for sixteenth-century Jews, long ago scattered from Jerusalem by the Romans and more recently shunted from Spain, to read history's tea leaves optimistically. History's pattern seemed to vindicate the ancient Greeks: an ever recurring cycle, often of tragedy and humiliation.

Yet, the Safed kabbalists taught, it was the Jews' duty not merely to suffer history's misfortunes in passive vigil for the Messiah, but to strive to bring the Messiah into their midst. They were called to accomplish *Tikkun olam,* the "perfecting" or "setting straight" of a disordered world where evil too often conquers good. Humans were tasked and privileged to restore the perfect order that had reigned on that seventh day when God finished His creative work and pronounced it all very good. The Jews would accomplish this awesome task by praying with a pure heart and virtuous intent, by wishing no evil on another, and by following God's commandments. Moses Cordovero exhorted his followers to understand that "in everyone there is something of his fellow man. Therefore, whoever sins, injures not only himself but also that part of himself which belongs to another."

Indeed, each human act of goodness or evil figured into the great drama of salvation history by hastening or delaying the hoped-for redemption. Every single moment of every single life was endowed with supreme significance. It was no longer the Messiah's task to achieve redemption and humans' merely to wait, hope, and pray for it, but the whole Jewish nation was swept up into that task of healing the world of that catastrophe whereby evil had entered the world. Tens of thousands of Sephardim, descendants of these exiles from Spain, live and pray in Jewish communities scattered all over the globe, many of them, like these Safed mystics of long ago, undertaking the prayer and good works that redeem a fallen humankind.

What does medieval Spain teach us about history? Are we going forward, or trapped in a meaningless cycle, or merely lurching about from generation to generation, foolishly deceiving ourselves whenever we imagine we have discerned in events some pattern where none really exists? Though much has changed in the centuries since seventh-century Isidore pondered Spain's history, not everything has. In 1834 the Inquisition was abolished in Spain; in 1966 Spain's Constitution formally established the principle of religious toleration; in 1978 the government proclaimed Spain a country without a state religion. Muslims, Christians, and Jews continue to believe in the same One God. Today, even though few Muslims and fewer Jews call Spain their home, all three faiths are practiced freely there, as for so many centuries in medieval Spain. The optimistic can only regard this as a sign of humanity moving forward.

Isidore of Seville's encyclopedia taught us to count more efficiently on our fingers; Pope Sylvester dazzled contemporaries with Hindu-Arabic numerals and his superabacus; Spaniards today brandish pocket calculators packing power to solve problems that all medieval Spain's Christian, Muslim, and Jewish mathematicians together could never have tackled. Isidore imagined a world surrounded by the ocean sea and populated with headless Blemmyes and one-legged Sciopodes; Alfonso's multifaith translation teams prepared the celestial maps and configured the astrolabes that enabled sixteenth-century navigators to remap that primitive, poorly understood world sketched out by Isidore; today, astrolabes are arcane museum pieces, and astronauts and chauffeurs navigate with previously unimaginable precision by global positioning satellite systems. Who can behold human knowledge surging forward and possibly parrot Aristotle's morose plaint that "each art and science has often been developed as far as possible and has again perished," a conjecture that seems more wrongheaded with each passing generation.

And yet.

Those same global positioning systems that so comfort chauffeurs also target munitions far more lethal than the swords, rocks, and spears with which Fernando III assaulted Seville and Córdoba. Has humanity progressed when one fighter pilot needs but seconds to obliterate more fellow humans than a Reconquest army could slay in a lifetime? Or when sophisticated aeronautical equipment enables suicide-pilot fanatics to immolate two great towers and thousands within them in September 2001? Or when a cell phone's exquisite electronics help madmen to shred trains and the lives of Spanish commuters in March 2004?

In one undeniable respect there is terrifying truth in Aristotle's claim that all we've achieved in every art and science could perish. If the twenty thousand years or so of human history is reduced to a day, in the last ten minutes of that long day we've acquired and multiplied at a frightening pace the capacity to exterminate our species and reduce our earthly habitat to a lifeless husk, annihilating along the way those few remaining manuscripts of Isidore's encyclopedia, those Romanesque churches lining the Santiago pilgrimage route, the silver casket protecting Santiago's remains in Compostela's cathedral, the grand Umayyad mosque from which rises Córdoba's cathedral, the Nasrid Alhambra where Ferdinand and Isabella marked the end of Muslim Spain, and all else that we consider the patrimony of our shared human civilization.

Aristotle never foresaw the terrible power we would someday harness, nor did the medieval Spaniard Ibn Tufayl, who nonetheless presciently proclaimed humanity's duty "not to root out a whole species." Ibn Tufayl's Hayy could withdraw to his isolated island and contemplate God in solitude. No such solitary island remains. Instead, technology has shrunk the globe and transformed our whole world into medieval Spain: we Jews, Christians, Muslims, believers of all other faiths, and those who profess none are now and forever thrown together by technology, whether that reality delights or dismays us. We can neither wish away the religious other nor pretend he or she does not exist.

The globe has become one of those medieval Andalusian villages, where we buy from and sell to each other, brush against one another in streets and alleys, marvel at or recoil from each other's beliefs and habits, hear the cry of muezzin and cantor and chorister, and find that the music, words, and ideas of Muslim, Christian, and Jew have seeped into a pooled cultural groundwater. Humanity in the twentieth century empowered itself to become copreservers of God's universe. And so, as those Safed mystics observed, redemption or catastrophe now lies with us.

What will we make of our new medieval Spain? Will we realize humanity's potential to live and work harmoniously alongside those who worship differently, as medieval Spaniards did at their best? Or will we, like them, veer off into a violent thicket, forever imbibing the poison of our own resentments? Our troubled age has sometimes mirrored medieval Spaniards at their very worst: killing the innocent in God's name, expelling the "infidel," rallying coreligionists by slandering other faiths, refusing to understand our neighbor's sacred beliefs, and infringing his or her right to worship God freely. Wherever such acts trample human dignity and freedom, no just and lasting peace can be possible. Resentment and anguish, for a time submerged, inevitably erupt anew in violence that mimics the pessimistic cycle of history imagined by the ancients: "and new wars again shall arise, and a new Achilles go to Troy."

Still, even in medieval Spain's saddest stories one finds not the stulti-fying air of inevitability but the realization that humans could have chosen to act differently. Those ancients who imagined history's ever-repeating cycle were only observing what they and predecessor genera-tions had wrought by misusing what may be God's most wondrous gift: entrusting humans with free choice and, as a result, stewardship over the created world's destiny. Medieval Spain teaches that history's pattern is shaped by us, not imposed by gods. We choose to adopt San-tiago the Killer's ever-resentful posture, where each backward glance through history is a prelude to settling old scores. Or, we choose Santi-ago the Pilgrim's optimistic journey forward, glancing back to learn the lessons from our past that might enable reconciliation in our future.

All three faiths counsel adherents to look forward toward this brighter future, where, as Maimonides describes, "there will be no famine, no war, no envy, no strife . . . and the land shall be full of the knowledge of the Lord, as the waters cover the sea." That happier fu-ture will not come to pass through some lucky turn of history's wheel, but when we each play a part in what the kabbalists called *tikkun olam,* the "setting straight" of our disordered world.

It is true, as Isidore of Seville surmised, that "the remainder of the age is known to God Alone." But it is equally true that the One God worshipped by Muslims, Christians, and Jews alike has endowed us with the freedom to shape the remainder of this age, to make of it a never-ending cycle of antagonism or to leave old antagonisms behind to undertake hopeful common pilgrimage forward.

Epilogue

A small pilgrim hostel, perched high in the Pyrenees at Roncesvalles, has welcomed Compostela-bound pilgrims for nearly a millennium. It was founded by a twelfth-century bishop distressed over tales of pilgrims perishing in snow drifts or devoured by wolves. Some of the thousands who take rest there in any year have trekked from as far as Italy, Germany, or central Europe. They're elated at reaching Roncesvalles after conquering the Pyrenees, the route's steepest ascent. Ahead lies only the final leg of their pilgrimage to Santiago de Compostela, a final leg that will stretch some 500 wearying miles.

A thirteenth-century poem sings of this hostel's legendary hospitality, where pilgrims are fed, enjoy clean beds, and have illnesses tended, hair trimmed, and filthy feet bathed by religious and lay helpers determined to bestow the same love and service on all who visit. The poet marvels, "Its doors are open to all, well and ill, not only to Catholics, but to pagans, Jews, and heretics, the idler and the vagabond and, to put it shortly, the good and the wicked."

That well-intended welcome reads today as a curiously mixed message. The hostel's "doors are open to all," bidding genuine, indiscriminate welcome. Yet non-Christians can be forgiven for reading it ambiguously, lumped together as they are into a dubious pile of "pagans, Jews, and heretics, the idler and the vagabond." Still, the sentiment considerably improves on another motto so famously associated with Roncesvalles. There, legend has it, France's valiant Prince Roland was cut down in a treacherous Muslim ambush, his blood sanctifying those very same defiles still trod today by Santiago pilgrims. Before Roland leads France's pride into certain death at infidel hands, he rallies knight colleagues with the simple reassurance, "The pagans are wrong and the Christians are right." As if to underscore the point,

King Charlemagne later rounds up some hundred thousand Muslims and

> takes the pagans up to the baptistery
> If there is anyone who withstands Charles
> He has him hanged or burned or put to death.

No modern Christian and virtually no medieval Christian would have cheered Charlemagne's gruesome style of winning converts. But neither Christians, Muslims, nor Jews can easily disavow Roland's indelicately phrased sentiment that "we" are right and the "others" are wrong. For each religion's core beliefs contradict dogmas proclaimed by the others. Those contradictions are logically irreconcilable, nor can any serious believer paper them over by pretending that the defining tenets of his or her faith don't really matter. Either Jesus is Messiah, or Jesus is not. Either Muhammad was the Messenger of God, or Muhammad was not.

God knows how medieval Spaniards suffered over the stubborn incompatibility of their beliefs, pummeling each other across the width and breadth of the Iberian Peninsula for centuries. A similarly ugly drama still plays itself out all over God's creation. Even if most Christians, Jews, and Muslims today live harmoniously alongside their neighbors, in countless cities, towns, and villages coexistence is wary, resentful, and fragile. Ironically, nowhere is this more evident than in Jerusalem, that holiest of cities revered by Jew, Muslim, and Christian alike. If the Holy Land's spectacularly horrific interfaith clashes are nowhere equaled in intensity, they are faintly echoed everywhere in bruising clashes that have convulsed Bosnia, India, Nigeria, New York City, East Timor, Istanbul, Tunis, Pakistan, and Paris. Need one go on?

Divided by doctrinal differences, Muslims, Christians, and Jews nonetheless must stand together before God to explain what seems a supreme and supremely perverse irony: that these common spiritual descendants of Abraham, these believers in the same One God, these adherents of faiths that exalt peace above almost all other virtues have nonetheless lashed out against one another generation after generation after generation. Pope John Paul II once ruefully observed that "the world is waiting for a world of peace" from "believers, from the representatives of religion," from the three billion of us—fully one-half of the planet's citizens—who profess belief in the same one God. How much longer will the world have to wait? The God of Abraham created humans "in God's own image" and, we are told, gazed upon all creation and pronounced it "very good." What greater mockery of that God than to destroy in God's name those created in God's image.

Medieval Spain's great rationalists were wise and devout enough to know that they were incapable of thinking their way out of every dilemma posed by their respective faiths. Maimonides never tired of pointing out the human mind's limitations: because we finite humans do the reasoning, we will never fully plumb the Infinite God we worship. The Christian apostle Paul spoke in his own way of this intellectual myopia, promising that our shortsightedness would yield upon death to perfect beatific vision: "Now we see in a mirror dimly," he wrote, "but then face to face. Now I know in part; then I shall understand fully."

Spain's great medieval mystics, Moses de León and Ibn Arabi among them, instead believed that acute spiritual vision might be attained in an earthly lifetime and need not be deferred until death. And when these mystics crested the last rise of their spiritual ascent to clearer perception, the polarizing distinctions that set Christian against Muslim against Jew faded into insignificance, or so Ibn Arabi seemed to suggest:

> My heart has become capable of every form,
> it is a pasture for gazelles and a convent for Christian monks,
> And a temple for idols and the pilgrim's Ka'ba and the
> Tables of the Tora and the book of the Quran.
> I follow the religion of Love.

Most of us will never undertake this mystic ascent, and precious few of those who try will ever attain the spiritual summit described by Moses de León, Ibn Arabi, or John of the Cross. Only a tiny handful will be privileged to know in an earthly lifetime whether our irreconcilable dogmatic differences, once illuminated under the pure light of perfect Truth, will somehow be reconciled by some logic we Muslims, Christians, and Jews cannot humanly comprehend. Until then, we apparently suffer the tyranny of those brutally incompatible facts: either Jesus is the Messiah or Jesus is not; either Muhammad is the Prophet, or Muhammad is not.

Still, though no logic may resolve the differences that divide believers and no mystical illumination burn those differences into insignificance and no believer dishonor his or her cherished beliefs by proclaiming those differences inconsequential, yet all three faiths have shown believers a way to surmount such insurmountable obstacles. Following that way requires neither the intellect of a Moses Maimonides nor the mystical gifts of an Ibn Arabi. It is no new-found revelation but a path that had always lain open to medieval Spaniards, too often trampled in the heated urgency to enlist and gird Santiago for Christian Crusades against an equally belligerent Muslim enemy.

Today's pilgrims will find in Compostela a medieval articulation of this venerable pathway, and the journey to that town prepares their hearts to receive Santiago's message. They are moved to ponder that the pilgrim route trod by the living is also a graveyard for the dead. No one knows how many tens of thousands of medieval pilgrims, felled by old age or disease, lie forgotten in makeshift graves all along the route. Today's pilgrim symbolically bears their hopes throughout his or her journey. The Santiago-bound pilgrim passes other reminders of medieval Spain's travails, from the monastery of Leyre in Pamplona where St. Eulogius purportedly copied the bilious biography of Muhammad, to the Burgos Cathedral where El Cid is interred, to the church of San Isidoro de León where Isidore of Seville patiently awaits the resurrection of the dead. The pilgrim passes the Mudejar church of San Tirso, a reminder of fruitful collaboration between Christian and Moorish culture, and a few icons of Santiago Matamoros, a reminder of painful collision between these two cultures.

We modern pilgrims through humanity's complicated journey owe it to past generations to reflect on these episodes from our shared past. But it mocks medieval Spain's lessons to the present when we wield the perceived injustices of the past as cudgels to justify new rounds of violence and hatred. That was exactly how these Spaniards erred, ever grinding past hurts into justification for retaliatory assaults.

Instead, the modern pilgrim must accept that he or she journeys through human history accompanied by Jews, Muslims, and Christians. Against the demagogues, zealots, fanatics, and terrorists who would forever divide us, the rest must find the courage to march forward on a shared journey. We must reject forever Santiago the Muslim Killer—and his hateful equivalent in any religion—to instead embrace the way that greets pilgrim arrivals at the great cathedral of Santiago the Pilgrim in Compostela. After reverencing the apostle's remains, many pilgrims proceed to the cathedral museum with its treasured manuscript of a twelfth-century sermon honoring St. James. For all the political savvy and diplomatic sophistry that promises us a more peaceful world, and for all the high-tech modern weaponry that too often gives the lie to that promise, inscribed on that fragile parchment is the simple, naïve, but only enduring formula for coexistence in a world of religious differences and the ultimate foundation of all peace with justice.

The sermon dwells on the custom of Santiago pilgrims to fasten a scallop shell to their outer garments, already a long-standing tradition in the twelfth century and one that continues to this day. It explains that pilgrims sew the shell to their capes, "and they wear them back to their own country with great exultation in honor of the apostle and in his memory and as a sign of such a great journey." The sermon explains the scallop shell's symbolic meaning: "Therefore, the two shields with which the fish is protected, one on either side, represent the two laws of charity with which the bearer must truly protect his life: that is, to love God above all things and to love one's neighbor as oneself."

Whether pilgrim to Compostela or pilgrim through life's everyday journeys, every believer faces the choice imbedded in this medieval sermon. Christian Spain chose to arm itself and its patron Santiago with the literal armor of hate-soaked warfare, as did those Moorish armies they opposed. Santiago the pilgrim instead invites all to journey through life armored only with the two shields of charity: "to love God above all things and love one's neighbor as oneself."

Medieval Spain's other great religious traditions extend the same invitation. As the unrelenting Christian advance during the fifteenth century presaged the imminent end of Muslim power in Spain, a Muslim judge prepared a digest of Islamic law to guide his coreligionists in their increasingly straitened circumstances. It began with this elegantly simple instruction:

> Worship the Creator alone, attributing to him neither image nor likeness,
> And honoring his chosen and blessed Muhammad.
> Desire for your neighbor [*proximo*] that good which you desire for yourself.

It's no coincidence that the great law of charity articulated by this Muslim judge mirrors the twelfth-century Christian sermon. For both are echoing the wisdom carried down from Mt. Sinai many centuries earlier by Moses. The Hebrew Scripture recalls Moses descending from the mountaintop bearing an unmistakable mark of the Pure Light that makes all truth plain: "The skin of his face shone because he had been talking with God." Deuteronomy records the greatest of the truths revealed to Moses atop that mountain: "Hear, O Israel: The Lord our God is one Lord; and you shall love the Lord your God with all your heart, and with all your soul, and with all your might." The Book of Leviticus proclaims its companion commandment: "You shall love your neighbor as yourself."

These two great commandments are reverenced in the faith proclaimed by today's Muslim, Christian, and Jewish descendants of Isidore, Tariq, El Cid, Maimonides, Almanzor, Alfonso, and Averroes, whether in Córdoba, Jerusalem, Bethlehem, or New York. To dishonor those commandments in God's name is to dishonor the One God who uttered them.

Acknowledgments

It's my great pleasure to thank some of many who blessed this work or my life with their support as I prepared this book.

Jim Fitzgerald shepherded the proposal to Free Press. I'm deeply grateful that Leslie Meredith took on the project and contributed valuable insight; Martin Beiser complemented her talents with a steady editing touch, frank opinions, good judgment, and plenty of encouragement. Dorothy Robinson, Stephen Karam, and Kit Frick were most helpful. I greatly appreciate Judith Hoover's painstakingly conscientious copyediting.

Many friends offered much valued support, ideas, or insights along the way, including Laurel Brien, Gerard Cameron, Gail Elia, Barbara Hack, Pat Hammond, Peter Honchaurk, Lou Jerome, Paul Kiernan, Therese Klay, Chris Lynch, Margaret Mathews, Charles McGovern, Rick Morris, Ramon de Oliveira, Pedro Prieto, George Simon, and Tony Thoman. One theme of this book is the need for us to engage other cultures with open hearts and minds, and I fondly recall those who once shepherded this American through the vagaries of life in Japan, Singapore, and England: Noriko Ohta, Jeannie Ang, Linda Tham, and Georgina Turnbull. My mother, sister, and brother, on the other hand, have always been, and still are, ever ready to shepherd me through the vagaries of life here in the homeland, for which I'm grateful. And it won't be long before my nephew Colin will be able to read his name here!

Most of the images in the book are drawn from the collection of the Hispanic Society of America. I'm especially grateful to Diana Liddy, who tirelessly and with good humor helped me find what I needed, and to her colleagues Marcus Burke, Patrick Lenaghan, and Menciá

Figueroa-Villota. The staff of Fordham University library were unfailingly helpful, particularly Betty Garity.

I was fortunate to study medieval history as an undergraduate with Joseph F. O'Callaghan, and I'm humbled that this great scholar carefully read the manuscript and offered valuable suggestions. I'm equally indebted to another renowned medievalist, Rev. Robert I. Burns, S.J., who kindly undertook a thorough reading and shared comments. I am indebted to a number of his Jesuit colleagues who brought their own academic expertise to some or all of the manuscript, including W. Norris Clarke of Fordham University, who offered helpful comments on medieval philosophy, and Patrick J. Ryan, president of Loyola Jesuit College in Abuja, Nigeria, who offered numerous observations from his perspective as a Christian scholar of Islam. James N. Loughran, president of St. Peter's College, was, as usual, a perceptive reader. I'm grateful to others who offered feedback on parts or all of the manuscript: Baher Foad, M.D., of the board of directors of the Brueggeman Center for Interreligious Dialogue; Edna Lief of Pace University; Gerard Biberman of the University of Scranton; Msgr. Guy Massie; Ella Glazer; and especially Rabbi Chava Koster of The Village Temple for her thorough reading and helpful insights.

The support and counsel of all the above made this a vastly better book than I could possibly have written on my own. Many inadequacies surely remain; for all of those I take full responsibility.

Notes

Epigraph

xi *Jews, Christians, and Muslims* Pope John Paul II, "Address to Participants in
    Sant'Egidio Interreligious Meeting," April 30, 1991, Rome, in Eugene J.
    Fisher and Leon Klenicki, eds., *John Paul II Spiritual Pilgrimage Texts on
    Jews and Judaism 1979–1995* (New York: Crossroad, 1995).

Preface

1   *"On their side 100,000* Demetrio Mansilla, *La Documentación Pontificia
    hasta Inocencio III (965–1216)* (Rome: 1955), p. 514, quoted in Joseph F.
    O'Callaghan, *A History of Medieval Spain* (Ithaca: Cornell University Press,
    1975), p. 248. King Alfonso VIII's claim was undoubtedly exaggerated for
    effect, as is typical of medieval war chronicles; the battle recounted, Las
    Navas de Tolosa, was nonetheless a slaughter on a terrible scale.

1   *settling old accounts* a letter signed by the Brigade of Abu Hafs al-Masri,
    quoted in Isambard Wilkinson, "Qaeda Suspected in Deadly Bombings in
    Madrid," *The New York Sun,* March 12–14, 2004, p. 1.

3   *"The pagans [Muslims] are wrong* Glyn Burgess, trans., *The Song of Roland*
    (New York: Penguin, 1984), no. 79/1015. (All citations from *Roland* are by
    laisse and verse in the Burgess edition.)

4   *"Whosoever kills an innocent* See Quran, Sura 5:32.

Introduction

5   *[who] do not keep* al-Bakri, in Charles Melville and Ahmad Ubaydli, *Chris-
    tians and Moors in Spain* (Warminster, U.K.: Aris and Phillips, 1988), vol. 3,
    p. 55.

5   *His 400,000 volume library* The 400,000 figure has struck some scholars as
    incredibly large. Though some doubt the accuracy of the figure, none
    doubt that the library dwarfed any other in western Christendom.

7   *"He is lost* Raymond P. Scheindlin, "Judah Abravanel to His Son," *Judaism*
    41 (spring 1992): 198.

8   *half of Israel's Jews* See "Sephardim" in Geoffrey Wigoder, ed. *The Oxford
    Dictionary of the Jewish Religion* (Oxford: Oxford University Press, 1997), p.
    620.

13 *"where God will wipe* Revelation 7:17. Revised Standard Version.

13 *"new wars again* Virgil, *The Aeneid,* in *Virgil's Works: The Aeneid, Ecologues,
    Georgics,* trans. J. W. Mackail (New York: Random House, 1934), p. 274.

Chapter 1

15 *"well-nigh everything* Ernest Brehaut, *An Encyclopedist of the Dark Ages:
    Isidore of Seville* (New York: Columbia University Press, 1912), p. 25.

15 *The written word* Estimates of Iberia's population during the medieval pe-
    riod vary widely, as do estimated breakdowns of the population by religious
    creed. Historians of medieval Europe, lacking census data or similar
    records, rely on tax rolls, the estimates of chroniclers, extrapolations from
    trade and agricultural information, and other imperfect sources. Further
    complicating any estimates is the impact of the devastating plagues that
    sometimes ravaged Europe, especially in 1348.

    Many historians estimate an Iberian population of between 3 and 5
    million at the time of the 711 invasion. Population estimates for 1492 tend
    to range between 7 and 10 million, with more estimates clustered in the
    range of 9 to 10 million. The lower figure of 7 million, derived from the
    work of the historian Josiah Russell, is driven by a more aggressive estimate
    of the effect of the 1348 plague (e.g., though Russell places only 7 million
    people in Iberia at 1450, he estimates a population of 9 million before the
    plague).

    Estimates of Iberia's Jewish population also vary widely. One low-end es-
    timate is based on Yitzhak Baer's examination of Castile's tax rolls at the
    end of the thirteenth century, implying that there were as few as 25,000
    Jews in all Iberia at that time. The more common estimate is a figure of ap-
    proximately 200,000 Jews at the time of the 1492 expulsion, though some
    estimates range as high as 800,000.

    For further discussion, two good places to start are L. P. Harvey, *Islamic
    Spain, 1250 to 1500* (Chicago: University of Chicago Press, 1990), pp. 6–9,
    which summarizes various research positions; and Joseph F. O'Callaghan,
    A History of Medieval Spain (Ithaca: Cornell University Press, 1975), pp.
    604–6; Pedro Chalmeta, "An Approximate Picture of the Economy of al-

Andalus," pp. 741–58 in *The Legacy of Muslim Spain,* ed. Salma Khadra Javvyusi (Leiden: E.J. Brill, 1992); Yitzhak Baer, *A History of the Jews in Christian Spain* (Philadelphia: Jewish Publication Society of America, 1961–66), 2 vols.; see esp vol. 1, pp. 189–197 for population of Jews in Spain; and Richard W. Bulliet, *Conversion to Islam in the Medieval Period: An Essay in Quantitative History* (Cambridge, MA: Harvard University Press, 1999), ch. 10, pp. 114–127.

16 *two in a year* David Ganz, "Book Production in the Carolingian Empire and the Spread of Caroline Minuscule" in Rosamond McKitterick, ed., *The New Cambridge Medieval History* (Cambridge: Cambridge University Press, 1995), vol. 2, pp. 791–792.

16 *fifteen pigs* Ibid., p. 793.

16 *devastating plagues ravaged* Paul Lagassé, ed. *The Columbia Encyclopedia,* 6th ed. (New York: Columbia University Press, 2000), p. 2241.

17 *"God raised [Isidore]* Sancti Braulionis, Caesaraugust. episcopi *Praenotatio librorum Isidori,* Migne, Patrologia Latina vol. 82, col. 65, in Brehaut, *An Encyclopedist,* p. 23.

18 *"An even number* Isidore of Seville, *Etymologiae,* bk, 3, ch. 5, no. 2; in Brehaut, *An Encyclopedist,* p. 127.

18 *"The Cynocephali are* Ibid., bk. 11, ch. 3, nos. 25, 17, 18, 19, 24; pp. 219–220.

18 *"Other fabulous monstrosities* Ibid., no. 28; p. 220.

19 *"after it comes* Ibid., bk 3, ch. 52, no. 1; p. 148.

19 *"skillful in the business* Ibid., bk 12, ch. 8, nos. 1–2; p. 232.

19 *"The world grows old* Eamon Duffy, *Saints and Sinners: A History of the Popes* (New Haven: Yale University Press, 1997), p. 48.

20 *"probably each art* Aristotle, *Metaphysics,* bk. 12, 1074b, 10–11, in Jonathan Barnes, ed., W. D. Ross, trans., *The Complete Works of Aristotle: The Revised Oxford Translation,* 2 vols. (Princeton: Princeton University Press, 1984), vol. 2, p. 1968.

20 *"whose king is truth* Augustine's letter to Marcellinus, epistle 138, in *Saint Augustine: Letters, Vol. 3, #131–164,* trans. Sister Wilfrid Parsons, S.N.D. (New York: Fathers of the Church, 1953), p. 50.

21 *"The remainder of* Isidore, bk. 5, ch. 39, no. 42; in Brehaut, *An Encyclopedist,* p. 182.

21 *"Of all the lands* Isidore of Seville, *History of the Kings of the Goths,* prologue, in Kenneth Baxter Wolf, trans., *Conquerors and Chroniclers of Early Medieval Spain* (Liverpool: Liverpool University Press, 1990), p. 81.

23 *"30,000 pounds* Jennifer Laing, *Warriors of the Dark Ages* (Phoenix Hill: Sutton Publishing, 2000), p. 22.

23   *"wanted to obliterate* Isidore, *Goths,* no. 15, in Wolf, *Conquerors,* p. 89.

25   *"With the help* Ibid.

26   *"After many victories* Isidore, *Goths,* in Baxter Wolf, *Conquerors and Chroniclers,* p. 80.

26   *according to their own nuanced* See Sura 19:21, and John L. Esposito, *What Everyone Needs to Know About Islam* (Oxford: Oxford University Press, 2002), pp. 31–32, for discussion of the virgin conception and birth as understood by Muslims.

27   *"the pride* Isidore, *Goths,* in Wolf, *Conquerors,* p. 82.

27   *"In the arts of war* Ibid., no. 69, in Wolf, *Conquerors,* p. 109.

Chapter 2

29   *mutilation of his own* Alberto Ferreiro, ed. *The Visigoths: Studies in Culture and Society* (Leiden: Brill, 1999), p. 133.

30   *"had to be cut off* Raúl González-Salerno, "Catholic anti-Judaism in Visigothic Spain," in Alberto Ferreiro, ed., *The Visigoths Studies in Culture and Society* (Leiden: Brill, 1999), p. 128.

30   *Gibraltar (Jabal Tariq* Though Gibraltar is undoubtedly a picturesque landmark from which to begin an invasion, some contemporary historians believe the invasion actually began closer to modern Cartagena and consider accounts citing Gibraltar as later poetic invention.

30   *"Whither can you fly* Ahmed ibn Mohammed al-Makkari, *The History of the Mohammedan Dynasties in Spain,* 2 vols., trans. Pascual de Gayangos (New York: Johnson Reprint Corporation, 1964), vol. 1, p. 271.

31   *"boil their flesh* Ibn al-Qutiyya, quoted in Colin Smith, ed. *Christians and Moors in Spain,* 3 vol. (Warminster, U.K.: Aris and Phillips, 1988), vol. 1, p. 5.

32   *Nothing of Muhammad's* John L. Esposito, *Islam: The Straight Path* (Oxford: Oxford University Press, 1988) is a key source for the exposition of Islam's basic tenets and early history as presented in this chapter.

33   *"The same religion* Quran 42:13, *The Holy Qur'an,* trans. Abdullah Yusuf Ali (London: Wordsworth Editions, 2000), p. 411.

35   *"Ye are the best* Quran, 3:110, p. 49.

36   *"Take not the Jews* Quran, 5:51, p. 88.

36   *"Let those fight* Quran, 4:74, p. 68.

36   *"To him who fighteth* Ibid.

37   *"I am the Lord* Exodus 20:2–3.

37   *"And those who don't* Theodosian Code, 16.1.2, in Henry Bettenson, ed.,

Documents of the Christian Church (London: Oxford University Press, 1943), p. 31.

38 *"And dispute ye not* Quran 29:46.

38 *The latter [Theodomir]* Al-Himyari, *Kitab al-Rawd al-Mitar,* 132–33, in Joseph F. O'Callaghan, *A History of Medieval Spain* (Ithaca: Cornell University Press, 1975), p. 94.

40 *In one particularly gruesome episode* Abdulw[a]hid Dhan{u}n T[a]ha, *The Muslim Conquest and Settlement of North Africa and Spain* (Routledge: London, 1989), p. 216.

41 *"Heed my warning* The Chronicle of Alfonso III, no. 9, in Wolf, *Conquerors,* p. 166.

41 *"turned back on those* Ibid., no. 10, p. 167.

41 *"Do not think this* Ibid., p. 168.

41 *"no other food* al-Makkari, *Mohammedan Dynasties,* vol. 2, p. 34.

Chapter 3

43 *"as they were looking* Acts 1:9.

43 *"You shall be my witnesses* Acts 1:8.

44 *"his face shone* Matthew 17:2.

44 *"bid fire come* Luke 9:54.

45 *"Command that these* Matthew 20:21.

45 *"Could you not watch* Matthew 26:40.

45 *"tongues as of fire* Acts 2:3.

45 *"I hope to see* Romans, 15:24.

46 *"his most holy remains* Richard Fletcher, *Saint James's Catapult: The Life and Times of Diego Gelmirez of Santiago de Compostela* (Oxford: Oxford University Press, 1984), p. 57.

51 *"The Franks were unwilling* Colin Smith, "The Geography and History of Iberia in the Liber Sancti Jacobi" in Maryjane Dunn and Linda Kay Davidson, eds., *The Pilgrimage to Compostela in the Middle Ages: A Book of Essays* (New York: Garland, 1996), p. 29.

51 *wily Compostela cleric* For a general discussion of Pseudo-Turpin, see H. M. Smyser, *The Pseudo-Turpin* (Cambridge, MA: The Medieval Academy of America, 1937).

52 *"writing-tablets* Lewis Thorpe, trans., *Einhard and Notker the Stammerer: Two Lives of Charlemagne* (London: Penguin, 1969), p. 79.

53 *"Santiago is . . . one* Al-Makkari, *Mohammedan Dynasties,* vol. 2, p. 193.

Chapter 4

56 *"the spirit of error"* Anonymous, *Istoria de Mahomet,* in Kenneth B. Wolf, "The Earliest Latin Lives of Muhammad," pp. 89–101, in *Conversion and Continuity, Indigenous Christian Communities in Islamic Lands, Eighth to Eighteenth Centuries,* ed. Michael Gervers and Ramzi Jibran Bikhazi (Toronto: Pontifical Institute of Mediaeval Studies, 1990), pp. 98 99.

56 *"dogs followed his* Ibid., p. 99.

56 *"It was appropriate that* Ibid.

58 *"Now hand down* Eulogius, *Memoriale Sanctorum,* 2.4, in Kenneth Baxter Wolf, *Christian Martyrs in Muslim Spain* (Cambridge: Cambridge University Press, 1988) p. 25.

58 *"killing all Christian* Ibid., 3.7.4; p. 19.

59 *"If stupid and idiotic* Paul Albar, *Vita Eulogii,* 5.15, in Wolf, *Christian Martyrs,* p. 61.

61 *"For when the psalmody* Eulogius, *Memoriale Sanctorum,* 1.21, in Wolf, *Christian Martyrs,* p. 101.

61 *Even Eulogius's own* Jessica Coope, *The Martyrs of Cordoba: Community and Family Conflict in an Age of Mass Conversion* (Lincoln: University of Nebraska Press, 1995), p. 21.

62 *"Bishop Reccafredus* Paul Albar, *Vita Eulogii,* 4, in Edward P. Colbert, *The Martyrs of Cordoba (850–859): A Study of the Sources* (Washington, DC: Catholic University of America Press, 1962), p. 176.

62 *"Bishop Reccafredus moved his tongue* Eulogius, *Memoriale Sanctorum,* 2.15.2, in Wolf, *Christian Martyrs,* p. 59.

62 *"I saw the skin* Eulogius, *Documentum Maryriale,* 21, in Wolf, *Christian Martyrs,* p. 66.

62 *"The news of your* Ibid.

63 *By the turn* For a discussion of the trend toward conversion to Islam in al-Andalus, see Richard W. Bulliet, *Conversion to Islam in the Medieval Period: An Essay in Quantitative History* (Cambridge, MA: Harvard University Press, 1979).

63 *"elevated with honors* Eulogius, *Memoriale,* 2.i.1, in Colbert, *Martyrs of Cordoba,* p. 194.

63 *"Do not all the Christian* Paul Albar, *Indiculus,* 35, in Colbert, *Martyrs of Cordoba,* p. 301.

64 *". . . a set of men* al-Makkari, *Mohammedan Dynasties,* vol. 1, p. 65.

64 *"God be praised* Ibid., p. 81.

64 *"His countenance inspired* Ibid., p. 94.

66 *"the soft down* Ibid., p. 119.

66 *"both men and women* Ibid., p. 120.

66 *"all wore their hair* Ibid., p. 120.

66 *"[took] away the fetid* Ibid.

66 *"through which the linen* Ibid.

66 *"change of clothing* Ibid., p. 121.

66 *"[the Christians] do not wash* al-Bakri, in Melville, *Christians and Moors,* vol. 3, p. 55.

67 *Thanks to Arab ingenuity* See Thomas F. Glick, *Irrigation and Society in Medieval Valencia* (Cambridge, MA: Belknap Press of Harvard University Press, 1970).

67 *Spanish agricultural and water* Ibid.

67 *"And [we] beheld Crónica* of King James, quoted in Colin Smith, *Christians and Moors in Spain* (Warminster: Aris & Phillips, 1989), vol. 2, p. 49.

68 *"not a single Christian* Ibn Khald[u]n, *Muqaddimah,* trans. F. Rosenthal (New York: Pantheon Books, 1958), vol. 2, p. 42.

69 *"all kinds of rare* al-Makkari, *Mohammedan Dynasties,* vol. 1, p. 210.

69 *"basins of different shapes* Ibid., p. 208.

69 *"pure gold and silver* Ibid., p. 237.

69 *"trembl[ing], thinking the* Ibid., p. 237.

69 *"carpeted with most costly* Abbot John of St. Arnulph, quoted in Colin Smith, *Christians and Moors in Spain, vol. I, 711–1150* (Warminster: Aris & Phillips, 1993), pp. 71–73.

Chapter 5

72 *"have a most subtle* MS San Lorenzo del Escorial, codex Vigilanus, lat. D.I.2, fol. 9v//*The Introduction of Arabic Learning into England* Charles Burnett (London: British Library, 1997), p. 12.

77 *The Britons Adelard of Bath* In fact, there is no documentary evidence that Adelard studied in Spain; many historians have concluded he did because his famous translations of al-Khwarizmi drew from an Iberian edition of the work.

Chapter 6

79 *"to send down confusion* al-Makkari, vol. 2, p. 193.

79 *"were we to enumerate* Ibid., p. 193.

80 *"None of the Moslem* Ibid., p. 193.

80   *"nobody could have* Ibid., p. 195.

81   *"send down confusion* al-Makkari, vol. 2, p. 193.

82   *"Go from your country* Genesis 12:1–2.

82   *"strangers and exiles* Hebrews 11:13.

82   *"If they had been thinking* Hebrews 11: 15–16.

83   *"Three times a year* Deuteronomy: 16:16.

83   *"went to Jerusalem* Luke 2:41.

84   *"so many people* Jonathan Sumption, *Pilgrimage: An Image of Medieval Religion* (London: Faber & Faber, 1975), p. 116.

84   *busiest long-distance highway* Ibid., p. 116.

85   *Roger da Bonito* Ibid., p. 100.

85   *another pilgrim went* Ibid., p. 107.

85   *"barefoot and naked* Diana Webb, *Pilgrims and Pilgrimage in Medieval Europe* (London: J.B. Tauris, 1999), pp. 52–53.

85   *another adulterer,* Ibid.

87   *A man struggling* "The Miracles of Saint James," pp. 57–96, in *The Miracles of Saint James: Translations from the Liber Sancti Jacobi,* trans. Thomas F. Coffey, Linda Kay Davidson, and Maryjane Dunn (New York: Italica Press, 1996), pp. 70–72.

87   *a sailor named Frisonius* Ibid., pp. 72–73.

87   *an Italian named Bernard* Ibid., p. 77.

87   *another Italian was healed* Ibid., p. 77–78.

87   *"could contain himself* Ibid., p. 84.

87   *"showed his scars* Coffey, *The Miracles,* no. 17, p. 89.

87   *"oblivious, raging, idiotic* "The 'Veneranda Dies' Sermon," pp. 8–56, in *The Miracles of Saint James,* p. 32.

87   *"for the sake of ravishing* Ibid., p. 36.

88   *"Since a multitude* Innocent IV, *Les Registres d'Innocent IV,* ed. E. Berger, quoted in Webb, 101.

89   *The famous twelfth-century sermon* "The 'Veneranda Dies' Sermon," *The Miracles of Saint James,* pp. 8–56.

89   *"show [pilgrims] the best* Ibid., p. 34.

89   *"very large on the outside* Ibid., p. 35.

90   *"their legs and arms* Ibid., p. 41.

90   *"They do not want* Ibid.

90   *"seated on its banks* The Pilgrim's Guide to Santiago de Compostela, trans. William Melczer (New York: Italica Press, 1993), p. 94.

90   *"If you saw them* Ibid., p. 94.

90   *"The Navarrese also* Ibid. p. 95.

91   *"fat as pigs and* Hieronymus Munzer in 1496, quoted in Jonathan Sump-

tion, *Pilgrimage: An Image,* p. 167.

91 *"For great joy* Webb, p. 71.

91 *"the highest achievement* "Samuel Ha-Nagid" in Cecil Roth, ed., *Encyclopedia Judaica* (Jerusalem: Keter Publishing House, 1971), vol. 14, p. 816.

Chapter 7

94 *two dozen petty Muslim kingdoms* These are typically known as the "taifas" or "party" states after the various factions who seized control across al-Andalus. Some historians estimate that there were as many as forty such states in the most chaotic period of taifa rule. For a general discussion of this period and a listing of the kingdoms, see David Wasserstein, *The Rise and Fall of the Party Kings* (Princeton: Princeton University Press, 1985).

95 *"Spanish Jews were,* Salvador de Madariaga, *Spain: A Modern History* (New York: Praeger, 1958), p. 18.

95 *third-century tombstone* "Spain" in Roth, *Encyclopedia Judaica,* vol. 15, p. 220.

96 *"left them in charge* al-Makkari, vol. 1, p. 280.

96 *"This practice became* Ibid.

97 *"Turn your eyes* Abu Ishaq, in Olivia Remie, ed., *Medieval Iberia: Readings from Christian, Muslim, and Jewish Sources* (Philadelphia: University of Pennsylvania Press, 1997), p. 98.

97 *"the David of my age* Leon J. Weinberger, trans., *Jewish Prince in Muslim Spain: Selected Poems of Samuel Ibn Nagrela* (University, AL: University of Alabama Press, 1973), p. 1.

97 *"This cursed man* Ibn Hayyan, quoted in Ross Brann, *Power in the Portrayal: Representations of Jews and Muslims in Eleventh- and Twelfth-Century Islamic Spain* (Princeton: Princeton University Press, 2002), p. 36.

97 *A monarch will not* The Monarch's Favors, in Leon J. Weinberger, *Jewish Prince* p. 61.

98 *"And the fire* The Battle of Alfuente, in ibid., p. 26.

98 *"And the Lord heard* Ibid., p. 26.

98 *"And He blew* Ibid.

99 *Samuel served as* nagid For a discussion of the role, see "Nagid" in Roth, *Encyclopedia Judaica,* vol. 12, p. 758.

99 *Joseph, all that I,* Weinberger, *Jewish Prince,* p. 63.

100 *With your life* A Letter on the Eve of the Battle of Lorca, in ibid,, p. 63.

100 *He [Granada's king]* Abu Ishaq, in Bernard Lewis, *Islam in History: Ideas,*

Men and Events in the Middle East, 2nd ed. (Chicago: Open Court, 1993), pp. 168–169.

Chapter 8

105   *"Better be a mule* al-Makkari, vol. 2, p. 273.

105   *"agreeable to God* Ibid., p. 273.

106   *daughter-in-law, Zaida* For more on the alliance, Sancho, and Zaida, see Colin Smith, *Christians and Moors,* vol. 1, pp. 104–105.

107   *"They displayed the symbol De Expugnatione Lyxbonensi: The Conquest of Lisbon,* ed. and trans. Charles Wendell David (New York: Columbia University Press, 1936), p. 133.

109   *Still, ten thousand Crusaders* Brian Moynahan, *The Faith: A History of Christianity* (New York: Doubleday, 2002), p. 239.

109   *"the blood of the Saracens* Ibid., p. 239.

110   *"We wrote to you* Letter of Pope Paschal II, quoted in Joseph F. O'Callaghan, *Reconquest and Crusade in Medieval Spain* (Philadelphia: University of Pennsylvania Press, 2003), p. 34.

110   *but ideas emerge* Historians are divided on the impact of the Almoravid model on the Crusader ideal. For a summary (and somewhat skeptical conclusion) concerning the Almoravid influence, see Joseph F. O'Callaghan, "The Affliation of the Order of Calatrava with the Order of Citeaux," in *The Spanish Military Order of Calatrava and Its Affiliates: Collected Studies* (London: Variorum Reprints, 1975), esp. pp. 176–178.

111   *Rubet ensis* Walter Starkie, *The Road to Santiago: Pilgrims of St. James* (New York: E. P. Dutton & Company, 1957), p. 42.

111   *"The brethren should* The *Rule of the Spanish Order of St. James 1170–1493: Latin and Spanish Texts, edited with Apparatus Criticus,* trans. Enrique Gallego Blanco (Leiden: E.J. Brill, 1971), rule 99.

111   *"beat[ing] [one's] wife* Ibid., rule 127.

112   *He was flogged* Ibid.

113   *Sheep and cattle ranching* For a more detailed discussion of Spain's medieval frontier history, see various works of Charles Julian Bishko, including *Studies in Medieval Frontier History* (London: Variorum Reprints, 1980).

114   *3 million sheep* O'Callaghan, *A History,* p. 617.

114   *animal had become extinct* Paul Lagassé, ed. *The Columbia Encyclopedia* 6th ed. (New York: Columbia University Press, 2000), p. 1318.

115   *"remain, held as a* James William Brodman, *Ransoming Captives in Crusader Spain: The Order of Merced on the Christian-Islamic Frontier* (Philadelphia: University of Pennsylvania Press, 1986), p. 111.

Chapter 9

121 *"There is no castle* Burgess, *Roland,* no. 1/4–5.

122 *"To try to bring* Ibid., no. 31/404–405.

122 *"High are the hills* Ibid., no. 66.

122 *"It is our duty* Ibid., no. 79/1009–1012.

122 *"splits his breast* Ibid., 93/1200–1201.

122 *"He smites both his eyes* Ibid., no. 106/1355–1356.

123 *"and gave a feeble* Ibid., no. 156/2104.

123 *"bear the count's soul* Ibid., no. 176/2396.

123 *"does not love God* Ibid., no. 1/7–8.

124 *"Rushing down on* Einhard and Notker the Stammerer, *Two Lives of Charlemagne,* trans. L. Thorpe (Harmondsworth: Penguin, 1969), pp. 64–65.

125 *"hoist Mohammed on high* Burgess, *Roland,* no. 68/853–854.

125 *"May Muhammad, who* Ibid., no. 195/2711–2712.

125 *"The pagans are wrong* Ibid., no. 79/1015.

125 *"Out in front* Ibid., no. 114/1470–1474.

125 *"Help us now* Ibid., no. 89/1129, 1134–1135.

125 *"As penance he* Ibid., no. 89/1138.

126 *"Vast are the forces* Ibid., no. 190/2630.

126 *"They are a race* Ibid., no. 239/3247, 3249–3250.

126 *"Charles, summon your* Ibid., no. 298/3994, 3998.

127 *"had no wish to go* Ibid., no. 298/3999.

127 *"God . . . how wearisome* Ibid., no. 298/4.

127 *"the rocks are dull-hued* Ibid., no. 66/815–816.

127 *His victory notwithstanding* Scholars have grasped at more sinister interpretations. Medieval chronicles vaguely allude to some enormous sin in the king's past, and some scholars have in turn conjectured (with little basis) that Roland is not Charlemagne's nephew but a son born of an incestuous union. In this interpretation, the gloom that never lifts from *Roland's* Charlemange is the never-spoken but ever present awareness of his unnatural act. Charlemagne's guilt is only compounded when Roland's self-sacrifice symbolically expiates his father's trespass against nature.

Chapter 10

129 *"Tears streamed* Rita Hamilton and Janet Perry, trans., *The Poem of the Cid* (New York: Penguin, 1984), no. 1, p. 1.

129 *"I give Thee thanks* Ibid., no. 1, pp. 8–9.

130 *"Per Abbat wrote it* Ibid., no. 152/3732.

130 *Whoever shaped* See Joseph J. Duggan, *The Cantar de Mio Cid: Poetic Creation in Its Economic and Social Contexts* (Cambridge: Cambridge University Press, 1989) and A. D. Deyermond, *Mio Cid Studies* (London: Tamesis Books, 1977). Both outline various scholarly viewpoints on the poem's authorship, date of composition, means of transmission, and other debates that continue to occupy academicians.

131 *"beat[ing] them with* Hamilton, *Cid* no. 128/2736–2746.

131 *"we are raised* Ibid., no. 141/3299–3300.

132 *"Because you [infantes]* Ibid., no. 146/3367–3369.

132 *"It was an honor* Ibid., no. 143/3313–3314.

132 *"May such a fate* Ibid., no. 152/3706–3707.

132 *"Today the Kings* Ibid., no. 152/3724–3725.

133 *"The Spanish kings* Anonymous, *Historia Silense,* ch. 8, in *The World of El Cid: Chronicles of the Spanish Reconquest,* trans. Simon Barton and Richard Fletcher (Manchester, England: Manchester University Press, 2000), p. 30.

134 *"the dwelling of all* Ibn Har[i]q, in *Hispano-Arabic Poetry and Its Relations with the Old Provencal Troubadors,* trans. A. R. Nykl (Baltimore: J. H. Furst, 1946), p. 331.

134 *"what a good vassal* Hamilton, *Cid,* no. 1/20.

134 *"The Cid comes* Ibid., no. 82.

135 *"pains as when* Ibid., no. 18/374.

136 *"[I] came here* Ibid., no. 116/2371–2372.

136 *"until, on my good* Ibid., no. 24.

136 *"When the Cid* Ibid., no. 46/853–856.

137 *"Had he been a* Burgess, *Roland,* no. 72/899.

137 *"for the love* Hamilton, *Cid,* no. 126/2658.

138 *"to become a convert* Burgess, *Roland,* no. 272/3674.

138 *"with iron hammers* Ibid., no. 272/3663.

138 *They take the pagans* Ibid., no. 272/3668–3671.

138 *precursor of the Crusades* O'Callaghan, *A History,* p. 197.

138 *"[He] therefore decided* al-Makkari, *Mohammedan Dynasties,* vol. 2, p. 266.

139 *"it was announced* Ibid., 277.

139 *"It was an invariable* Ibid.

139 *"The devil . . . out* Quoted in Colin Smith, *Christians and Moors,* p. 85.

139 *"the Emperor of the* Scholars debate whether in fact Alfonso employed this title. For a discussion of the controversy, see Angus MacKay and M'Hammad Benaboud, "Yet again Alfonso VI, 'the Emperor, Lord of [the adherents of] the Two Faiths, the Most Excellent Ruler': A Rejoinder to Norman Roth," *Bulletin of Hispanic Studies* vol. 61, no. 2 (April 1984), pp. 171–179.

140   *"Alfonso began to govern"* al-Makkari, vol. 2, p. 264.

140   *"Seeing that he"* Ibid.

Chapter 11

144   *"Thou [Jesus] didst allow"* Hamilton, *Cid*, no. 18/346–347.

145   *Jewish Golden Age* See, for example, "Spain" in Roth, *Encyclopedia Judaica*, vol. 15, p. 227.

145   *"the most illustrious figure"* "Maimonides, Moses" in Roth, *Encyclopedia Judaica*, vol. 11, p. 754.

145   *"the outstanding representative"* Jane S. Gerber, *The Jews of Spain: A History of the Sephardic Experience* (New York: The Free Press, 1992), p. 79.

146   *"had become so bold"* Al-Bayan al-Mugrib, I, 204 in O'Callaghan, *History of Medieval*, p. 286.

147   *"I am obliged"* Maimonides, letter to Rabbi Samuel Ibn Tibbon, in Fred Rosner, M.D., *Sex Ethics in the Writings of Moses Maimonides* (New York: Bloch, 1974), p. 4.

147   *"even while lying"* Ibid., p. 5.

147   *"regimen that is"* Treatise on Cohabitation, ch. 1, in ibid., p. 17.

147   *"a wondrous secret"* Ibid., p. 27.

148   *"acute fever, sticking"* Maimonides, *Medical Aphorisms*, in Fred Rosner, M.D., *The Medical Legacy of Moses Maimonides* (Hoboken, NJ: KTAV Publishing, 1998), p. 91.

150   *"seeing the abundance"* David C. Lindberg, ed., *Science in the Middle Ages* (Chicago: University of Chicago Press, 1978), p. 65.

150   *"wise man who"* Ibid.

151   *Salamanca was still using* María Teresa Herrera, "Medicine" in E. Michael Gerli, ed., *Medieval Iberia: An Encyclopedia* (New York: Routledge, 2002), p. 554.

151   *The physician to tenth-century* Margarita Castells, "Medicine in al-Andalus until the Fall of the Caliphate," in *The Formation of al-Andalus, Part 2: Language, Religion, Culture and the Sciences,* ed. Maribel Fierro and Julio Samsó (Ashgate: Variorum, 1998), p. 395.

151   *"Let calcine [i.e., burn]"* Charles H. La Wall, *Four Thousand Years of Pharmacy: An Outline History of Pharmacy and the Allied Sciences* (Philadelphia: J.B. Lippincott, 1927), p. 124.

152   *"Although their [the physicians']"* Avicenna's *Canon,* quoted in Danielle Jacquart, "Medical Scholasticism," in Mirko D. Grmek, ed., *Western Medical Thought from Antiquity to the Middle Ages* (Cambridge, MA: Harvard University Press, 1998), p. 218.

153   *"To consult physicians* Roy Porter, *The Greatest Benefit to Mankind: A Medical History of Humanity* (New York: Norton, 1997), p. 110.

153   *"[We] order and strictly* Norman P. Tanner, S.J., ed., *Decrees of the Ecumenical Councils, Vol. I* (New York: Sheed and Ward, 1990), decree 22, p. 245.

154   *"Against dysentery, a bramble* La Wall, p. 123.

155   *"Comparing the air* Maimonides, *Regimen of Health,* ch 4, no. 2, in Fred Rosner, trans., *Moses Maimonides' Three Treatises on Health: Maimonides' Medical Writings* (Haifa. Maimonides Research Institute, 1990), p 74.

156   *"One must pay attention* Ibid., ch. 3, no. 13, p. 61.

156   *"These situations can* Ibid.

Chapter 12

157   *"A person should not sleep* Maimonides, *Book of Knowledge: Laws of Human Temperaments,* ch. 4, no. 5, in Rosner, *Three Treatises,* p. 193.

158   *"Seven pairs of all clean* Genesis 7:2.

159   *"a man who first reads* Maimonides, *Mishneh Torah,* introduction, 5a, quoted in Ralph Lerner, *Maimonides' Empire of Light: Popular Enlightenment in an Age of Belief* (Chicago: University of Chicago Press, 2000), p. 140.

159   *"In that era* Moses Maimonides, *Mishneh Torah,* b. 14, ch. 5, 12, no. 4, ed. Philip Birnbaum (New York: Hebrew Publishing Co., 1967), p. 329.

159   *"The things that are now* Ibid.

159   *"Let us make man* Genesis I:26.

160   *"which no other creature* Maimonides, *The Guide for the Perplexed,* 2nd ed., trans. M. Friedlander (New York: Dover, 1956), p. 14, emphasis added.

160   *"harmonize the law* Moses Maimonides, *Treatise on Resurrection,* trans. Hillel Fradkin, in Lerner, *Maimonides' Empire of Light: Popular Enlightenment in an Age of Belief,* p. 52.

160   *"formed man of dust* Genesis 2:6–7.

160   *"and the writing was* Exodus 32:16.

160   *"Most ignorant of human* Maimonides *Treatise on Resurrection,* in Lerner, pp. 155–156.

161   *soul, freed of the meddlesome* In fact, Maimonides postulated a rather complicated theory of afterlife: body and soul would *temporarily* be reunited after a bodily resurrection, but the body would eventually die once again, giving way to an eternal afterlife enjoyed by the spiritual intellect (or soul) alone. See the "Treatise on Resurrection" and related commentary in Ralph Lerner, *Maimonides' Empire of Light.* Also, "Maimonidean Controversy" in Roth, *Encyclopedia Judaica,* vol. 11, p. 776.

161   *"Their hope had turned* Ha-Yarhi, in Bernard Septimus, *Hispano-Jewish*

Culture in Transition: The Career and Controversies of Ramah (Cambridge, MA: Harvard University Press, 1982), p. 41.

161 *"Only their souls* Ibid.

161 *"And many of those* Daniel 12: 2.

161 *"In what way is the soul* Meir ha-Levi Abulafia, in Septimus, *Hispano-Jewish* p. 58.

162 *The controversy featured* Ibid., p. 66.

162 *"Our knowledge," he wrote* Maimonides *Guide,* p. 85.

162 *"endeavor to extol* Ibid., p. 83.

162 *"Commune with your own heart* Psalm 4:4; Maimonides, *Guide,* p. 85.

162 *"When a person contemplates* Maimonides, *Mishneh Torah,* in Isadore Twersky, *Introduction to the Code of Maimonides* (New Haven: Yale University Press, 1980), pp. 215–216.

163 *"Companions with beautiful* Quran 56:22, 465–466.

Chapter 13

165 *"God's commands, and* Daniel Defoe, *Robinson Crusoe,* ed. A. Ross (London: Penguin, 1965), pp. 222–223.

166 *"allowing mankind to fall* Ibn Tufayl's *Hayy Ibn Yaqz[u]n,* trans. Lenn Evan Goodman (New York: Twayne, 1972), no. 146, p. 161.

166 *"amassing of wealth* Ibid.

167 *"outstanding character, brilliant* Ibid., no. 147, p. 162.

167 *"most men are no better* Ibid., no. 153, p. 164.

168 *"[He] imitated the* Ibid., no. 115, p. 146.

168 *"Thus he could eat* Ibid., no. 112, pp. 144–145.

169 *"If the function of philosophy* Abu'l Walid Muhammad ibn Rushd, "The Definitive Statement Determining the Relationship Between Divine Law and Human Wisdom," in *Two Andalusian Philosophers,* trans. Jim Colville (London: Kegan Paul International, 1999), p. 76.

169 *"then scriptural interpretation* Averroes, *Definitive Statement* in Ibid., p. 81.

169 *"is to bar the door* Ibid., p. 80.

169 *bulwarks of Islamic Law* For a broader discussion of the foundations of Islamic Law and its history, see Esposito, *Islam: The Straight Path,* pp. 69–88.

170 *early tenth century* Jim Colville *Two Andalusian Philosophers* (London: Kegan Paul International, 1999), p. xvi.

170 *"You who have eyes* Ibid., p. 76, quoting Quran 54:2.

170 *"The ability of women* Averroes' *Commentary on Plato's Republic,* ed. and trans., E. I. J. Rosenthal (Cambridge: Cambridge University Press, 1956), p. 166.

170 *"it is not impossible* Ibid., p. 165.

171 *"So seems to be the case* Ibid., p. 223.

171 *"rediscovery of the philosophical* Etienne Gilson, *History of Christian Philoso-phy in the Middle Ages* (New York: Random House, 1955), p. 278.

172 *"most perfect and glorious* John of Jandun in "Latin Averroism" in Berard L. Marthaler, ed. *New Catholic Encyclopedia,* 2nd ed. (New York: Gale, 2003), vol. 1, pp. 936–937.

174 *whether to stone to death* For analysis of *sharia* and such a case in Nigeria, see Patrick J. Ryan, S.J., "Ready to Cast the First Stone" in *America,* vol. 187, no. 17 (Nov. 25, 2002), pp. 12–14.

174 *"a landmark in the history* Gilson, *History of Christian,* p. 408.

174 *"Behold, the man* Genesis 3:22.

175 *"Turn from thy fierce wrath* Exodus 32: 12.

Chapter 14

177 *"This is the Imam* Ibn Al 'Arabi, *al- Fut[ū]h[ā]t al-makkiyyah* I, p. 153, in R. W. J. Austin, trans., *The Bezels of Wisdom* (New York: Paulist Press, 1980), p. 7.

177 *"Yes and No.* Ibid., p. 2.

179 *"would spin around* Goodman, *Hayy ibn Yaqzan,* no. 116–117, pp. 146–147.

179 *"At last it came* Ibid., no. 121, p. 149.

179 *"From of old no one* Isaiah 64:4.

179 *"What no eye has seen* 1 Corinthians 2:9.

179 *"so devoted to the* R. W. J. Austin, trans., *Sufis of Andalusia: The R[u]h al-quds and al-Durrat al-f[a]khirah of Ibn Arabi* (Berkeley: University of Cali-fornia Press, 1971), p. 134.

180 *"never settled in any* Ibid., p. 138.

180 *"nights were spent in prayer* Ibid., p. 92.

180 *"one of the lovers* Austin, *Bezels of Wisdom,* pp. 3–4.

180 *"I have penetrated* Austin, *Bezels,* p. 91.

181 *"You [created beings] are* Ibid., p. 94.

181 *"He praises me* Ibid., p. 95.

181 *"greatest mystical genius* Arthur J. Arberry, *An Introduction to the History of Sufism* (New Delhi: Orient Longman, 1942), p. 58.

181 *"yearns for itself* Austin, *Bezels,* p. 274.

181 *"The Beloved longs to see me* Ibid., p. 273.

181 *"Thus . . . the man yearn[s]* Ibid., p. 274.

182 *"My heart has become capable* Reynold A. Nicholson, trans., *The Tarjuman*

al-Ashwaq: A Collection of Mystical Odes by Muhyi'ddin ibn al-'Arabi, II, 13–15 (London: Theosophical Publishing House, 1978), p. 67.

Chapter 15

183 *Devotees of mysticism* See Catherine Swietlicki, *Spanish Christian Cabala: The Works of Luis de Leon, Santa Teresa de Jesús, and San Juan de la Cruz* (Columbia: University of Missouri Press, 1986).

183 *both said to have been* For St. Teresa, see Norman Roth, "Conversos," in Gerli, *Medieval Iberia,* p. 255.

183 *"If I told them* Daniel Chanan Matt, trans., *Zohar: The Book of Enlightenment* (New York: Paulist Press, 1983), p. 4.

184 *For much of the sixteenth* Gershom G. Scholem, *Major Trends in Jewish Mysticism,* 3rd ed. (New York: Schocken, 1941), p. 156.

184 *"He is hidden* Matt, *Zohar,* p. 65.

185 *"Male and female He created* Ibid., p. 56.

185 *"Any image that does not* Ibid., p. 55.

185 *"He is now male and female* Gershom G. Scholem, ed. *Zohar: The Book of Splendor* (New York: Schocken, 1949), p. 34.

185 *"It is his duty* Scholem, *Zohar,* p. 35.

188 *"We avail ourselves of what* Averroes, *Definitive Statement,* in Colville, pp. 78–79.

Chapter 16

191 *But medieval Spain would cast* Twelfth-century Queen Urraca of Castile is one of few notable exceptions.

193 *The battle of Las Navas de Tolosa* See, for example, O'Callaghan, *A History,* pp. 245–249.

193 *chained to one another* Derek W. Lomax *The Reconquest of Spain* (New York: Longman, 1978), p. 127.

193 *"On their side* Demetrio Mansilla, *La Documentación Pontificia hasta Inocencio III (965–1216)* (Rome: 1955), 514, quoted in Joseph F. O'Callaghan, *A History of Medieval Spain* (Ithaca: Cornell University Press, 1975), p. 248.

194 *"taste of disaster* Ibn 'Idhari, *al-Bayan al-mughrib,* in Colin Smith and Ahmad Ubaydli, eds., *Christians and Moors in Spain* (Warminster: Aris and Phillips, 1988), vol. 3, p. 145.

194 *Sevillians were slowly starving* see Joseph F. O'Callaghan, *Reconquest and*

Crusade in Medieval Spain (Philadelphia: University of Pennsylvania Press, 2003), p. 144.

194   *"had the appearance of a great Primera crónica general de España* of Alfonso X, quoted in Olivia Remie-Constable, ed., *Medieval Iberia: Readings from Christian, Muslim, and Jewish Sources* (Philadelphia: University of Pennsylvania Press, 1997).

194   *"destroy[ing] all amenities,* Ibid., p. 145.

195   *launched the severed* O'Callaghan, *Reconquest,* pp. 138–139.

195   *"stagger[ed] around like drunkards,* Remie-Constable, p. 145.

197   *It is chiseled in Latin,* Sepulcros del Arco, 107, 230–231, quoted in Joseph F. O'Callaghan, *Alfonso X and the Cantigas de Santa María: A Poetic Biography* (Leiden: Brill, 1998), p. 55.

Chapter 17

199   *"with esteem,"* "Declaration on the Relationship of the Church to Non-Christian Religions," in Walter M. Abbott, S.J., ed., *The Documents of Vatican II* (New York: Herder and Herder, 1966), p. 663.

199   *"urged all . . . to strive* Ibid.

199   *"Mindful of her common* Ibid., p. 666. Though it's common to refer to decrees of the ecumenical council, in fact conciliar decrees are formally promulgated not by the council members but by the pope.

199   *"damnable mixing* Norman P. Tanner, S.J., ed., *Decrees of the Ecumenical Councils, Vol. 1* (New York: Sheed and Ward, 1990), decree no. 68, p. 266.

199   *"by mistake Christians join* Ibid.

200   *"That such persons* Ibid.

200   *Within a few years* Jeffrey Richards, *Sex, Dissidence and Damnation: Minority Groups in the Middle Ages* (London: Routledge, 1990), p. 109.

200   *Jews in Paris* Norman Roth, *Jews, Visigoths, and Muslims in Medieval Spain: Cooperation and Conflict* (Leiden: E. J. Brill, 1994), pp. 115, 167–168.

200   *"Jews of your diocese* Honorius III to Archbishop of Toledo, Nov. 24, 1221, in Solomon Grayzel, *The Church and the Jews in the XIIIth Century: A Study of Their Relations During the Years 1198–1254, Based on the Papal Letters and the Conciliar Decrees of the Period* 2nd ed. (New York: Hermon Press, 1966), p. 169.

200   *"beg and earnestly* Ibid., p. 207.

200   *"one round patch of yellow* Gregory IX to Thibaut I of Navarre, in Ibid., p. 217.

200   *"in large measure neglected* 1228, Council of Valladolid, in Ibid., p. 319. "In large measure" neglected throughout Iberia, though by no means com-

pletely neglected: in the realms of Aragon, King Jaime I had imposed the badge in 1228. See Jeffrey Richards, *Sex, Dissidence and Damnation: Minority Groups in the Middle Ages* (London: Routledge, 1990), p. 108.

200   *"serious misfortune may befall* Honorius III to Archbishop of Toledo, March 20, 1219, in Grayzel, p. 151.

200   *"choose rather to flee* Ibid., p. 151.

202   *First established by Muslims* See the introduction to James F. Powers, trans., *The Code of Cuenca Municipal Law on the Twelfth-Century Castilian Frontier,* (Philadelphia: University of Pennsylvania Press, 2000).

202   *"whoever may come* Powers, *The Code of Cuenca Municipal Law on the Twelfth-Century Castilian Frontier*, I, no. 10, p. 31.

202   *"The Moors of Chivert* Chivert Charter, in Robert Ignatius Burns, S.J., *Medieval Colonialism: Postcrusade Exploitation of Islamic Valencia* (Princeton: Princeton University Press, 1975), p. 142.

202   *When French armies* Ibid., p. 144.

203   *"to which both Christians* James I regulation of 1258, quoted in Burns, p. 51.

203   *The King Jaime who* It is also worth noting that the royal treasury extracted a licensing fee for awarding each municipality's bakeoven permit, one of myriad ways for medieval monarchs to augment their perennially constrained financial resources.

203   *As the harvest approached* Elena Lourie, "Anatomy of Ambivalence: Muslims under the Crown of Aragon in the Late Thirteenth Century," in *Crusade and Colonisation: Muslims, Christians and Jews in Medieval Aragon* (Hampshire: Variorum, 1990), p. 17.

204   *The most intimate* James F. Powers, "Frontier Municipal Baths and Social Interaction in Thirteenth Century Spain," *American Historical Review* 84, no. 3 (June 1979), pp. 649–667, is a fascinating treatment of communal baths on the Iberian frontier.

204   *Christian men used Teruel's* Powers, "Frontier Municipal Baths and Social Interaction in Thirteenth Century Spain." For women bathers, see Heath Dillard, *Daughters of the Reconquest: Women in Castilian Town Society, 1100–1300* (Cambridge: Cambridge University Press, 1984), p. 148.

204   *The five hundred Jews* See Teofilo F. Ruiz, *Crisis and Continuity: Land and Town in Late Medieval Castile* (Philadelphia: University of Pennsylvania Press, 1994), p. 273.

204   *A medieval census reveals* Teofilo F. Ruiz, *Crisis and Continuity*, p. 277–278.

205   *Indeed, they supplied their healing*, Ibid., p. 275.

205   *"slaughter beasts in our markets* Remie-Constable, *Medieval Iberia*, p. 98.

205   *Christian butchers in Valencia* In 1301. See Lourie, *Anatomy of Ambivalence*, p. 58 n. 178; Burns, *Medieval Colonialism*, p. 46.

205 *The "second Moses" suggested,* Roth, *Jews, Visigoths,* p. 183.

205 *The fourteenth-century Muslim* Ibid., p. 132.

205 *In nearby Borja* John Boswell, *The Royal Treasure: Muslim Communities Under the Crown of Aragon in the Fourteenth Century* (New Haven: Yale University Press, 1977), p. 68.

206 *A late thirteenth-century Tarazona* Lourie, *Anatomy of Ambivalence,* p. 69.

206 *Witness the poignant story* Grayzel, *Church and the Jews,* p. 97.

207 *Slave owners of all three* Lourie, *Anatomy of Ambivalence,* p. 71.

207 *"I have a girl among* Ibn Haddad, in Melville, *Christians and Moors,* vol. 3, p. 75.

207 *"By the hand of the* Norman Roth *Jews, Visigoths, and Muslims in Medieval Spain: Cooperation and Conflict* (Leiden: E. J. Brill, 1994), p. 191.

207 *But more than a few medieval* Mark D. Meyerson, *The Muslims of Valencia in the Age of Fernando and Isabel: Between Coexistence and Crusade* (Berkeley: University of California Press, 1991), p. 221.

208 *"If you know how to preserve Primera crónica general,* quoted in Joseph F. O'Callaghan, "Image and Reality: The King Creates His Kingdom," in Robert I. Burns, S.J., ed., *Emperor of Culture: Alfonso X the Learned of Castile and His Thirteenth-Century Renaissance* (Philadelphia: University of Pennsylvania Press, 1990), p. 15.

Chapter 18

209 *Thanks to the military* For Alfonso X's inherited domains, see Joseph F. O'Callaghan, "Image and Reality: The King Creates His Kingdom," in Robert I. Burns, S.J., ed., *Emperor of Culture: Alfonso X the Learned of Castile and His Thirteenth-Century Renaissance* (Philadelphia: University of Pennsylvania Press, 1990), p. 16.

211 *one Muslim chronicler* Ibn Abi Zar. See O'Callaghan, *A History,* p. 376.

211 *"no renewal of clothes* Chronicle of Alfonso X, trans. Shelby Thacker and José Escobar (Lexington: University Press of Kentucky, 2002), p. 227.

211 *"falling dead in the streets,* Ibid., p. 228.

211 *"so few and injured,* Ibid., p. 229.

212 *painful degenerative cancer* O'Callaghan, *Poetic Biography,* p. 132.

212 *(A fifteenth-century Muslim* See Ibid., p. 69.

212 *heart be removed* Ibid., p. 98.

213 *wiser Alfonso revolutionized* For a collection of essays examining Alfonso's wide-ranging cultural contributions, see Robert I. Burns, S.J., ed., *Emperor of Culture: Alfonso X the Learned of Castile and His Thirteenth-Century Renaissance.*

215 *"Whoever puts his backside* James F. Powers, trans., *The Code of Cuenca Municipal Law on the Twelfth-Century Castilian Frontier* (Philadelphia: University of Pennsylvania Press, 2000), ch. 12, no. 29, p. 91.

215 *One learns when a man Las Siete Partidas,* trans. Samuel Parsons Scott, ed Robert I. Burns, S.J. (Philadelphia: University of Pennsylvania Press: 2001), vol. 3: partida 3, title 28, law 22, p. 827.

215 *"nasty, brutish, and short* Thomas Hobbes, *Leviathan,* Richard Tuck, ed. (Cambridge: Cambridge University Press, 1991), pt. 1, ch. 13, p. 89.

215 *"kill both parties* Parsons Scott, *Siete Partidas,* 7, 17, 14, vol. 5, p. 1417.

215 *"complains of great hunger* Ibid., 4, 17, 8, vol. 4, p. 962.

216 *"eat his son without* Ibid.

216 *Even though Jesus had famously* Mark 12:17.

217 *"go to the door* Parsons Scott, *Siete Partidas,* 3, 11, 21, vol. 3, p. 641.

217 *"by that God than Partidas,* title 11, law 21, vol. 3, p. 641.

217 *"all the accusations* Ibid., p. 1303.

217 *"the marvelous and holy acts* Ibid., title 24, laws 1–11, vol. 5, p. 1433.

217 *"We have heard* Ibid., 7, 17, 2, vol. 5, p. 1433.

217 *"stealing children* Ibid.

217 *"where the name of God* Ibid., law 4, p. 1434. For further background, see Dwayne E. Carpenter, "Tolerance and Intolerance: Alfonso X's Attitude towards the Synagogue as Reflected in the Siete Partidas," *Kentucky Romance Quarterly* 31, no. 1 (1984): pp. 31–39.

217 *"by observing their own law Partidas,* pt. 25, law 1, p. 1438.

218 *"for no one can love* Ibid., 7, 24, 6, vol. 5, p. 1435.

218 *"Where a Christian* Ibid., pt. 7, p. 1435.

218 *"insane* Ibid., pt. 25, law 4, p. 1439.

218 *"undergarments made from it* Kathleen Kulp-Hill, trans., *Songs of Holy Mary of Alfonso X, the Wise* (Tempe: Arizona Center for Medieval and Renaissance Studies, 2000), no. 327, p. 397.

218 *cited more frequently in the Quran,* Esposito, *What Everyone Needs,* p. 31.

219 *One Muslim general, Cantiga* 46, p. 62.

219 *Holy Mary of Salas revives, Cantiga* 167, p. 202.

219 *In another poem* Ibid., *Cantiga* 205, p. 246.

219 *"Both companies* Ibid., *Cantiga* 344, p. 418.

219 *"were greatly amazed Cantiga* 344, p. 418.

219 *"Holy Mary brings* Ibid.

219 *"[Mary's] enemies, whom Cantiga* 348, p. 424.

219 *"struck him such a blow Cantiga* 6, p. 11.

219 *Another Jew casts, Cantiga* 4, p. 6.

220 *"[he] sat down there Cantiga* 34, p. 45.

220   *"shall take any medicine* Parsons Scott, *Siete Partidas,* pt. 7, title 17, law 8, p. 1436.

220   *While parceling spoils* Joseph F. O'Callaghan, "The Mudejars of Castile and Portugal in the Twelfth and Thirteenth Centuries," in James M. Powell, ed. *Muslims under Latin Rule, 1100–1300* (Princeton: Princeton University Press, 1990), p. 43.

220   *"Jews enjoyed their greatest* Albert I. Bagby Jr., "The Figure of the Jew in the Cantigas of Alfonso X," in Israel J. Katz and John F. Keller, eds., *Studies on the Cantigas de Santa María: Art, Music, and Poetry* (Madison, WI: Hispanic Seminar of Medieval Studies, 1987), p. 235.

221   *Still, religious celebrations sometimes* Henry Kamen, *The Spanish Inquisition: A Historical Revision* (New Haven: Yale University Press, 1998), p. 4.

221   *Such interfaith merrymaking* Montgomery-Watt, *History,* 159.

221   *a church council in Valladolid* see W. Montgomery Watt, *A History of Islamic Spain,* (Edinburgh: Edinburgh University Press, 1996), p. 159.

221   *a rabbinical ruling admonished* Norman Roth, *Jews, Visigoths, and Muslims in Medieval Spain: Cooperation and Conflict* (Leiden: E.J. Brill, 1994), p. 182.

221   *"[Receiving] presents at Christmas* Melville, *Christians and Moors,* vol. 3, p. 31, quoting fifteenth-century collection of legal judgements compiled by al-Wansharishi.

221   *"At the celebration of* al-Andara Melville, p. 121.

222   *"set out from the church,* Kamen, p. 4.

222   *"Following [the artisans] Crónica de Juan II,* quoted in Olivia Remie Constable, *Medieval Iberia,* p. 318.

222   *"the Jew can find salvation,* Kamen, p. 5.

222   *"Who knows which is the better,* Ibid.

222   *"the good Jew and the,* Ibid., p. 6.

222   *"The good Jew would be saved* John Edwards, "Religious Faith and Doubt in Late Medieval Spain: Soria c. 1450–1500," *Past and Present,* no. 120 (August 1988), p. 16.

222   *"sincere believers in the one* Friar Alonso de Mella, in Colin Smith, *Christians and Moors in Spain, vol. 2, 1195–1614* (Warminster, U.K.: Aris and Phillips, 1989), p. 135.

223   *"We truly recognized* Ibid.

223   *"In the name of Our Lord* Richard Fletcher, *Moorish Spain* (New York: H. Holt, 1992), p. 140–141.

223   *"In the name of Allah* Ibid.

223   *"his life and light," the* Yitzhak Baer, *A History of the Jews in Christian Spain,* 2 vols. (Philadelphia: Jewish Publication Society of America, 1961–66), vol. 2, p. 275.

224   *"whose king is truth* Augustine's letter to Marcellinus, epistle 138, in *Saint Augustine: Letters,* vol. 3, no. 131–164, trans. Sister Wilfrid Parsons, S.N.D. (New York: Fathers of the Church: 1953), p. 50.

Chapter 19

227   *His brother's bloated, stinking* O'Callaghan, *A History,* p. 427.

228   *a third of its population* "plague" in Paul Lagassé, ed. *The Columbia Encyclopedia,* 6th ed. (New York: Columbia University Press, 2000), p. 2241.

228   *Half of the Cerrato region's* Statistics were compiled as part of the mid-fourteenth-century census known as the *Becerro de Behetrías*; see Teofilo Ruiz, *Crisis and Continuity, Land and Town in Late Medieval Castile* (Philadelphia: University of Pennsylvania Press, 1994), p. 325.

228   *"All the Jews in my realms* Richard L. Kagan, "The Spain of Ferdinand and Isabella," in James R. McGovern, ed., *The World of Columbus* (Macon, GA: Mercer University Press, 1992), p. 32.

229   *"out of a thirst* López de Ayala, in *Crónica de Enrique III,* 1391, 20; quoted in O'Callaghan, *A History* p. 537.

229   *as many as half of Spain's* It is impossible to judge precisely either the exact size of the Jewish population at this time or the number of conversions in the wake of 1391. One meticulous discussion and analysis is B. Netanyahu, *The Marranos of Spain from the Late 14th to the Early 16th Century,* 3rd ed., (Ithaca: Cornell University Press, 1999), pp. 238–248.

231   *Like so many medieval* María Isavel del Val Valdivieso, "Isavel, Infanta and Princess of Castile," in David A. Boruchoff, *Isabel La Católica, Queen of Castile: Critical Essays* (New York: Palgrave Macmillan, 2003), p. 51.

232   *record of anti-Semitism* See Henry Kamen, *The Spanish Inquisition: A Historical Revision,* (New Haven: Yale University Press, 1998), pp. 16–17.

233   *"[It] has for some time* Kamen, *Spanish Inquisition,* p. 49.

234   *Castile's population was roughly* Richard L. Kagan, "The Spain of Ferdinand and Isabella," in James R. McGovern, ed. *The World of Columbus* (Macon, GA: Mercer University Press, 1992), p. 22.

235   *as if the message wasn't clear,* Kamen, *Spanish Inquisition,* p. 54.

235   *as non-Christians they were* See B. Netanyahu, *The Origins of the Inquisition in Fifteenth Century Spain* (New York: Random House, 1995), p. 1087.

235   *nearly 2,500 Toledans,* Kamen, p. 57.

236   *"If a man does not abide* John 15:6.

236   *The converso María Díaz* Renée Levine Melammed, "Judaizing Women in Castile: A Look at Their Lives before and after 1492," in Menachem Mor and Bryan F. Le Beau, eds., *Religion in the Age of Exploration: The*

Case of Spain and New Spain (Omaha: Creighton University Press, 1996), p. 19.

237   *Beatriz González of Toledo* Ibid., p. 20.

237   *Constanza Núñez donated* Renée Levine Melammed, *Heretics or Daughters of Israel?: The Crypto-Jewish Women of Castile* (Oxford: Oxford University Press, 1999), p. 26.

237   *Blanca Rodríguez of Guadalajara* Melammed, "Judaizing" in Mor, pp. 20–21.

237   *"Holy Mary, Mother of God* Henry Kamen, *The Spanish Inquisition: A Historical Revision* (New Haven: Yale University Press, 1997), p. 42; emphasis added.

237   *Up to two thousand conversos* Scholarly estimates vary, sometimes considerably, on these figures. See, for example, Henry Kamen, *The Spanish Inquisition,* pp. 59–60, and Levine Melammed, *Heretics or Daughters of Israel?,* p. 14.

237   *8 million Europeans* Moynahan, *The Faith: A History,* pp. 476–477. Estimates vary widely, with some historians putting the death toll closer to 14 million.

238   *which almost certainly included* Though it is often suggested that Torquemada himself was descended from converts, this seems unlikely. For a discussion of both Torquemada and the likely converso origins of his uncle, Juan de Torquemada, see B. Netanyahu, *The Origins of the Inquisition,* pp. 431–434, 1250.

240   *"all the common people The Capitulations of 1491,* in L. P. Harvey, *Islamic Spain, 1250–1500* (Chicago: University of Chicago Press, 1990), pp. 315–321.

240   *"wicked Christians who Judaized* The Chapter of Expulsion of 1492, in Edward Peters, "Jewish History and Gentile Memory: The Expulsion of 1492" in *Jewish History,* vol. 9, no. 1 (Spring, 1995), p. 25.

241   *"seek always and by* Ibid.

241   *"To order the said Jews* Ibid., p. 26.

242   *and between 150,000 and 200,000* Estimates of this number vary widely. For a careful discussion of the sources, see Haim Beinart, *The Expulsion of the Jews from Spain,* trans. Jeffrey M. Green (Oxford: The Littman Library of Jewish Civilization, 2002), pp. 284–290.

242   *one Christian cowherd* Beinart, *The Expulsion,* p. 514.

242   *forbade Jews from removing* Chapter of Expulsion, in Peters, *Jewish History,* p. 27.

243   *"in much travail and misfortune* Beinart, *Expulsion,* p. 524.

243   *Upon reaching the port* Ibid., p. 244.

243 *Hundreds of young Jews were herded* See Rui de Pina, "Chronicle of King João II" in David Raphael, ed. *The Expulsion of 1492 Chronicles* (North Hollywood: Carmi House, 1992), p. 151.

244 *extraordinary Abrabanel family* Sometimes spelled Abravanel. For a detailed discussion of the best known of the Abrabanels, see Benzion Netanyahu, *Don Isaac Abravanel: Statesman and Philosopher,* 5th ed. (Ithaca: Cornell University Press, 1998).

244 *kidnap and baptize* See Raymond P. Scheindlin, "Judah Abravanel to His Son," *Judaism,* vol. 41 (spring, 1992), p. 191.

245 *"Time with his pointed shafts,* Raymond P. Scheindlin, "Judah Abravanel to His Son," *Judaism* 41 (spring 1992): 190–199.

Chapter 20

248 *"There were not so many* Benjamin Keen, trans., *The Life of the Admiral Christopher Columbus by His Son, Ferdinand* (New Brunswick, NJ: Rutgers University Press, 1959), p. 38.

248 *"would be going downhill* Ibid., p. 39.

249 *"all of the profit* Columbus's diary quoted in Hector Avalos, "Columbus as Biblical Exegete: A Study of the Libro de las Profecías," in *Religion in the Age of Exploration: The Case of Spain and New Spain,* ed. Bryan F. LeBeau and Menachem Mor (Creighton, NE: Creighton University Press, 1996), p. 70.

250 *"Therefore ask their Pope* Anonymous, from *Hispano-Arab Poetry: A Student Anthology,* trans. James T. Monroe (Berkeley: University of California Press, 1974), p. 384.

250 *"It was the fear of death,* Ibid.

251 *"as a memorial of* John Edwards, *The Spain of the Catholic Monarchs 1474–1520* (London: Blackwell, 2000), p. 223.

251 *"God made me the messenger* G. B. Spotorno, *Memorial of Columbus* (London, 1823), p. 224, in Pauline Moffitt Watts, "Prophecy and Discovery: On the Spiritual Origins of Christopher Columbus's Enterprise of the Indies," *American Historical Review* 90 (February 1985): 73.

251 *"according to the account* John Boyd Thacher, *Christopher Columbus: His life, his works, his remains, as revealed by original printed and manuscript records, together with an essay on Peter Martyr of Anghera and Bartolomé de las Casas, the first historians of America,* 3 vols. (London: G.P. Putnam's Sons, 1903–4), p. 662.

252 *"the well-being of Spain* Chronicle, in Baxter-Wolf, *Conquerors,* p. 166.

253 *"Your Highness ought not* Samuel Eliot Morison, *Admiral of the Ocean Sea: A Life of Christopher Columbus* (Boston: Little Brown, 1942), p. 279.

254 *"for two thousand and three* Daniel 8:14.

254 *"Destroyers of the Mohammedan* Americo Castro, *The Spaniards: An Introduction to Their History,* trans. Willard F. King and Selma Margaretten (Berkeley: University of California Press, 1971), p. 205.

257 *"one of the most significant* Lawrence Fine, trans., *Safed Spirituality: Rules of Mystical Piety, The Beginning of Wisdom* (New York: Paulist Press, 1984), p. xiii. See his introduction for a broader discussion of the key Safed kabbalists and the movement more broadly.

258 *"in everyone there is* Gershom G. Scholem, *Major Trends in Jewish Mysticism,* 3rd ed. (New York: Schocken Books, 1941), p. 279.

259 *"each art and science* Aristotle, *Metaphysics,* bk. 12, no. 8, 1074b, 10–11, trans. W. D. Ross, in *The Complete Works of Aristotle: The Revised Oxford Translation,* ed. Jonathan Barnes (Princeton: Princeton University Press, 1984), vol. 2, p. 1698.

261 *"there will be no* Birnbaum,. *Mishneh Torah,* p. 329.

Epilogue

263 *"Its doors are open* Quoted in Jack Hitt, *Off the Road: A Modern-Day Walk Down the Pilgrim's Route into Spain* (New York: Simon & Schuster, 1994), p. 24.

263 *"The pagans are wrong* Burgess, *Roland,* no. 79/1015.

264 *takes the pagans up* Ibid., no. 272/3668–3671.

265 *"the world is waiting* Pope John Paul II, "Address to Participants in Sant'-Egidio Interreligious Meeting," April 30, 1991, Rome, in *Spiritual Pilgrimage: Texts on Jews and Judaism 1979–1995,* Eugene J. Fisher and Leon Klenicki, eds., (New York: Crossroad, 1995).

265 *"Now we see in a mirror* 1 Corinthians 13:12.

265 *"My heart has become capable* A. Nicholson Reynolds, trans., *The Tarjuman al-Ashwaq: A Collection of Mystical Odes* by Muhyi'ddin ibn al-'Arabi Ed. from three mansucripts with a literal version of the text, XI, 13-15 (London: Theosophical Publishing House, 1978), p. 67.

267 *"and they wear them* "The 'Veneranda Dies' Sermon," in *The Miracles of Saint James: Translations from the Liber Sancti Jacobi,* first English translation with introduction by Thomas F. Coffey, Linda Kay Davidson, and Maryjane Dunn (New York: Italica Press, 1996), p. 25.

267   *"Therefore, the two shields* Ibid.

268   *"Worship the Creator alone* From Ice de Gebir's Sunn[i] Breviary, in L. P. Harvey, *Islamic Spain, 1250–1500* (Chicago: University of Chicago Press, 1990), p. 88.

268   *"The skin of his face* Exodus 34:29.

268   *"Hear, O Israel: The Lord* Deuteronomy 6:4–5.

268   *"You shall love your neighbor* Leviticus 19:18.

Suggested Reading

A comprehensive digest of the extensive body of scholarly literature dedicated to any one of the fields noted below would run to many pages. Following is an introductory guide to a cross-section of English-language works on topics treated in this book. Though many of the works are academic studies, all are accessible to generalist readers who possess a basic background on the period. Readers should also consult the endnotes for other sources that have been instrumental in preparation of this book, including, importantly, the editions of translations used for primary sources quoted throughout.

General Histories

Joseph F. O'Callaghan, *A History of Medieval Spain* (Ithaca: Cornell University Press, 1975) remains the standard general history. Raymond Carr, ed., *Spain, a History* (Oxford: Oxford University Press, 2000) is an alternative to O'Callaghan for those who want a shorter work that spans the whole period; essays by noted scholars, good illustrations. Salma Khadra Jayyusi, ed., *The Legacy of Muslim Spain* (Leiden: E. J. Brill, 1992) is a collection of scholarly essays sprawling over one thousand pages. Readers interested in delving in detail into topics will almost undoubtedly find relevant essays here. Olivia Remie Constable, ed., *Medieval Iberia: Readings from Christian, Muslim, and Jewish Sources* (Philadelphia: University of Pennsylvania Press, 1997). Another series of excerpted primary sources is *Christians and Moors in Spain,* esp. vol. 3, ed. Charles Melville and Ahmad Ubaydli (Warminster: Aris & Phillips, 1988), and vol. 1, ed. Colin Smith and Ahmad Ubaydli. Richard Fletcher, *Moorish Spain* (New York: Henry Holt, 1992) and *The Quest for El Cid* (London: Hutchinson, 1989). Gabriel Jackson, *The Making of Medieval Spain* (London: Thames and Hudson, 1972) is a short, highly readable work, with over one hundred illustrations. Vivian B. Mann, Thomas F. Glick, and Jerrilynn D. Dodds, eds., *Convivencia: Jews, Muslims, and Christians in Medieval Spain* (New York: George Braziller, 1992) is a lavishly illustrated large-format book focusing primarily on cultural contributions of the period. María Rosa Menocal, *The Ornament of the World: How Muslims, Jews, and Christians Created a Culture of Tolerance in Medieval Spain* (New York: Little, Brown, 2002) is a general history from the noted Yale scholar. Maribel Fierro and Julio Samsó, eds., *The Formation of al-Andalus. Part 2: Language, Religion, Culture and the Sciences* (Ashgate: Variorum, 1998) is especially strong on medicine and astronomy. María Rosa Menocal, Raymond P. Scheindlin, and Michael Sells, eds., *The Literature of al-Andalus* (Cambridge, England: Cambridge University Press, 2000) includes important essays by leaders in field. Michael Sells's essay on mysticism is especially to be noted. José Rubia Barcia, *Américo Castro and the Meaning of Spanish Civilization* (Berkeley: University of California Press, 1976) is a collection of essays that will introduce readers to this famous interpreter of Spanish history who developed the idea of *convivencia*.

The Ninth-Century Córdoba Martyr Movement

Two scholarly, readable, and short works are Jessica A. Coope, *The Martyrs of Cordoba: Community and Family Conflict in an Era of Mass Conversion* (Lincoln: University of Nebraska Press, 1995) and Kenneth Baxter Wolf, *Christian Martyrs in Muslim Spain* (Cambridge, England: Cambridge University Press, 1988).

Judaism: The Jewish People in Spain

Jane S. Gerber, *The Jews of Spain: A History of the Sephardic Experience* (New York: Free Press, 1992) is a splendid, easy-to-read history, perhaps the most accessible short work for generalist readers looking to learn about Jewish history in Spain's medieval era. Barry W. Holtz, ed., *Back to the Sources: Reading the Classic Jewish Texts* (New York: Summit Books, 1984) provides an easy-to-read introduction to those seeking to understand the role and significance of sources ranging from the Hebrew Bible through the Talmud and kabbalah texts. B. Netanyahu, *Don Isaac Abravanel: Statesman and Philosopher,* 5th ed. (Ithaca: Cornell University Press,1972) is a biography by the scholarly author of other important works on the Jewish experience in Spain during the late medieval era. Robert Garfield, "A Forgotten Fragment of the Diaspora: The Jews of Sao Tome Island, 1492–1654," in Raymond B. Waddington and Arthur H. Williamson, eds., *The Expulsion of the Jews, 1492 and After* (New York: Garland, 1994). Leon J. Weinberger, trans., *Jewish Prince in Muslim Spain: Selected Poems of Samuel Ibn Nagrela* (University, Alabama: University of Alabama Press, 1973). Yitzhak Baer, A *History of the Jews in Christian Spain,* 2 vols. (Philadelphia: Jewish Publication Society of America,

1961–66) remains one of the most comprehensive and authoritative treatments, along with E. Ashtor, *The Jews of Muslim Spain,* 3 vols. (Philadelphia: Jewish Publication Society: 1973–84). Renée Levine Melammed, *Heretics or Daughters of Israel? The Crypto-Jewish Women of Castile* (Oxford: Oxford University Press, 1999). David M. Gitlitz, *Secrecy and Deceit: The Religion of the Crypto-Jews* (Philadelphia: Jewish Publication Society, 1996). Isidro G. Bango, *Remembering Sepharad Jewish Culture in Medieval Spain* (Madrid: State Corporation for Spanish Cultural Action Abroad, 2003) is a beautifully illustrated exhibition catalogue accompanied by helpful historical summary.

Islam; Muslim Spain

Salma Khadra Jayyusi, ed., *The Legacy of Muslim Spain.* John L. Esposito's works will provide generalist readers an excellent introduction to Islam; see his *Islam: The Straight Path* (Oxford: Oxford University Press, 1988) and *What Everyone Needs to Know about Islam* (Oxford: Oxford University Press, 2002). Seyyed Hossein Nasr, *The Heart of Islam: Enduring Values for Humanity* (San Francisco: Harper San Francisco, 2002) is an eloquent introduction highlighting key themes. Robert Ignatius Burns, S.J., *Islam under the Crusaders: Colonial Survival in the Thirteenth-Century Kingdom of Valencia* (Princeton: Princeton University Press, 1973). Kaled Abou El Fadl, *The Place of Tolerance in Islam* (Boston: Beacon Press, 2002) does not deal with the medieval period, but interesting essays address themes underlying this book. For further insight on the Muslim philosophers covered in this book, see George F. Hourani, *Reason and Tradition in Islamic Ethics* (London: Cambridge University Press, 1985), and the many relevant works by Oliver Leaman, including *An Introduction to Medieval Islamic Philosophy* (Cambridge, England: Cambridge University Press, 1985), and *A Brief Introduction to Islamic Philosophy* (Cambridge, England: Polity Press, 2000), and his specialized treatments of Maimonides and Averroes.

Moses Maimonides

Fred Rosner, *The Medical Legacy of Moses Maimonides* (Hoboken, NJ: KTAV Publishing House, 1998) is one of many readable treatments of Maimonides' contributions to medicine and ethics seen through the eyes of a medical doctor. Maimonides, *Medical Aphorisms,* in Fred Rosner, M.D., *The Medical Legacy of Moses Maimonides* (Hoboken, NJ: KTAV Publishing House, 1998). Ralph Lerner, *Mai-*

monides' Empire of Light: Popular Enlightenment in an Age of Belief (Chicago: University of Chicago Press, 2000) masterfully exposes in a short work key Maimonidean themes, complementing primary text excerpts with explanatory matter. Menachem Kellner, *Maimonides on Judaism and the Jewish People* (Albany: State University of New York Press, 1991). A special issue of *American Catholic Philosophical Quarterly* 76 (winter 2002), *Maimonides,* ed. Daniel H. Frank, includes essays by various Maimonides scholars examining the philosophical dimensions of his work. Daniel Jeremy Silver, *Maimonidean Criticism and the Maimonidean Controversy, 1180–1240* (Leiden: E.J. Brill, 1965) lays out key Maimonidean ideas and the positions of his critics in prose accessible to nonscholars.

Reign of Ferdinand and Isabella, Columbus, the Inquisition

Felipe Fernández-Armesto, *Columbus and the Conquest of the Impossible* (London: Phoenix Press, 1974) is typical of this author's scholarly, provocative, and readable works. Menachem Mor and Bryan F. Le Beau, eds., *Religion in the Age of Exploration: The Case of Spain and New Spain* (Omaha: Creighton University Press, 1996). Robert Garfield, "A Forgotten Fragment of the Diaspora: The Jews of Sao Tome Island, 1492–1654," in Raymond B. Waddington and Arthur H. Williamson, eds., *The Expulsion of the Jews, 1492 and After* (New York: Garland, 1994). James R. McGovern, ed., *The World of Columbus* (Macon, GA: Mercer University Press, 1992). Two authors who have written widely, and at times controversially, about the Inquisition era in Spain are Henry Kamen, *The Spanish Inquisition: A Historical Revision* (New Haven: Yale University Press, 1997) and John Edwards, *The Spain of the Catholic Monarchs 1474–1520* (London: Blackwell, 2000). See also Renée Levine Melammed, *Heretics or Daughters of Israel? The Crypto-Jewish Women of Castile* (Oxford: Oxford University Press, 1999). Haim Beinart, *The Expulsion of the Jews from Spain,* trans. Jeffrey M. Green (Oxford: Littman Library of Jewish Civilization, 2002) is a painstakingly researched work that offers a window into the expulsion through details gathered from Inquisition records and other sources.

Alfonso X and the *Cantigas de Santa María*

Robert I. Burns, S.J., ed., *Emperor of Culture: Alfonso X the Learned of Castile and His Thirteenth-Century Renaissance* (Philadelphia: University of Pennsylvania Press, 1990) is a collection of scholarly essays. Kathleen Kulp-Hill, trans., and Connie L. Scarborough, introduction, *Songs of Holy Mary of Alfonso X, the Wise*

(Tempe: Arizona Center for Medieval and Renaissance Studies, 2000). Israel J. Katz and John E. Keller, eds., *Studies on the Cantigas de Santa María: Art, Music, and Poetry* (Madison, WI: Hispanic Seminar of Medieval Studies, 1987). John Esten Keller and Annette Grant Cash, *Daily Life Depicted in the Cantigas de Santa María* (Lexington: University Press of Kentucky, 1988) is a learned study filled with delightful color reproductions from a medieval edition of the *Cantigas*.

Medieval Philosophy

Frederick Copleston, C.S.J., has written a masterful introductory series on the history of Western philosophy: *A History of Medieval Philosophy* (Notre Dame: University of Notre Dame Press, 1990) covers the period of this book. Another interpretative history, a bit dense in patches, is Etienne Gilson, *History of Christian Philosophy in the Middle Ages* (New York: Random House, 1955). Despite its title, there are good chapters on Islamic and Jewish thinkers and a thoughtful treatment of the condemnations of 1277.

Moses de León, Ibn Arabi, Mysticism

Gershom G. Scholem's studies of Jewish mysticism, though well over fifty years old, remain authoritative guides. Learned yet readable works include *Major Trends in Jewish Mysticism* (New York: Schocken, 1941) and *Zohar: The Book of Splendor*, ed. Gershom G. Scholem (New York: Schocken, 1949). Daniel Chanan Matt, trans., *Zohar: The Book of Enlightenment* (New York: Paulist Press, 1983) combines excerpts with a short yet valuable introduction. R. W. J Austin, trans., *The Bezels of Wisdom* (New York: Paulist Press, 1980).

Art

John O'Neill, ed., *The Art of Medieval Spain* (New York: Metropolitan Museum of Art, 1993). Vivian B. Mann, Thomas F. Glick, and Jerrilyn D. Dodds, eds., *Convivencia: Jews, Muslims, and Christians in Medieval Spain* (New York: G. Braziller and Jewish Museum of New York, 1992). Jerrilynn D. Dodd, ed., *Al-Andalus: The Art of Islamic Spain* (New York: Metropolitan Museum of Art, 1992), and Isidro Bango, ed., *Remembering Sepharad Jewish Culture in Medieval Spain* (University of Washington, 2004). All four of these oversized books, beautifully illustrated with valuable essays, were produced in conjunction with museum exhibitions.

Reference Works

Two recently published reference works are immensely valuable resources for generalists: E. Michael Gerli, ed., *Medieval Iberia: An Encyclopedia* (New York: Routledge, 2002), and Norman Roth, ed., *Medieval Jewish Civilization: An Encyclopedia* (New York: Routledge, 2003).

Santiago de Compostela Pilgrimage, Pilgrims and Pilgrimage

Diana Webb, *Pilgrims and Pilgrimage in Medieval Europe* (London: J.B. Tauris, 1999) is a fascinating general survey; it deals less with Santiago de Compostela than with examples from Britain. Jack Hitt, *Off the Road: A Modern-Day Walk down the Pilgrim's Route into Spain* (New York: Simon and Schuster, 1994) blends history of the pilgrimage into a firsthand account of a pilgrimage trip to Santiago; it is one of many pilgrimage memoirs. William Melczer, *The Pilgrim's Guide to Santiago de Compostela* first English translation with introduction (New York: Italica Press, 1993) is a good brief introduction to the medieval context of the pilgrimage and a good outline of the pilgrimage itself. Annie Shaver-Crandell and Paula Gerson, *The Pilgrim's Guide to Santiago de Compostela: A Gazeteer* (London: Harvey Miller Publishers, 1995) is an extensively illustrated guide to the various churches and hostels en route, including French stretches of the route. Too heavy for a backpack! Walter Starkie, *The Road to Santiago: Pilgrims of St. James* (New York: E.P. Dutton, 1957) is another pilgrimage memoir blending historical background with the author's experiences.

Science and Medicine in the Middle Ages

David C. Lindberg, ed., *Science in the Middle Ages* (Chicago: University of Chicago Press, 1978). Roy Porter, *The Greatest Benefit to Mankind: A Medical History of Humanity* (New York: Norton, 1997) is a lavishly illustrated, learned survey that touches on contributions of medieval Muslim physicians both in and beyond Spain. George Sarton's *Introduction to the History of Science* (Baltimore: Williams and Wilkins, 1931) is a classic, exhaustive multivolume effort, a reference resource rather than a popular history. Vol. 2 covers Moses Maimonides, Ibn Rushd, and other medieval thinkers.

Women in Medieval Spain

Three works that shed light on this underresearched field are Heath Dillard, *Daughters of the Reconquest: Women in Castilian Town Society, 1100–1300* (Cambridge: Cambridge University Press, 1984); Louise Mirrer, *Women, Jews and Muslims in the Texts of Reconquest Castile* (Ann Arbor: University of Michigan Press, 1996); and Renée Levine Melammed, *Heretics or Daughters of Israel? The Crypto-Jewish Women of Castile* (Oxford: Oxford University Press, 1999).

Miscellaneous Topics

F. E. Peters, *The Monotheists: Jews, Christians, and Muslims in Conflict and Competition* (Princeton: Princeton University Press, 2003) is an excellent two-volume scholarly introduction to each of these three religions, their development, and belief systems. E. A. Thompson, *The Goths in Spain* (Oxford: Oxford University Press, 1969) is for those who want to delve into the Visigoth era. Robert Barlett and Angus MacKay, eds., *Medieval Frontier Societies* (Oxford: Clarendon Press, 1989) contains interesting scholarly essays on the frontier in Spain and elsewhere, treating the customs and institutions of frontier life. Derek W. Lomax, *The Reconquest of Spain* (New York: Longman, 1978) is a concise, excellent history of the campaigns and context of the Christian Reconquest of Iberia. A more recent work on the topic is by the noted scholar Joseph F. O'Callaghan, *Reconquest and Crusade in Medieval Spain* (Philadelphia: University of Pennsylvania Press, 2003). Olivia Remie Constable, *Trade and Traders in Muslim Spain: The Commercial Realignment of the Iberian Peninsula, 900–1500* (Cambridge: Cambridge University Press, 1994). James T. Monroe, trans., *Hispano-Arab Poetry: A Student Anthology* (Berkeley: University of California Press, 1974). Brian Moynahan, *The Faith: A History of Christianity* (New York: Doubleday, 2002) is a hefty one-volume survey. James Brodman *Ransoming Captives in Crusader Spain: The Order of Merced on the Christian-Islamic Frontier* (Philadelphia: University of Pennsylvania Press, 1986). David Nicolle, *The Crusades* (London: Osprey, 2001) is a bite-sized introductory history with a bibliography that directs readers toward more comprehensive sources on this massive topic. David Nicolle, *Medieval Warfare Source Book,* esp. Vol 2: *Christian Europe and Its Neighbours* (London: Cassell Group, 1996) is a comprehensive introduction. Joseph J. Duggan, *The Cantar de Mio Cid: Poetic Creation in Its Economic and Social Contexts* (Cambridge: Cambridge University Press, 1989) situates the poem in its historical context and concisely introduces readers to various scholarly contentions concerning its authorship, date of composition, and means of transmission. James F. Powers, trans., *The Code of Cuenca Municipal Law on the Twelfth-Century Castilian Frontier* (Philadelphia: University of Pennsylvania Press, 2000) offers a fascinating glimpse of frontier life through a medieval law code.

Credits

Photo credits

Photos no. 1 through 15 appear courtesy of The Hispanic Society of America, New York. Drawn primarily from The Hispanic Society's superb collection of late nineteenth- and early twentieth-century photographs, the vintage images capture the timeless appeal of Spain's medieval heritage. Photos no. 16 through 18 are courtesy of the Collection of the Museo Nacional del Prado, Madrid.

Cover Image

King Alfonso the Learned (d. 1284) aspired to bring the world's wisdom to Spain. His court scholars translated Arabic treatises to produce one of Europe's first comprehensive manuals for chess, dice, backgammon, and other table games (*Libro de Ajedrez, Dados, y Tablas*). The manuscript's many illuminations include this depiction of a Muslim and a Christian playing chess, an apt symbol for the cooperation, conflict, and exchange of ideas between Muslim and Christian cultures during the medieval era. The image is courtesy of Biblioteca Monasterio del Escorial, Madrid/Index/Bridgeman Art Library.

Excerpts in the Text

Poem of El Cid: courtesy of Manchester University Press. *Song of Roland:* courtesy of Penguin Books Ltd. [Penguin Group (UK)]. "Judah Abravanel to His Son": courtesy of the American Jewish Congress. *Ibn Tufayl's Hayy Ibn Yaqzan,* by Muhammad Ibn Tufayl, Twayne Publishers, © 1972: courtesy of Twayne Publishers; reprinted by permission of The Gale Group.

Index

About the Author

Chris Lowney (www.chrislowney.com) is author of *Heroic Leadership: Best Practices from a 450-Year-Old Company That Changed the World,* the acclaimed history chronicling the transformation of sixteenth-century Jesuits into their era's most successful company. As a Jesuit seminarian, Lowney earned degrees in medieval history and philosophy. He later joined J. P. Morgan & Co., serving as a managing director on three continents. At least twenty percent of *A Vanished World*'s royalties will be donated to charities providing education, social, or health-care services in the developing world.